"What I'm trying to encapsulate with these mere words is the absolute utter charismatic *hipness* of Bernie Wolfe, a man who knows more about everything there is to know about than any other writer I've met."
—*HARLAN ELLISON*

"Wolfe is best remembered for his novels of the late '50s; twenty years before that, just out of Yale where he was anything but a Yalie and hoping to become a wordsmith, he spent a year writing on consignment for someone called Barneybill Roster who was fronting (or was he) for a Tulsa oil millionaire. He completed his first 'Eros-ive novel' in two weeks; wrote four more, and then went on to pornographize the great books and quit after 11 months, 10,000 dollars richer. Wolfe is one of the more voluble sorts—believes in the 'grand spatter business' like Celine and Henry Miller (the latter appears here too) and he can soup up a line so that it comes out this way: 'So the slobbered appetites of the cradle hang on undented and undaunted in the sophisticated eroticisms that infantile Libido ultimately gets channeled into.'"
—*KIRKUS*

"As to the books of Bernard Wolfe, his extraordinary imagination, his range of styles and genres, should alone qualify him for a conspicuous role in 20th century American literature."
—*THOMAS BERGER*

"An autobiography such as was never seen before beneath the moon."
—*BEN RAY REDMAN*

"His humor is uproarious . . . one is reminded of Ade or Leacock or Benchley (or all three)."
—*BOSTON SUNDAY GLOBE*

"Wolfe writes in the mixture of the styles of Joyce and Runyon . . ."
—*SAN FRANCISCO CHRONICLE*

MEMOIRS
OF A NOT
ALTOGETHER SHY
PORNOGRAPHER

First printed by Doubleday & Company, Inc. 1972
First Pharos Editions printing 2016

Library of Congress Cataloging-in-Publication Data is available.
ISBN 978-1-940436-26-5

Cover and interior design by Faceout Studio

Pharos Editions, an imprint of Counterpoint
2560 Ninth Street, Suite 318
Berkeley, CA 94710
www.pharoseditions.com
www.counterpointpress.com

Printed in the United States of America

SELECTED AND INTRODUCED BY
JONATHAN LETHEM

MEMOIRS OF A NOT ALTOGETHER SHY PORNOGRAPHER

by

BERNARD WOLFE

PHAROS EDITIONS | AN IMPRINT OF COUNTERPOINT | BERKELEY

INTRODUCTION BY
JONATHAN LETHEM

Bernard Wolfe's *Memoirs of a Not Altogether Shy Pornographer* comes into your hands as a book-out-of-time. Such republication efforts as these always collapse the shallow literary present into a more complicated shape, making a portal through history—who is this lost writer, we ask ourselves, and what is this lost book? But also: what views of a lost cultural landscape might be available through the portal this particular lost writer and lost book represents?

Make no mistake, the case of Bernard Wolfe is an especially interesting one, not least because, even in 1972, in the pages of his memoir when it rolled fresh off the presses into the hands of god-knows-how-few readers, Wolfe already presents himself as a man-out-of-time, in ways both helpless and defiant. Wolfe's career was bizarrely rich: from time as Leon Trotsky's personal secretary to stints in the Merchant Marine, as ghostwriter for Broadway columnist Billy Rose and author of early-TV-era teleplays, as editor of *Mechanix Illustrated*, and as exponent of the theories of dissident psychoanalytic guru Edmund Bergler (whose homophobia was obnoxious, but whose discarded theories strongly anticipate later thinking, and who could be seen as a kind of "lost American Lacan," if anyone was digging for one), to his glancing participation in the realm of American science fiction, and his role as amanuensis, to jazzman Mezz Mezzrow, in writing a memoir depicting a prescient version of "hipsterdom" and which became a kind of bible of inner-urban American slang—Wolfe was practically everywhere in twentieth-century culture.

Yet Wolfe was also nowhere, in the sense that the present interest attaching to him doesn't stem from the notion of "reviving" a writer with an earlier purchase on either popularity or the embrace of literary critics of his time. Wolfe had neither. A few of his books sold a bit; *Limbo* has kept an obscure reputation within science fiction and bobbed back into print a few times. Yet for his hyperactivity, Wolfe had little traction, and in 1972 was hardly a writer whose memoirs any publishers were likely to be clamoring for. Wolfe, restless, fast-producing, and seemingly impervious to indifference, wrote one anyway. When he did it was surely the "pornographer" of the title that drew Doubleday's interest in publishing the result.

What the reader meets here is both fascinating and truly eccentric. The book is a writer's-coming-of-age narrative, but a highly unsentimental one, describing Wolfe's location of a habit and a craft and a discipline and a capacity, much more than it details his discovery of any definite sense of purpose as a writer. Wolfe's vibrant intelligence, which picks up and turns over any number of vital subjects as if they were rocks concealing scuttling insect life, rarely settles on introspection, let alone seeks a tone of confession or remorse or self-doubt, such as we'd expect from nearly any memoir lately. Despite this, there's a terrible poignancy to the material concerning his father's spiraling mental illness, and the bizarre ironies attaching to Wolfe's own role as a New Haven-townie-gone-to-Yale who gets a psychiatric fellowship at the same institution in nearby Middletown where his father is a semi-comatose inmate. Of course, a commissioning editor, nowadays, would have insisted that Wolfe punch this material up, goose it emotionally, and put it in the foreground (a contemporary point of comparison might be Nick Flynn's fine *Another Bullshit Night in Suck City*). The same imaginary editor would surely, I think, have asked Wolfe to excise so much of the fading political context from the book, but for various reasons one can guess this book wasn't so much edited as it was simply written and published. It's in the politics that one can feel how deeply, and restlessly, Wolfe was, by 1972, testifying from an already-lost world. His passionate and still unresolved commitment to Marxism, a commitment betrayed (of course, and in so many different ways) by twentieth-century historical reality, remains the lens through which he views the "labor" of writing, and the social relations into which he projected himself as a hungry young writer in the wartime years.

Despite his engagement with history, there's no attempt to make a wide-screen historical panorama of his book—what enters of political and cultural context does so through individual experience. Wolfe also doesn't trouble much over the question of censorship, despite the great battles over *Ulysses*, *Lolita*, "Howl", and others that he'd certainly be capable of drawing into the mix. Apart from Henry Miller, and one other generationally important writer who comes in as a bizarre punch line, late in the book, Wolfe doesn't drop names. He doesn't situate his writer's life in terms of movements or generations, apart from dividing his future efforts from the drab proletarianism he sees as the Marxist writer's obligated legacy.

That the "labor" young Wolfe found for himself was to create exotic, gussied-up porn novels for the private delectation of gentlemen-collectors, or maybe just one gentleman-collector—talk about your lost worlds!—is a perverse irony of which the book makes its primary meat. Not that the memoir is salacious in any way (in fact, Wolfe can seem prim), but the situation forms a puzzle for the young writer, one the older Wolfe's still captivated by: how did I get here and what could it possibly mean? The book is a portrait too, a poison-pen portrait, of the disappointed, pretentious, and disingenuous publisher/go-between for the porn novels, who Wolfe calls "Barneybill Roster." In his luxuriant and fascinated distaste for this man, Wolfe himself resembles Henry Miller in the grip of one of his long denunciatory ranting episodes, like his great novella *A Devil In Paradise*. This brings us to the matter of the book's style—the weird, cavorting, punning, ruminative, aggrieved and deeply humane style that was Wolfe's own. Like many things in the book, Wolfe's astonishing and peculiar voice is deeply individual, but also historically characteristic. It shows, to me, the way Joyce's influence, but also Henry Miller's, was essential in the development of so much colorful "voice" in mid-century writers as seemingly otherwise unallied, or even divergent, as Mailer, Kerouac, Brautigan, Pynchon, Philip Roth, and so forth. Wolfe, in his novels, never quite rose into that company—his restless and motley enthusiasms may have catapulted him in too many directions, and he may simply not have had the luck or even the desire to apply such fixity to the novelist's art—he's almost a monologuist, a stand-up man, like Lenny Bruce or Lord Buckley. But the fellow who writes, here, "Words are problem-prongs" was a great man of language, and it's a gift to be able to read him again. Wolfe lives.

— JONATHAN LETHEM

MEMOIRS
OF A NOT
ALTOGETHER SHY
PORNOGRAPHER

CONTENTS

To

Thomas Berger

CHAPTER 1

PREPORN/WHAT'S WHAT

You never know exactly why you got hired for a job. You put yourself in the boss's shoes, you think back to what a fine froth of a boy you must have looked when first you bloomed into his office, babyass cheeks, glassied shoes, neatened nails, cutlery creases in the trousers, morning-mown hair, famously faked work record, panache of a free and independently wealthy soul who's totally unpressured and going more for inspiration than occupation—you still don't know.

I did my time in pornography, as this book will tell. In, not for. I didn't print, illustrate, shoot, exhibit, sell, act in, pose for, or slobber over it, I wrote it, one fat and flamy volume after another. It was far and away the best job I'd ever, by age 24–25, found, and I thought myself smiled on by the gods, if smirkingly, and I prayed it might go on forever. But I never could figure out why they saw me as qualified for this line of work, and actually took me on, those being depression times—the soup lines long, and the competition for all jobs tough.

I went on the payroll well after the Munich Umbrella Caper and in the wake of the Maginot Line Erasure.

My stint in the porno business is not to be rated on the Richter Scale with nation mashings, no. But it could be argued, as here I won't bother to argue, that all these items are parts of one picture, and maybe the business wouldn't have been flourishing so, and therefore might not have had an opening for me, if there hadn't been a lot of Munichs and Maginots happening and in the air.

I was a spic and span lad, all right, toothsomely shaved, barbered, shined and suited. A word about that word "suited." I was wearing a hand-tailored suit of velvety cashmere, lined with what appeared to be a fabric woven of filamented platinum. When J. Press delivered it to the Yale student who'd had it made to custom, the cost was something like $250, enough in those days to feed a family for months. When it was sold to me by my friend Attilio, the Western Union messenger boy, days after it had been handed to its original owner, judging by its mint condition, the price had come down to $12.50, suggesting that this fellow was more interested in rapid turnover than heavy return.

I never was told how that choice garment came to the Western Union messenger so soon after it arrived at the student's rooms. I figured it this way. Most likely Attilio had delivered a telegram to the dormitories. Most likely it contained good news, maybe word from a girl up in Vassar that she would be coming to the thé dansant or that she was back in the flow of things after all and not to worry. The student had probably wanted to give my friend a nice tip. There probably wasn't any loose change around. But J. Press cashmere suits? These were all over the place. Attilio, by the way, was always getting tips of suits, camel's-hair coats, wristwatches and bags of golf clubs from the Yale students. He must have brought them lots of cheerful bulletins from Vassar.

So for Pierson Quadrangle I was smashingly well suited. This tells us nothing about why the porno people took one look at me and decided I was similarly suited for them. Porno is not the most nepotistical power pyramid around when it needs new blood, but neither does it bend over backward to make openings for rank beginners. Some ranknesses it doesn't have use for. A few.

. . .

I refuse to believe that luck was the whole or even the main story. I think it was a matter of talent too. I think I had a thousand rare gifts tailormade (like the cashmere suit for the Yale student) for this kind of work and those in charge were smart enough to spot them. What puzzles me is how.

Whether or not I was a writer I could do the things that writers do and that the porno people wanted done. I had the looked-for talents, if not the vocation. The thing that shook me was that my employers could see them when they were nowhere on display.

I thought for a long time they were seeing things and trying to suck me into their hallucination. They did convince me, finally. They paid me good money for my products and everybody knows that money talks louder than words, loud enough sometimes to drown out all other sounds; including those of your own doubts.

A voyage of self-discovery. Shit to the moon and back, we'd better find a way to talk to each other for a change, that isn't language that can get some human facts across it's writing. The sort that people who write do more than writers.

Say I entered into the porno world shapeless, nameless, a blob, a nobody, and came out of it wearing a badge of office that wouldn't rust too fast and could be accepted without giggle by the outside world and, more importantly, me. It wasn't a perilous sailing on the high inner seas, or a long and parched staggering across the baking deserts of alienation to the oasis of healed identity, or a mountain climber's inch-by-inch crawl up the sheer cliffs of inauthenticity to the sunny if austere peaks of inner-direction. No, sir, it didn't have any of the high-rise drama found so regularly in poets' trips and so rarely in real-life ones, it can't be called anything so dramatic as discovery if that means some moment of rosy epiphany dispatched from stage-wise heavens with a Jack Lemmon sense of timing, say, rather, it was a game of slow-motion tag, that's closer. Not all the way there, but close enough. A game I came out of with an identification tag on me that was useful and even comforting.

Not all labels are to be sneered at. The ones that are transparent so they can't be used as masks, and give real names instead of aliases and real addresses you can be sent home to in case you're hit by a truck or get clouded by amnesia, they can do something for you. Get you back where you're known and belong, should you stray. Jog your memory as to your rank and serial number if you get a little hazy, as everybody does at times.

Nobody's ever going to prove himself a writer by doing porno for the commercial market but it's a hell of a good place to go to find out in a hurry if you can write. Some people take correspondence-school exams, some enter limerick contests, some keep composing letters to the editor—I tried my wings at porno, as will unfold here, and wump, I was airborne. If I was lucky to come across the porno barons in their time of need, they had an equally charmed moment, were really on the sunny side of the hedge, the day they found me needy and therefore available to them.

My hat's off to those sharp-eyed people for seeing my stashed merits and drawing my attention to them.

The Eastern Seaboard was overrun with people not so sharp-eyed. Twentieth-Century-Fox said no, absolutely not, neither now nor in this lifetime, to my request for a post in their New York publicity office. Yale University Press, while granting that the subject might with profit be looked into sometime during the next hundred years by somebody who knew something about it, had turned down my project for a study of the tendency in even the most Jacobin of revolutions to lurch on to Thermidor. Over and over Time-Life had informed me that they had no openings I could fill and did not see a time in the next decades when they might have a space that odd-shaped.

That bothered me, since a lot of Yale graduates had the impression that the strongest qualification you could have for a staff job at Time-Life, next to writing sentences backward, was to be a Yale graduate, and I was. (I could also write sentences backward.) I was, of course, also a Jew (more accurately, was called that by others who seemed fairly sure of themselves), the son of a factory worker, and for some years a Trotskyite, moreover a recent member of Trotsky's household staff, traits which very few Yale graduates could boast, especially in that rich mixture, especially those who made their way to Time-Life. If Henry Luce's proconsuls failed to see the virtues in me that the porno people later spotted and bid for, the burden of explanation is on them, not me.

They didn't need me and were determined not to make room for me on all the magazines and newspapers in the Greater New York Metropolitan Area. They'd forged a policy of keeping me at a safe distance from all the Madison Avenue ad agencies, all the radio stations, small independents as well as big network affiliates. When I answered classified ads for trade papers and house organs, ghosting agencies and vanity presses, for jobs composing mail-order brochures, how-to-do manuals, throwaways, comic books, seed catalogues, they scrupulously did not let me hear from them.

There was a terrible depression on, sure, but even national calamity didn't explain why all of American industry, even, as you'll see in a minute, the sectors that made and sold things other than words, had gotten together to lock one man out. Say they did have grounds for suspicion when a Jew, a Yale graduate, a son of the proletariat and a recent Trotsky boarder showed up on their doorsteps all in one person. They still had no right to assume so automatically that the one reason a man so configurated would want to get on their premises was to blow them up—that's stereotyped thinking and not in the American spirit of judging a man by what he can do rather than by what he came out of.

. . .

Most of the economy was still creaking along but one branch of it, war industry, was beginning to buzz. I went to a Manhattan employment agency that specialized in factory work. They said military-hardware plants were looking for technical writers. Was that in or around my line? I informed them that I'd taken a course in engineering drafting at Yale, that the blueprint hadn't been drawn that I couldn't read, that if they wanted the plain facts blueprints were my favorite reading matter.

Next morning I was sitting in the personnel office of a giant electronics firm over in New Jersey, so close to the Secaucus pig farms that you had to keep blowing your nose so they couldn't tell you were holding it.

The manager gave me a blueprint. He wondered if I'd be good enough to point out what I recall as the intermeshing backup reverse-feed alternate-bypass switch-trip voltage-trap breaker circuit. Partial to curves of all types, I put my finger fast on an ingratiating cluster of chicken tracks in a circular pattern.

No, he said, this element wasn't part of the wiring system. Then I got the whole truth: it didn't have *anything* to do with the internals of this piece of apparatus, in fact what I was pointing to was one of the ball-shaped feet the console rested on, the right front one just this side of the tuning dial. The chicken tracks, I now saw, were just the draftsman's indication of the roughened texture given to the foot's plastic surface for a better purchase.

The reference to tuning interested me. What did this dial tune, I asked, a radio set?

Not exactly, he said, this was a control unit for the sonar sounding system for a submarine, useful in locating other subs and traveling torpedoes it would be good to know about. Besides, if I didn't mind his mentioning it, what I now had my finger on wasn't the tuning dial, it was the manufacturer's trademark embossed on the casing.

Letdown, though I tried not to show it. For a quick minute I'd had the happy thought that I might be getting into the radio end of the up-and-coming communications industry, if only in the manufacture of consoles.

The manager asked if at some time in my early life I might have experienced a trauma with liquids, say a swimming accident that left me leery of waters over my head or any reminder of them. He thought this might be a possibility because the suggestion of deep waters seemed to panic me to the point of incoherence, not a good state of mind in which to study electronic circuits for sub-surface vessels nine to five. He wondered if a man with my emotional setup wouldn't have a happier life writing assembly and operating manuals for a talking-doll factory, say, or the people who make Lionel trains.

I was in his palled eyes every inch a writer, that highly specialized type of writer who can't read, and he wanted every inch ejected from his office so it could go back to smelling no worse than Secaucus.

Once, only once, I scared up some action from the help-wanteds.

A publisher was looking for a bright young man wanting to go places, good starting salary, unlimited opportunity, fast advancement. Said bright young man had to have a good plot mind and a knack for snappy dialogue. I knew I had a nimble plot mind, I'd been plotting for years to keep eating and so far wasn't losing weight. I had proof of my knack for snappy dialogue in the number of times I'd been removed from rooms by other people who countered with *their* knack for it. Anyhow, I got off a letter full of unrestrained enthusiasm for myself. A man with a voice to dislocate seismographs called to invite me down for an interview.

The address was on the Lower East Side, just off Delancey Street. It turned out to be a fifth-floor loft that had to have seen better days, otherwise it would have been condemned by the building inspectors the day the roof went on. This I estimated was around the time Peter

Stuyvesant was being fitted for his fourth or fifth pegleg. Possibly Peter was one of the building inspectors. The shredding wooden floor had a lot of holes that looked like knotholes but could have been pegleg perforations. The room was bare and dusty and smelled of printer's ink. From another one to the rear came a labored chinking sound, the sort small printing presses make.

The man who greeted me had no part that was not alarmingly pendulant. All his tissues seemed to have been systematically displaced downward, as in a melt suddenly interrupted, giving the queer impression that forehead was where nose should be, nose where lips, wrists where fingertips, and so on—a landslide of a man. His outstanding feature was his nose, I mean it stood out as though it was ready to leave home and had already taken the first step, yet what I remember most is the lips, they were really in love, constantly kissing and moving apart like a fish's.

There was something fishy about this man all around; if you looked through the window of the big aquarium at Marineland and spotted him lazing along with the carp and manta rays you'd have thought he was at home, except for the matching argyle sweater and socks. I guess he wanted something in him to match, his eyes certainly didn't, one was dramatically blackened. Our conversation went like this:

"How're you at dialogue, kid?"

"I use it all the time."

"We'll start again. How are you at dialogue?"

"I keep up my end."

"Suppose you had to keep up both ends."

"I'd keep them up and play them both against the middle and have one hand free to write some dialogue for you. That's a sample."

"That's a sample. Tell you what to do with that sample. You go make up some more, then take that one and chew it and swallow it before the cops get their hands on it. You'll have ptomaine for a few days but that's better than the electric chair. You think you could tell a whole quick-moving story in dialogue, say 15, 20 lines at the most?"

"If spoken by people with 15 or 20 things to say, sure."

"I see you're a wiseass but I'll tell you, we could have some use for a wiseass. We specialize in fumy stuff around here and maybe with a lot of coaching a hotshot joker like you could come up with a tickle line or two. You acquainted with the Tijuana Bibles?"

"I've heard a lot goes on in those border towns but not much that calls for religious reference works."

"These bibles they don't use, they make, and fast as they come off the presses they go over the border."

"Oh. You're in bibles on the manufacturing end. Well, I could be very useful to you there, I'm not familiar with the Tijuana Bibles but I've read a lot of others and if you want some more bibles written I'm your man. I've made a study of how to get in the right frame of mind to write messianic copy, you think yourself into the position of the Pied Piper, say, or a white hunter, or the soldier who walks point in a patrol, any frontrunner type, then you think a halo around your haircut and start looking upward more than sideways or over your shoulder, and pretty soon some real leadership prose starts—"

"Put the stopper in, kid, you could sprain your tonsils. I'll explain it to you, Tijuana Bible's a nickname for a certain type funnies, like so."

The thing he took from his desk drawer to pass across was a comic book, in full color, on paper that upped five or six grades could have been used for Kleenex. All the characters, I saw as I leafed through, were known American ones, but their words as captured in the balloons oven their heads were all in Spanish, more, they'd all lost their clothes, every last button and string, and were heel-kickingly happy about it, judging from the shrapnel they all were generating—ripples, shimmers, shooting stars, pows, bams and exclamation points, judging further from the interpersonal antics they were engaged in with all portions of

their bared anatomies. These carefree cutups didn't have any problem
relating to others, they were relating in every way the epidermis allows,
variously coupling, tripleting, communing, nosing, mouthing, finger-
ing, backbending, splitting, three-decker-sandwiching. Moon Mullins
was ringmaster for a tightly interwoven daisy chain that Dagwood was
working hard to unravel. (Thanatos forever trying to undo Eros's best
work, where will it end.) Mickey Mouse had had a knockdown fight
with Minnie Mouse. He'd decided to cut all troublemaking females out
of his life and go it on his own. Just now he was exploring the insertive
possibilities in a slab of Swiss cheese while over on the far side, unknown
to him, Minnie was energetically reaping the benefits of his probes. The
Katzenjammer Kids were here revealing themselves as powerhouse-
jammers. The object of their ramrod affections was none other than Little
Orphan Annie. Aided and abetted by a slavering Daddy Warbucks, they
were using that diminutive Brillo-haired lady as a human pincushion,
entering her at every passageway as though to make the point, long
before Sartre, about there being no exits. I took no pleasure in what was
being done to that little slip of a girl though I'd always thought she was
too big for her britches (now missing) and needed to be taken down a
few pegs for her protofascist leanings.

"—by the carload down there," the man was saying. "The art work's
right on the nose, sure, they draw fine, but where they fall down is with
the continuity, see, the talk give and take, their dialogue writers don't
cut the mustard—"

"I've often wondered about that."

"About what?"

"Why any mustard should be cut. Most mustard, if you cut it it's
back in one piece the second you take your knife out, so I don't—"

"You're a smartski. You're a button buster, no doubt about it. All
right, here's where a weisenheimer like you could come in. We take over
the drawings but leave the Spanishy crap out of the balloons and fill

in our own lines in English. We need people to write the lines. Bright young fellows who can turn a phrase without it saying ouch. We can pay for the words pretty good because we get all this art work for free, we lift it from these thieving Mexes so we come out way ahead on the graphics end. You by any chance read Spanish, kid?"

It happened I did, and said so. I'd taken Spanish in high school and applied myself a lot more than I did later in college to engineering drafting. He handed me another comic book, this one with the Spanish balloons intact.

"Here you got a Tijuana original we're right now in process of knocking off. Study the human situation, the dramatic setup, then read the dogass words those chumps put in and you'll see our problem." I studied the human situation. This was a full-page drawing he'd opened the book to, one featuring Popeye the Sailor Man and his girlfriend Olive Oil. They, too, had separated themselves from their clothes and were respectively, balls naked and pudendum naked. (Will Wimlib's study of the sexism permeating our language be complete without a close look into the circumstance that we have all sorts of lively terms for male nudity but none, none at all, for female?) Popeye had insinuated himself into Olive Oil from the rear. His footloose organ was exiting from her mouth to the tune of maybe two feet worth. She looked slack-jawed and crosseyed, understandably; he was puffing absorbedly on his corncob. The exchange they were having went:

POPEYE: Don't you worry about me running short, little cactus flower, in case you need a few more feet I got plenty to spare, I just ate two whole cans of spinach.

OLIVE OYL: You might run through another yard or so if it's not too much trouble, my heart, that should be enough to mop the floor with where you spilled all that spinach juice, you're sure a sloppy eater.

I thought that was damn good writing, if a little wordy, considering the limited possibilities. The text was not prurient and I found it to have redeeming social value. It didn't capitalize in an obvious way on the setup. It didn't try to put any icing on the already rich cake. It showed an original turn of mind, a free-wheeling imagination ready to work against the given materials, which takes courage. I couldn't see how these lines could be improved on but the man for some reason was not satisfied.

"Well, sonny boy, let's see what you can do," he now said. "Take this page. As you see it's a proof of the same drawing but with the balloons blank. O.K., you fill them in. Give us some lines that grow out of this interesting situation and sort of round out the visual picture, tell some kind of a little story. Here's a pencil. Don't rush, I got all afternoon, we'd rather have it right than Tuesday."

My plot mind had retired to the old soldier's home. My knack for snappy dialogue was out on some street-corner selling apples. After several false starts this was the best I could think of to write in those balloons:

POPEYE: Where do you stand on a third term for Franklin D. Roosevelt?

OLIVE OYL: Is that with one "o" or two, I never seem to remember.

The man studied my effort. He studied it for quite some time. He looked out the window and whistled soundlessly, which is said to be an ominous sign. His one black eye appeared to be getting blacker.

"All right," he said. "I'm counting to five. I'd count to one but I'm not primarily a murderer. When I get to five should you not have your smart ass halfway down the stairs it'll be leaving by this window—"

I was in rapid transit. I was never to know just who had given him that black eye but there were all sorts of possibilities, any one of the Tijuana publishers he stole from, any one of the American cartoonists they stole from, any of the bright young men he gave his balloon-inflating tests to, the NAM (for the way he maligned a pillar-of-the-community capitalist like Daddy Warbucks), the American CP (for his demeaning of an honest proletarian like Popeye), come to think of it, even Little Orphan Annie, for assorted indignities.

That man—when I picture him today I see him with argyle hair, too—did not know his own business. He was of the opinion that I lacked the golden touch for porno. Wait till you hear.

Why did I keep going after jobs in the word industry? Well, what are you going to do when non-word industry up and down the land keeps slamming its doors in your face?

One sector of it, the war plants (they were beginning to acquire a more amiable face by being called defense plants) was, if I can put it this way, going great guns. But every time I showed up they had to exert themselves to keep from leveling all those guns at me. My plight had something to do with my being a college graduate. That biographical detail was everywhere, and especially by people in hiring positions, taken to be an ID, not just a clue as to where I'd spent the four years after high school.

They were good Manicheans, those personnel people, last-ditch dualists; where they saw any trace of psyche they wouldn't allow for the merest soupçon of soma. Assuming that college had pumped my head too full, they also took it for granted that my body had somehow gotten lost in the cerebral shuffle and dropped off, and bodies were the items in short supply in their booming defense plants, and over-bred heads they were making short shrift (an organic-food variety of shortbread) of. Language was where I had to get some occupational footing because language was where I was dumped by the industrial body-snatchers.

All the things I've just said are true but not the truth. There had been signs along the way that words and I were a good deal more than kissing cousins, were, indeed, as Damon to Pythias, Sears to Roebuck.

Item. From any number of people who were around at the time, presumably with hands pressed to ears, had come the report that I was speaking whole sentences, loudly and firmly, before my first birthday. I'll save my main comment on this noisy prodigality until later. Here I'll record the one thought that at that time, somewhere along in 1916, I probably didn't have much to say, just the urge to say it well, fully, emphatically—some well-chosen words, no doubt, as to how badly things were already going, and how much worse they could be expected to get, and how this was in no way my doing, indeed went counter to all my plans and objectives, and how the swarms of people out there on all sides whose doing this transparently was were all bobbing and weaving in the most disgusting manner to dodge the responsibility, and how they'd probably be getting away with their who-me act if I hadn't been endowed with the set of tonsils to denounce them and itemize their assorted shoddinesses for the world to shudder at. A few such marginalia from a beginner with lynxy eyes and none of that existential passivity toward the given, the latest form of do-nothing stoicism.

Item. An English teacher in New Haven's Hillhouse High assigned us to write a page or two of description with a warning to avoid trite subjects like trees, snowflakes, flowers, bunny rabbits and sunsets. She seemed to take a particularly dim view of sunsets. I sat down and composed a piece of surging, singing prose about a nightfall to end all nightfalls, a lyrical accolade which was in one part a forerunner of today's psychedelic light shows, in another an anticipation of Hiroshima.

I was determined, you see, to get it established that for such as me no subject was trite, my flashing prose would make the most overdone matters all shiny and new. Somewhere in France at just about that time, and unknown to me, James Joyce was recording his immortal line, "I can do anything I want with words." In this early essay, I see now, I was making the same statement.

My aim, it has to be faced, was not altogether literary. This teacher, by name Nora, was very young, very blond, and luscious, which New England teachers of English at that time were conspicuously not. If I thought I could do anything with words one of the things I most meant to do was make her aware of my presence, pay attention. I thought it worked but I wasn't sure. Nora did give my paper an "A." She also wrote in the margin, "If we have more sunsets like this, sunrises are going to go out of business."

Item. As a result of such virtuosity I became president of the Hillhouse Writers Club, then editor of the class book and the literary annual. I can't remember much about the first honor except that I somehow made use of it to get excused from gym, maybe on the grounds that in born writers the head has so overshadowed and sapped the body as to render it unfit for physical exertions. (A lesson about the literary life I've never forgotten: it can, if you work it right, get you exempted from lifting things, including yourself.)

Unwilling to compromise on quality, I undertook to fill the pages of the literary magazine with the best prose around, my own. My first appearances in print were in this annual. One item was an essay entitled "On Being Lazy," a treatise elaborating on all the delights of not working, designed, clearly, to annoy the many Yankee partisans of the work ethic who presided over the school. Another contribution was a short story about a gifted young student who has to work nights in a factory. He's in a state of exhaustion. One night he sinks down on a comfortable leather belt to take a catnap, whereupon the belt is somehow activated to feed him into a grinding machine. The factory was pretty much modeled after the one my father worked in, and the high-potential young student had a variety of things in common with me, indicating, I suppose, how far back my paranoia about American industrialization took hold.

This story was by all standards a piece of proletarian literature, though the term had not yet come into currency. Two short years later writers by the hundreds had shed their Brooks Brothers gabardines for blue denim work shirts and the Proletarian Novel was swamping the American literary scene. Nowhere, however, in that massive body of workingclass literature will you find one word acknowledging the high-school junior who sparked the movement. But that's always the fate of the frontrunner. No prophet is so scorned in his own country as the one whose pioneering work is taken over lock, stock and barrel by his plagiaristic countrymen.

I contented myself with the knowledge that of the 100 or so prole-cult novels that flooded the bookstalls few came up to the literary level of my early effort, and practically none added anything to my innocent-victim thematization of the contest between nice young lads and carnivorous old free-enterprise machines.

(That wasn't meant cynically. I'm still of the opinion that our means of production are really consumers, savage meat-eaters, even, I would now add, when the social relations of production have been drastically changed—in form, anyhow. It has dawned on me, though, that young fellows who try to catch 40 winks on a shaft-driven transmission belt, no matter how worthy and no matter how tired, are, to put it mildly, mastication-prone.)

Item. There was a national essay contest for high school seniors. I entered it and won it. My subject, since I was oriented toward science to get away from letters, rather, from the kinds of people who usually teach letters, was, the future of soil-conditioners in American farming. Or, "Whither Fertilizers?" Something in that line. I made up a joke about this contest—maybe you can't make a silk purse out of a sow's ear but you sure can get together a big pile of horseshit and come up with a prizewinning essay.

I was breathing hard in anticipation of some cold, hard cash. What they handed me was a leather-bound commemorative volume honoring a dean at Harvard who'd been helpful to several generations of incipient writers when they were undergraduates, among them John Dos Passos. The dean's name was Riggs, or Briggs, or Griggs. I'm pretty sure it wasn't Tetrazzini. I've never read that book. Not that I had anything against this dean—what put me off was that they should give me payment in kind, instead of the kind payment of money.

It simply did not make sense, in or out of the Great Depression, to reward words with words. This seemed to imply that the most important thing for an incipient writer to do was read, not eat. That committee on awards turned its collective back on the strong possibility that neither reading nor writing was going to be feasible for me if I suffered from malnutrition, and in those days an awful lot of people, including writers both incipient and well-launched, were doing just that.

I don't know if that copy of the commemorative volume is still around. Maybe it's buried in a carton in my brother's cellar outside New Haven, I haven't seen it in decades. I rather wish I had it now, I'd like to read about Dean Riggs, or Briggs. I understand he was very nice to John Dos Passos. For some years I've been trying to be nice to incipient writers at UCLA and I'd be interested to see how our techniques compare.

Item. So we can say that at 15 I was by any definition an incipient, as well as malnourished, writer. Further proof came in my first year at Yale when I won some sort of freshman essay contest. My subject this time was the development of the esthetic of realism, which my survey traced, hastily and in big jumps, from the early cave drawings to Norman Rockwell and Raymond Chandler.

This time, too, I got not a penny, just a voucher entitling me to $25 worth of books at Whitlock's Book Store. I pleaded with the people at Whitlock's to convert that useless piece of paper to negotiable currency but those incorruptible Yankees—whose enthusiasm for steady habits (Connecticut had way back nicknamed itself "The Land of Steady Habits") did not seem to extend to eating—wouldn't hear of it. I finally took my payment in Modern Library novels, sat up several nights devouring them two or three at a time, there being little else around to devour, then sold them for whatever I could get. With the proceeds I bought a meal ticket at the Greek's on Chapel Street, where they offered a marvelous thick and crusty breaded veal cutlet drowned in tomato sauce with a heap of spaghetti and two fat buttered rolls for 35 cents.

For once, however devious the operation, I'd managed to convert award-winning words into food, and you will not mistake my meaning when I say it whetted my appetite.

Item. Words finally did bring in some moneys at college. With my good friend Johnny Dorsey I started a ghosting agency for people like football players who had no time to write essays and term papers and who in any case had probably so sapped their heads by overnourishing their bodies that they couldn't write anything. (If the Manicheans have at times kept me from employment, at other times they've made profitable work for me.) We charged four dollars a page if the client was satisfied to squeak by, but hiked the price to six if he wanted a guaranteed "B" or better.

I must say that when we gave a grade guarantee we stood behind our product and we never missed. This can be interpreted in a couple of ways. It might mean that we were incredibly talented writers. It may, on the other hand, suggest that Johnny Dorsey and I knew a lot of the young reading assistants who graded papers for the professors, were alert to their crochets, and got good at assessing their tastes. For a couple of years there Johnny and I ate well at the Greek's, and any number of varsity members did their double-shift wingbacks at the Yale Bowl with an easy mind.

Item. After some pointless months in the Yale Graduate School I quit to take a teaching job in a school for women trade unionists which operated on the Bryn Mawr campus during the summers. Here I reached new heights of eloquence, though of the oral rather than written order, particularly when I addressed the noontime assembly on current happenings around the world.

One noon I lectured forcefully as to why the political tensions now mounting in Paris would have to explode with a military bid for power by the labor-hating fascists in the Croix de Feu. Two days after I made my categorical prediction there was a fascist uprising, Francisco Franco's in Spain. I quickly appeared before the assembly again to announce that my analysis of the class struggle in Europe had been absolutely right but that I'd gotten the country wrong, that was all. I overwhelmed these girls the first time and I overwhelmed them equally the second without shifting any essential gears.

Right after that I came down with a bad case of gastric poisoning and had to spend several days in the campus infirmary. Nobody visited me on my bed of pain to crow over what happens when a man has to eat his words (I thought I'd avoided that rather neatly) but oh, how my stomach hurt.

Item. After Bryn Mawr I hung around New York for a time producing for the Trotskyite publications (*The Militant* and *The New International*) words covering the Spanish Civil War, the one I'd misplaced geographically, plus book reviews and an article or two. I discovered that the best way to report any overseas war is to sit in a Greenwich Village room and redo the dispatches of the *New York Times* correspondents who are required by their task-master bosses to make personal appearances at the fronts. (The approach I picked up in this period was to stand me in good stead during World War II, in which I avoided personal appearances on a wide variety of fronts.) The technique is simple, you keep the facts cabled home by the front-line reporters, since you don't have any of your own to substitute for them, and just correct their blurred vision with Bolshevik-Leninist bifocals.

One piece I did for *The New International* was an exhaustive study of the theoretical errors vitiating all schools of criminology past and present. The thematic burden of this analysis was that the criminal in capitalist society is simply a revolutionary who through an oversight has neglected to join a Marxist party and coordinate his rebelliousness with other people's. It beats me how I happened to wander into the field of crime and its causes. It could be that more of the Puritan work ethic had seeped into my head than I realized and prolonged unemployment was making me feel like a criminal. Certainly writing articles on the unconscious politics of footpads and second-story men wasn't giving me any sense of gainful employment, whereas the criminal welcomes any opportunity to present himself as a politician—it's a promotion, though a slight one.

(This is in no way to make light of the current politicalization of our prison populations. That is progress all around. But if we want to keep our bearings, particularly those of us on the left, we'd better see the difference between prisoners who take to politics in a mighty striving for mind expansion and those—their numbers may not be negligible—who reach for politics as a handy, because fashionable, mask.)

I feel now that this analysis done in 1938 was defective in key respects. It seems to give less than the full story about a number of disorderly and impatient types, from the Boston Strangler to Charles Manson. I'm relieved, in retrospect, that my article did not bring a rush of recruits to the Socialist Workers Party from the chronic lawbreaking strata—if the Stranglers and Mansons ever decide to flock to a leftwing movement their comrades will have to put on bulletproof vests and hire bodyguards to see them home from meetings.

My real point is that the words I was turning out in this period, if totally wrong, were uniformly effective. My comrades thanked me many times for setting them straight on both the Spanish Civil War (which they never knew I had located in France) and the blind alleys all criminologists but me had gotten themselves into.

Item. In the course of time I was invited to join Trotsky's small secretarial and household staff in Mexico, where he'd received asylum after being expelled from Norway by Trygve Lie's whimsically and skittishly socialist government. This was another nice, if not in any way remunerative, recognition of my dexterity with words—they needed somebody who knew English, could translate documents from French and German, prepare news releases and in general handle the press. It was clear to me that Albie Booth (star quarterback and captain of the Yale football team when I was in school) would not have qualified for this job, so it looked like my exemptions from gym had not been in vain. I won't dwell on my literary activities during this year in Mexico because, although my output was high, its form was minor: mostly postcards.

Item. When I got back from Mexico I was taken on by the Connecticut WPA Writers Project to head a research and writing team that was said to be preparing an ethnic study of the peoples of Connecticut for ultimate publication by the Yale University Press. More about this job later. I'll just point out here that I would never have gotten it if I hadn't appeared to the WPA bureaucrats as a writer, at least somebody who could write, and, further, if a good friend of mine hadn't happened to be doing the hiring. This appointment would have seemed sure proof of my literary calling if I hadn't observed, right after reporting for work, that Albie Booth could just as well have wangled the job and passed unnoticed no matter how much writing he didn't do, all the people present being too drunk or too hung-over to check on anything but the Alka-Seltzer.

I elected to do my main research in Yale's Sterling Library, where if the ethnic components of the Connecticut population were not highly visible the furniture was at least softly upholstered. I spent most of those 18 months sleeping in the splendid sofas of the Linonia & Brothers Reading Room. It was in this vaulted chamber, soothingly reminiscent of the Union League Club, that one day I picked up an avantgarde magazine from Paris and read Joyce's haunting sentence, "I can do anything I want with words."

My reaction to that chesty line should be recorded. I thought, here I am, ready, willing and able to do anything *anybody* wants with my words so long as they'll pay modestly for them . . . dying to get some words out tailored to the needs and interests of some market, any market at all . . . my full literary equipment is there on the block, and they're all too busy reaching for the Alka-Seltzer to take me up on it, make a bid, draw some guidelines, notice me at all.

You might say that under the circumstances, since I was drawing a paycheck every week—nothing great but enough to eat on—I might have used my great gobs of free time to do something I wanted with my unemployed words. But that was just the trouble. There was nothing I wanted to do with them, nothing I dared to do, except put them up for sale and lament the absence of buyers.

One more item, this going back to the Mexican days, and you'll have the background picture.

It wasn't a soft life we had in that broken-down villa in Coyoacán, then a backwash village outside Mexico City. It was, all in all, a radical departure from the sculpted panels and puffy pillows of Linonia & Brothers. We lived in a one-story house built around the thee sides of a patio, all of the single-file rooms opening on the internal garden. There was no heating system. When the panes of the French doors got broken they didn't get fixed. It turns cold nights on the Mexico City plateau, up 7,500 feet. You look to the snow peaks of Popocatepetl and you feel that snow in your bones, in your teeth.

We were often up nights in that drafty, unheated place, feeling the Popo snows. We had to be. In addition to the day's chores of paper work and seeing to security we, the members of the secretariat, kept a rotating guard shift through the night. There were three of us, a Frenchman, a Czech, and myself. *That* meant we split the night into three watches, early, middle, and late. That meant that every third night I could expect to be up through the most miserable hours from midnight to almost dawn, huddled in a soldier's ratty fur wraparound left over from Red Army days, blowing on my fingers, trying not to let the cold blow my mind.

Lots of nights I sat in the dining room at the 20-foot-long lemon-yellow wooden table that we used at one end for eating, at the other for our typewriters and papers, taking apart the Luger I'd been issued, then putting it together. I had no strong interest in the insides of a gun, though I'd never examined them closely before. The idea was to have some project, focus the head, keep busy. The cold wouldn't go away but it could, with strategy, he banished for periods to the outskirts of mind. I had to use my fingers somehow. I couldn't think of anything to do with them at the typewriter, having written all my postcards hours before and having no nobler literary projects in mind. I broke that Luger down till it couldn't be reduced any further except with an acetylene torch. Night after night I did this, getting it all apart, then getting it all together.

Once, very late, the Old Man came through the dining room on his way to the bathroom, and saw me with parts of the gun in my hands and more parts spread on the table. He was always alert to how the young people around him behaved with weapons, afraid that their tendencies to kid around and show off might make them careless.

His hands-off style wouldn't allow him any tone of chiding or lecture. He just said quietly and seriously, "You know, in the Revolution we lost more people than the enemy could claim credit for. Many young comrades killed themselves with their own guns and suicide was very far from their minds."

I said, "You don't have to worry about me, L.D., I always take the clip out and make sure the chamber's empty, there's no danger here."

I couldn't detail for him all the ways in which there was no danger. Minutes before he'd appeared, just as I was beginning to fit the barrel back into its housing, there'd been a whiffing noise and I'd watched some spring from the firing mechanism fly out the French doors. I was vague as to the spring's location in the innards of the gun and in the dark as to its function. But wherever it operated and whatever it did, I knew it was important. Just before the Old Man came in I'd proved to my satisfaction that the gun would not fire without this obscure coil. The perfect gun, you might say, for Russian roulette.

The Luger was never to fire again. That night, and many cold nights after that, I spent hours on my hands and knees around the cactus and pieces of Aztec statuary in the patio, looking for the spring. It was nowhere to be found.

I really don't want to talk about the state of our weaponry in Coyoacán. I'm simply drawing your attention to the fact that in that cold room on those cold nights I had to get my hands working at something. Since guns wouldn't do it for me indefinitely, sooner or later I had to face the fact that there was another piece of apparatus present whose springs wouldn't take flight so readily—a typewriter. And so began some writing on my nights of vigil because there was nothing else available to keep me from climbing the walls, which were black with tarantulas.

It was hard to get started. If in those days there was any relationship between me and words it was one in which we warily circled each other, unable to come together, unable to break it off and go our separate ways. As a result I was a little stiff with the writers who came visiting at our house. There were many—Jim Farrell, who was later my good and helpful friend, Michael Blankfort (later to be president of the Hollywood Writers' Guild, currently my neighbor in the Beverly Hills rat trap where I have my office, and am writing these notes), Herb Solow and Johnny Macdonald (both of whom wound up as editors on *Fortune*), Suzanne LaFollette, Benjamin Stolberg, Charles Rumford Walker, on and on. I felt a bit guilty to be presented to them as someone with a political identity, guiltier yet because my deepest urges were toward writing and I couldn't say a word about them. What was there to say? That I read like a demon? That I knew a shitpile of novels? What does such information communicate about a man except that he's an insomniac, and pretty anti-social to boot?

There was my problem. The fancy name for it these days is identity crisis—in those simpler times all we had to say about this shaky condition was, Shit or get off the pot. I had to appear as, and go through the motions of, a politico, at which I really wasn't very good, mainly I just repeated other people's phrases. I had to keep under cover those appetites and curiosities about which I could really hold forth because that's all I'd ever done about them, hold forth, not work with or build on. As a result I was invisible. When later my good friend Ralph Ellison brought out his novel *Invisible Man* I knew exactly what he was talking about, though my own long bout with invisibility had taken place in a nonracial context.

But, you know, writers were in a certain sense the niggers of the left movements. These days all groups that feel set upon like to apply to themselves the labels of the oppressed black—students talk about being treated like niggers, as being the Harlem of the young, and so on. Writers had plenty of reason to see themselves that way in revolutionary circles. They were looked down upon as cafeteria intellectuals, parlor activists, undisciplined and irresponsible bohemians. They were defined as incorrigibly petty-bourgeois, constantly slapped in the face with their non-prolism. In all respects that counted they were held to be inferior people who if they had any loyalty to the cause of social overhauling at all would allow their names and public weights to be used without ever presuming to question the hallowed fulltime politicos who used them. This anti-egghead arrogance was most vicious in Stalinist circles but it was by no means unknown among certain Trotskyites.

For example. Jim Cannon was the titular head of the tiny Trotskyite movement in those days. He had plenty of reason to feel grateful to Suzanne LaFollette. Suzanne was not in any sense a Trotskyite but she'd been sufficiently repulsed by the Moscow Trials to take an energetic lead in organizing what became known as the John Dewey Commission of Inquiry into the Moscow Trials. That Commission had spent weeks interrogating Trotsky in Coyoacán. (One of the main reasons I'd been sent to Mexico was to help prepare documents for these hearings.) Then it had returned to New York to prepare its two-volume report, which exonerated Trotsky from all charges made against him and established the Trials as complete judicial frame-ups. This was an enormous service to Trotsky and his followers, one they could never have performed for themselves. I had come back to New York to help Suzanne get the documents and verbatim transcripts in order for the publishers, Harpers.

Although spending most of my time with Suzanne, once in a while I ran into Jim Cannon. He was always more curious than I thought he had any right to be about what was going on with Suzanne and her associates from minute to minute. The Commission's Report was getting put together, it was going to clear Trotsky and indict the Stalinists, that was all Cannon had any call to be concerned about, but his questions didn't end there. I sensed he was irked that a group of brainy people working on matters vital to him were beyond his control.

At one point he cornered me to insist that a certain formulation in the Report be worded in a certain way. There was no world-shaking principle involved, it really didn't matter one way or the other, but I saw he was dead serious about this, meant it as a test of strength. When I next saw Suzanne LaFollette I passed on Cannon's views without comment. Suzanne was smart enough to see that the issue was trivial in itself and that Cannon was simply trying to flex his bureaucratic muscles a bit with the heavy heads. She gave me a message for Cannon which I took some pleasure in delivering: under no circumstances would the passage in the Report be worded his way, further, he was to lay off, the Commission was in no sense an arm of the Trotsky party and did not intend to let itself be so used.

Cannon's craggy face clouded over when I repeated Suzanne's words. His cheeks got very red. His tight lips moved just enough to say, "Those pigfuckers."

I thought of a man capable of calling literary people pigfuckers because they didn't accept total dictation from him, of such a man rising to the top position in a new workers' state. I thought of how intellectuals might fare under his short-tempered regime. (Workers too.) I was very sure I'd be in bad trouble if I were among those intellectuals. This was not speculation. We'd had 10 years of Stalinism in Russia. We'd seen a lot of valuable writers disappear into Siberia, from Victor Serge to Isaac Babel. (Serge was to appear again but not Babel.) And many others of no proven value, many not even visible, like me.

So—I was ashamed of the incipient writer in me on several interlocking grounds. On the one hand, because he wasn't getting anything done, he was being carefully sat on. On the other, because such an inner man, if he could get out, would not be an object of admiration in my circle of activists. I couldn't get him in the open, I was afraid of the hoots and catcalls he'd be greeted with if I did. Damned if you do and damned if you don't.

But he wasn't to be sat on entirely. It was too damned cold in that dining room in Coyoacán. I huddled there in the small hours with my detriggered Luger and began to write a short story. A young fellow is opening his eyes in a bare room. As they focus he begins to study the cracks and flakes on the ceiling. Lying on his cot, he traces all sorts of significant items on that dingy, crumbing rectangle.

As I remember I did a stunning job of bringing that decaying ceiling all the way to life. Cosmic overtones were discovered in the expanse of sooty plaster, proliferating symbols in each irregularity, each flyspeck. I wrote the opening pages of this story, then wrote them over, then recast them a third time, and that was just warm-up. The trouble was I couldn't get *past* that ceiling.

I know exactly why I lingered so. Once I'd exhausted the potential of that ceiling, milked it of all its meaning, I would have to go on to other matters, look into my main people, get a situation set up and some sort of story going, initiate some action—and I didn't have the least idea where to go once I left the ceiling and came down to earth.

The writing was more or less matchless. I think I'm safe in saying that the literature of the Western world contains few passages about ceilings so impactful. Writers know that some of their best writing gets done in this static mood, this kind of endless lingering over a trifle, inspired by a dread, really, of moving along, of plunging in. Far easier to stay put, meander, blow trivia up into larger—and more inert—than life elements.

This sort of writing is the literary equivalent of jogging in one place. Its source, I will insist, is a serious blockage, an inability to carry a project through to the end, see the people, grasp their situations, develop an interactive dynamic between them, get them into motion toward some culminative finale or at least some turning-point. The incapacity to move forward can generate a lot of sideways crawling.

I'm saying, in short, that a great deal of eloquent prose, at times extremely effective, is triggered by a massive writing block. So much for the simple souls who are undialectical enough to think that the writer who's dammed up doesn't produce words. Look at Hemingway. He made a whole new kind of literature, think of it what you will, out of the minimality that comes from chronic clogging. He made stoppage into a style. That's not to say that Thomas Wolfe was not a torrential bore.

So there were my endlessly rewritten pages about the forever disintegrating ceiling as observed inch by inch by the permanently immovable young man, all of them buried under piles of newspaper clippings and press releases about the Moscow Dials. And Eleanor Clark came visiting.

Eleanor (now, and for many years past, Robert Penn Warren's wife) was very young but already beginning to be known as a writer of talent. She was aside from that an editor at Macmillan's—all in all a figure from the literary world. She and the Czech were rummaging in the papers on the work table one afternoon when I was off in town trying to find out how many limonadas con tequila I could wash down with limonada con tequila. They found those pages about the ceiling and were struck by their lack of connection with the Moscow Trials or any-thing else this household was concerned with.

Thinking it over today, I suspect they liked the writing, though it gave no indication of going anywhere. Chiefly what impressed them was the painstaking evocation of a moribund ceiling. It was a whole new note in literature. Recent fiction had tended to slight ceilings, being fix-ated on sidewalks and gutters. When I met them later for a drink they asked a natural question—had I written those pages?

With the rapidity of a tic, a reflex, hand flying from hot stove, I said—no, what pages were they talking about? They described the pages. I said I'd never heard of them and had no idea where they might have come from.

When a grown man is accused of unzipping his fly in a kindergarten playground, if even the thought of so doing has crossed his mind once or twice, he will loudly and hastily deny it. It was in similar spirit that I washed my hands of any responsibility for those pages. The thing about furtive writers is that it is hard for them to make a clean breast of it in public, they being addicts of the dirty breast.

It was slashingly clear from the circumstances in our household that nobody else with access to our premises could have written those pages and deposited them on the dining-room table. A fair number of people in our circles, no doubt, had spent time in close proximity to ceilings of this order of decrepitude, but I was the only one who might be trying to recapture them on paper.

Eleanor was a sensitive and sensible girl. She understood without more being said that it was of burning importance to me to disown my words, though she couldn't have guessed at all the complicated emotions that led me to it. She changed the subject.

The minute I got back to the house that night I burned the pages. It's really too bad. That was a most superior rendition of a decomposing ceiling; I've never seen it equaled. I'm sure I could make good use of it in this or that book, now that I'm putting my name on my words. No matter what kind of story you're writing there's bound to be a ceiling in it somewhere, or room to work one in.

You're probably confused about the time element here. That would be because I am. This has been coming out in a jumble for the simple reason that that's how it came in, that's how the years happened and looked. I'm trying to give the facts as they showed up, in all their sprawl, not a writer's tidy-up, which always calls attention to the tidier and slights or distorts the facts.

There was no continuity in our lives in those days, just a stewing around with now this bobbing to the surface, now that—that's my point. If you want the truth I don't remember the porno months in the context of the calendar at all. They don't fit into the slot after Munich and Maginot, no, they stick in my head as the time I wasn't rolling my own. In those years we used to come together in somebody's room with several of those devices for rolling cigarettes out of cheap bulk tobacco, and play poker and roll, talk politics and roll, drink and roll, sometimes just smoke and roll. When I got into porno I gave up these homemades because I had enough money for store-boughts. During my porno months I was nice to myself, I treated myself to Murads and Melachrinos, so to me porno will always have the faintly musky odor of exotic Turkish tobaccos, will, as a matter of fact, suggest shapes oval rather than round.

Art makes order out of chaos, do they still teach that hogwash in the schools? It's liars who give order to chaos, then go around calling themselves artists and in this way give art a bad name. Here high up on their cerebral peaks are all the artists sifting and sorting out the facts and pasting them together any old way to show how neat it all is and how they're at the controls of the whole works, and there under their feet the facts go on tumulting and pitching them on their asses over and over, and what's the whole demonstration worth? Don't tell me the real artists are tidiers. Céline is in the grand spatter business. Henry Miller spatters too, though a good part of the time by plan, by program, and that's his tension. Hemingway held it all in his tight hand and pretended it was one packed ball of wax till the end, then his true spewing self came out and he spattered all right, spattered all his order-making brains over the living room, and the lie of having it all together was done for he arrived at the moment of going at his authenticity, his one moment of truth. When do you see Dostoevsky laying out his reality with a T-square?

No, the ones who want to make a big display of how they master facts through words, all they master most of the time is words. The words tend to get in the way of the facts. The words get to be lies because they don't reflect and illuminate the runaway facts, they conceal them. The worst thing about an art that's forever making packaged sense out of the world is that it leaves no room for the randomizing senselessness that pervades most of the daily scene. In Hemingway's neat print world held together and presided over by the code of grace under pressure there's just no room for graceless berserkers who with enough pressure blow their heads off—such unstyled people are even made fun of, and often are Jews.

What a new and exhilarating art we'd come to, finally, if artists set out to feature the amuckness of the world instead of their own imposed and irrelevant designs—an art that faced the simple roughhouse facts and told the plain ramble-scramble truth—revolutionary! This is by way of saying that I mean to tell this story, no world-shaker, I admit, I insist, in the hit or miss way it happened. If at times I seem to go everywhichway, well, that's pretty much how things were going back there at the tail-end of the rampageous Thirties, without let-up, around the clock, and it seems to me all that needs recounting, not rendering.

I hope I've shown you in these introductory words where I was before porno—nowhere. On the outer limits of all matters. Limbo. Beyond any pale you care to name. You will appreciate that porno came into my life not as a pardon or commutation of sentence, nothing that histrionic, but at least as an opportunity to discharge some words from that mass of language pent up and squirming in me, a needed bleeding in the last skinny nick of time.

It had to appear to me as a bountiful gift from the gods I did not believe in. I clutched at it as the drowning man at a cabin cruiser, one well stocked with supplies and, more important still, equipped with a powerful shortwave radio.

Somebody out there in the wide, wide world actually wanted me to write something. They wanted my words. They were more than ready to pay me for them.

I'd be eating, the precondition for writing. I would write, the only way I knew to eat. Words and money had finally been introduced to each other in my life and made partners in my head.

I suddenly felt wanted. Not, for once, by the authorities; they assuredly were much too busy looking for my employers.

I'm going to stop calling it porno. The vowel ending makes the stuff sound Italian or Spanish, something foreign and a little greasy, an importation, which is far from the facts. Without question this country has had its own homegrown or homespun pornography as long as it's had a Constitution, very likely as long as it's had printing presses.

I suspect that the Puritan fathers, by emphasizing how many things in this world were pornographic either in quality or potential, succeeded in calling the public's attention to this whole area of life. There's nothing like a negative endorsement from the clergy to get the public interested, stir up a good word of mouth, as they say in PR, when you're introducing a new product a bumrapping from a churchman is worth more than any special introductory offer, 30-day trial with no obligation to buy, money-back guarantee, 5,000 Blue Chip stamps for bonus, entry in the milliondollar sweepstakes with each box top—look how a Boston banning used to make any sappy book into a bestseller.

From here on in I'll call it porn. Porn has a very American ring to it. It sounds a little like corn and a little like pone, and cornpone's about as American as mom's apple pie, a product, by the way, which by a sort of backlash effect has made a lot of Americans run toward pornography pretty much for the same reason that the diabetic runs from sugar.

You see, then, what I've been trying to do in these opening pages, give you some picture of me preporn, preborn.

The setting: I was dividing my time between New York and New Haven (my home town, if I haven't made that clear). I'd be unemployed in New York for a while. I'd get out on the Boston Post Road and hitch a ride east. I'd be unemployed in New Haven for a time. I'd get out on the Boston Post Road and hitch a ride going west. I rolled a lot of homemades in both towns, maybe a few more in New Haven because I had my family there, and there were trees to walk under, and snow wasn't processed into a slushy gray muck 10 minutes after it fell. Then through some fluke I got a job in a factory up in Bridgeport. Then this girl Bettina wrote me from the Village. She'd run into this woman named something like Zoma or Zo-Zo. Zoma or Zo-Zo knew this fellow named Barneybill who had some things going. If I wanted to come down and meet Zo-Zo in order to get to meet Barneybill I might, it was just possible—read on, you'll find out how it all happened, how from the very pyorrheic jaws of crisis I snatched the loose tooth of identity. . . .

This is going to be hard, I feel myself tensing up, I'm not used to writing about myself. Not that I'm coy, I just get restless looking at the same thing day in, day out. I've got a short attention span, which discourages autobiography.

Some writers write nothing but successive editions of their autobi-ographies in various fake guises, telling even more lies than straight autobiographers do. I can't put myself in that self-circling frame of mind and don't warm up to people who do. (Céline excepted. Céline looks so hard and deep into his insides, he sees the whole damn world deposited there.) A page sprinkled with first-person pronouns puts me off. People whose subject is forever themselves seem to me to be operating under two handicaps, one, that they suffer from tunnel vision, two, that they don't have much to say, a characteristic of tunnel workers. On their horizons their own persons bulk so large as to blot out the world about, and without a not-me surround to point up where they end and the impersonal materials begin they can't even see themselves, their one subject. Writers who are eternally running round and round inside their own heads and recording each lap for posterity will eventually tamp down and deaden major portions of their brains, that delicate stuff isn't built to take a heavy foot traffic, it's there to be used, not trampled on.

Paradox: the more you comb through your insides the less you come up with to write about. Besides, there's more to look at out there than in here, and it's less fogged over. You've got to learn more from three billion people than from one, it's a matter of arithmetic. Again, it's the writers who keep their eyes on the world about who tell us the most about themselves. What's a man after all but his vision? Blinders and all? What's he going to convey to us about his vision if he keeps it trained on his own insides, which he'll never see? But I suppose every writer has to do this me-myself-and-I softshoe one time out, to show how versatile he is and that he hasn't got two left feet.

Stay with me, I'll get the hang of it. I think we can begin. . . .

CHAPTER 2

OLD BLUE

New Haven. Say it again, New Haven. No haven. No haven at all. No haven first of all from New Haven.

That gangling thin-muscled mopy perennial adolescent of a town, head cozied on West Rock, knees hooked over East Rock, groggy from too many pizzas and steamed clams, slow to grow up or get up, fuzz of Gothic spires at its middle for an uncordial pubic hair. The flinty headquarters, made up of unused bell towers and unnoticed turrets, would of course be the University, which is in the business of quartering heads.

The municipality is built around and revolves around, snaps to the orders from, dances to the tune of, Old Blue. There under the catastrophically out of place Olde Englishe steeples and parapets is the area's nerve-center. Its old brain and its new brain too. Should you not feel at home around seats of learning there's no place for you to sit down.

Spilled out there on scummed Long Island Sound east of Bridgeport with its foundries and aircraft plants, west of New London with its submarine yards, south of Hartford with its insurance companies and state government offices, New Haven has no great factory, no teeming naval base, no major business at all but Yale. Yale is the focus of its enterprise as of its anatomy.

It's not good for a town to be appendage to a center of higher learning. The high visibility and vast wingspread of the school make it look as though there's nothing lofting in life but learning. The impression is given that heads are what count, cultivated ones (that is, those *that can* afford cultivation), and bodies are of value chiefly to help the cultivation along. In practice that means town, the body, gets the menial chores done, the brawn and leg labor, so gown, the soaring head, can be free to ideate. Those who do the hauling and hammering in the neighborhood can't help feeling that worthiness lives elsewhere than in them, somewhere around the thrusting filigrees of stone they see only from a distance when they look up from their hand work.

New Haven is an extravagantly and doggedly Manichean community—its prime industry is the care and feeding of heads. The body that needs care and feeding too will find itself a shutout or a reject around here; at least it did back in the Depression, when bodies were often more pauperized than minds.

The University dominates all of the city's downtown, rolling out for blocks both west and north from the central Green, taking up precious acres that otherwise would be packed with houses, stores, factories and hangouts. The University therefore sidetracks or stops cold the natural laws of urban development.

We know what those laws are now, we've been learning. Left to unfold by its internal logic, the inner city has to suck all the pariahs and human dregs unto itself, all the expendables in the local population, while those with money and standing and mobility pack up and entrain for the outskirts, hoping they can keep a few steps ahead of the core's overbrimming blight.

The overlooked and shoved aside can't fulfill their urban destiny in New Haven. They can't crowd into the city's hub, can't take over all the way as they do in other places, even when the fugitives from their massing presence take off. The University does not encourage invasions of overwhelmingly body people into the precincts of the cultivated heads.

Universities should by rights be on the outer edges of cities, to point up the peripheral place of mind in a body-focused culture. In New Haven the University's focal position suggests a role for the intellect and the spirit which they don't truly have in the real world, the world just outside the campus; and memorializes the fiction by Gothically filling land that by natural law should be ghetto, a body-terrorized place.

It can't eliminate ghetto. It is all but ringed by ghetto. Ghetto touches Yale to the northwest and to the southeast. Ghetto not only abuts it, it pushes hard against it. The University pushes back with all its Gothic bulk.

To the west the body-obsessed hordes from the Dixwell-Ashmun ghetto are fended off by the Sterling Memorial Library, the Payne Whitney Gymnasium, the Law School, $50 million worth of stone from another, meaning-drained time. To the south the swarms from the Grand Avenue ghetto are kept out by the Hospital, the Medical School, the Institute of Human Relations. Proving, it would seem, that even those departments of the University concerned with the human body are more concerned with some bodies than with others, concretely, with the bodies of the well-off, which need the least attention.

The bodies of academics get the very best care in the academic world, though incidentally to the care of mind. The bodies that fill the ghettos on two spilling sides, though infinitely needful of all the kinds of attention there are, both physical and mental, are major threats to an institution that fosters the cultivated life of the mind. They have to be repelled—by the great stone edifices devoted to medical science, physical education, the law, human relations, etc.

This disfiguring of town by gown, this enthroning of mind values over a whole community with an accompanying downgrading of the rest of the human corpus, may not be as apparent in New Haven today as it was in the early and middle thirties when I was in college. But neither has it been altogether corrected. That would take a physical removal of the University, if not its junking.

Consider that Dick Lee went on from his job as publicity man for Yale to become the long-term mayor of New Haven. For his bold programs of urban redevelopment, which gave an entirely new face to the downtown areas, he won national and even international acclaim. In his extensive rebuilding he was always mindful of the interests of Yale and the local businesses affected, but his renewal specialists couldn't stop to worry about alternate housing and other community facilities for all the blacks displaced from the razed ghetto areas; there isn't enough money in federal allotments to cover everything; there have to be priorities in city planning; profile comes before people. As a result, New Haven, that backwash to the nation's tumults, that hive of tweedy nonchalance and buttondown good manners, got her ghetto riots when Detroit and Newark got theirs. It got its Bobby Seale trial, its Black Panther convocations. The spires and parapets remain firmly rooted in the 15th century but the people living in their shadows finally slammed into the 20th, with torches and guns.

When they built those Gothic mausoleums to entomb a past that was never really our past, back there before the Depression, the University's architects ran into a problem—the plaster they used on the internal walls appeared spankingly new, and therefore wrong. They hit upon a remedy, they mixed a soot of bone dust and other powders in with the plaster, to give a surface that looked ancient enough to belong to some time not this. That could tell us a lot about why Bobby Seale, a man very much of our times, a man rooted in no century but our own, finally showed up in New Haven.

The architects had another headache: the outside stone of these buildings looked brand-new too, suggesting that contemporary hands had something to do with the construction, and contemporaneity is death to venerableness, as everybody knows. Their solution was to treat the stone facings with some sort of chemical that made them look weathered by the centuries. Which gave rise to another puzzler: this treatment made the seals permeable, so that the walls leaked something fierce when it rained. No doubt this difficulty has been resolved too, thanks to the wonders of modem chemistry, a development since Gothic times.

This preoccupation of adult minds with the techniques of how to make new stone look old without the walls leaking also may throw some light on why Bobby Seale came to town. He was visiting with his friends and associates along Dixwell Avenue and Ashmun Street, an un-Gothic stone's throw from the Yale campuses, in a neighborhood where houses leak for more 20th-century reasons, such as lack of money to make repairs.

I went to Yale for five years but I never spent a night on its premises.

I'll have to take that back. There was the night I was reading in one of the uterine alcoves of Linonia & Brothers and dozed off. I'm not sure, but I think I was reading *Lady Chatterley's Lover,* I never could get into that book, I'm not that much interested in gardening. A careless night watchman locked me in and I was stuck until they opened the doors for the bookworms in the morning. That was pretty spooky. It's not good to be alone in the dark with so many books. Books properly are daytime companions. In the day you can keep your eye on them.

My point is that New Haven was my home, I lived there, and Yale was simply a place where I attended certain classes, as few as possible. My life of the mind took place partly on campus but my life of the sense was located entirely off. I was very much of the town, but the gown they insisted I was born to just never did fit me well.

I'll tell you how much I resisted their gowns. When the time came for me to graduate I couldn't face the business of renting and actually putting on one of those silly robes. I went to the dean and told him I couldn't make the commencement exercises because the International Ladies' Garment Workers Union was about to go on strike along the Eastern Seaboard and I'd gotten myself a job as a picket captain.

The dean did not take kindly to my news. He said it was an unpromising sign that I couldn't wait to begin my troublemaking until I got my degree. I said it was the stomachs of the seamstresses in the sweatshops that had caused the trouble by not getting enough to eat on sweatshop wages, I was only trying to help them solve the problem by advancing to a better diet. He said it was out of the question that a fellow bent on such mischief should be excused from the academic routine, I wouldn't get my diploma if I didn't show up for the ceremony and that was that. He added that if I was making such a fuss because it cost a few dollars to rent the cap and gown he himself, personally, was ready to lay out the rental fee.

I was so taken with the idea of one of these cultivated heads footing the bill that I agreed. I told him the rental agency charged five dollars where in fact it charged only three, so I made two dollars on the deal. I didn't put up too much of a fight because in truth I didn't have that picket-captain job with the ILGWU, I'd made a bid for it but all the openings were already filled. Things were so bad that I couldn't even get work going on strike.

Town, I'm saying, always loomed larger in my head than gown and mostly shoved gown aside. Town was my habitat, where I drank my beer and hung my hat, gown just a uniform that didn't conform to my true contours. That brings me back to the matter of my never living on campus.

You'd be right if you observed that I didn't have the money to live in a dormitory but you'd be dead wrong if you concluded that that was my reason for not living there. If I'd had the money of a Ford or a Rockefeller (there was a Ford in my class, Henry III, and a Rockefeller too, Winthrop, maybe, I never was clear on that) I still wouldn't have moved into a dormitory. I was delighted to live in furnished rooms in or near the ghettos, on Dixwell Avenue, Elm Street, College Place, Ashmun Street, Lake Place, Crown Street, Asylum Street, Davenport Avenue, and be where my friends were, and come and go without being checked by entry guards.

Yale's officialdom could not understand someone who was in their community but not of it, who was not a joiner. In their minds admission to their churned circle was such a boon and a blessing that anybody so honored had to embrace all that was offered. They couldn't make sense of my not wanting to march in their commencement parade and they had to misinterpret my reasons for living off campus.

They saw me as one more of the underprivileged townies. There were these deserving-but-poor scholarship lads out of the city's ranks who were dying to belong all the way but couldn't scare up the loot for all the privileges available on campus, starting with that of living in a college-unit dormitory. We paupers who were condemned to live away from gown, in town, among the peasants, the ivyless somaticists, had to be sorry. Yale set out to make us less sorry. Whether we liked it or not.

They have the residence-college system at Yale, Pierson being one closed unit, Calhoun another, and so on. Each college has its own dormitories and dining hall, its lounges, library, seminar rooms. The plan the officials came up with was to assign each off-campus student to the roster of one of these college units, on the theory that even if we couldn't sleep among our fellows we at least would have visitation rights, the opportunity to eat with our peers, participate in the college's doings, use its facilities. I was made an associate, or non-resident member, whatever it was called, of Calhoun.

The idea behind this insultingly social-work gesture was to make us feel wanted. What I felt was truly overlooked, I mean, not recognized, not made room for.

I felt violated. That they could have imagined for a minute I'd go for their insipid English roasts, served by a lot of underpaid black women in starched uniforms, most of them my neighbors, some of them the mothers of my friends, when nightly I enjoyed those fine pork-chop sandwiches smothered in hot sauce that they featured in the hash joints along Dixwell Avenue, and had the bonus of my real friends eating with me—that I took for the wildest sort of arrogance.

The bureaucrats of the Wasp-élite world don't read the minds of bottomdogs as acutely as they think. They suffer from the social-worker's fallacy that the lower a man is on the social scale the more of a stereotype he is and therefore more of an open book to sophisticated high-individuation minds like their own. They are victims of what has been called occupational psychosis (also known as trained incapacity)—a blindness that comes from too much stilted insight.

I never set foot in Calhoun before I was coopted to its membership list without my permission, and I never did after. So much for the ability of the University, that beehive of explorations in humanistic individualism, to spot and give scope to this or that individual.

Maybe if I'd gone to Yale in good times I'd have responded to its ways better and fitted into its life more. But I started college in 1931, when people all over the country were standing in lines, sometimes at soup kitchens, sometimes at banks that were about to close down without returning their depositors' hard-earned savings.

I remember the Bank Holiday the way other Yale graduates remember ski holidays at Klosters or Bad Gastein. I had to miss some of my classes because I was needed to spell my mother in the line that stretched clear around the block from her bank on Temple Street. The bank was about to shut its doors. It had announced that it would pay off its depositors a few cents on the dollar while its ready cash lasted. (I wondered what its unready cash was up to.) My mother wasn't able to stand in that line for two whole days. She had a job scrubbing floors somewhere—depressing, how often the soap-operatic note appears in American biographies—and she couldn't miss work.

So, as I say, I missed some classes, mostly in Chaucer, which I didn't mind—*The Canterbury Tales* didn't have much to say to me at a time when the moneys you'd scraped together to put in what you took for a bank appeared to have been dropped into a hole with no bottom, though you suspected somebody was down there filling his sneaky bags. My mother had something better than $100 in her account, saved up over many months. What the bank deigned to give us was $20 or so.

You can see why I couldn't view Yale as something separate and apart from the Depression. I had to take the University and the Panic as different facets of the same slimy, howling mess. More than once the thought crossed my mind that in ways I wasn't yet smart enough to figure out Yale was a central component of the whole system that was diverting my mother's earnings as a slavey into somebody else's anonymous pockets.

I graduated from Yale in 1935, and left Graduate School in 1936, years in which there were almost daily riots at relief offices around the country, some of which I took part in as an organizer for the National Unemployed League. In short order after entering the world of work, I was informed that the only employment around was for body laborers, and precious little of that. However, Yale had disqualified me for any sort of employment but head employment, of which there was none. Everywhere they were drawing the hard-and-fast Manichean line across the windpipe and announcing that everything above that line was perfectly splendid and worth endless leisurely cultivation and everything below it was for lesser, less endowed people to concern themselves with, mostly non-Anglos, certainly non-Wasps, until, of course, the Depression came along and it was a buyer's market for bodies and a lot of them had to be dumped.

Rooted in town as I was, I had no way of relating to a life all gown. Most of my classmates could hole up and never see the life outside. They could, if they so chose, arrange their lives so that they would never from year to year even brush against the squelched and squirming, untutored protoplasms surrounding their tight little island of cerebrators.

Going from dormitory to classroom to library to football field to happy Vassar weekends, you're moving much too fast to notice the faceless mass out of whose systematic exploitation your fun and frolic get cushily financed. Occasionally, sure, you'll leave a tip or a bauble for the black man who serves you your meals in the dining hall or the Polish lady who makes your bed up or the Irish guard at the dormitory entrance. But they don't grow to human dimensions in your mind, which is too filled as it is with poetry and lacrosse schedules, they're there mainly as props and devices, good ones, worth five bucks at the Yuletide season, certainly.

My mother was never one of those campus maids but that was just her bad luck. She'd applied many times for the job. There was always a long waiting list. She never had the luxury to wait. Of course I couldn't reconcile town and gown in my life or in my mind. Every time I stepped on campus I had the creepy feeling that I was in enemy territory.

There are two ways you can handle a split life. You can just fall apart. Or you can keep your eye on your two halves and keep running back and forth between them, giving one enough spin to keep it going for a while, then the other. The second technique takes a certain agility, and you have to develop a good wind, but it can be done.

You don't have to like the game. You can hold a low opinion of its rules, which they set up without consulting you. But if it's the only game in town you've only got one choice, to play or not to play. In times of more flourish they put it, to be or not to be.

My father chose not to be, not to play.

For 19 years he'd had a good and secure job in a very large factory where they made all sorts of printing presses, some for branches of government like the Treasury Department—the Harris, Seibold & Potter Company in Shelton, 10 miles from New Haven. Starting out in the paint department, he'd risen to be foreman, but he never went over to the management side; he belonged to the workers' union and when it went out on strike he went out. Management never got around to firing him for his union loyalty because when there was no stiike he ran the paint department well, besides, if they'd tried to fire him the workers would have gone out on strike over *that*.

Then came the Stock Market Crash of 1929. All businesses took a nosedive (along with a fair number of the businessmen), including Harris, Seibold & Potter. Maybe there was less demand for printing presses because in times of economic downturn there just aren't many things to print except forms for overdue bills and eviction notices. In any case, the factory shut down, and my father was suddenly without a job.

He'd been living a split life all along. For one thing, there was a certain gap between his occupation and his desire to play the violin, which he did well. But with that degree of twoness he could cope, since for ideological as well as human reasons he enjoyed his comradeship with the other factory hands; also, he could play his violin evenings and weekends. Now came a much more serious fission—on one hand was his urge to feed his family, keep up payments on the house, and do something out in the world that he got some pats on the back for; on the other, his sudden termination of all function, his drop into a total vacuum, his loss, as they like to say these days, of identity, as much as he had.

Overnight he'd been broken to pieces and he had no desire to juggle the fragments. Any world that would do that to a man, he was profoundly convinced, was just not worth bothering with. He resigned from the human race and all its doings. He went into the bedroom, pulled down the shades, and there in the darkness sat on a chair facing the wall.

I can't say I altogether blamed him. The way things were going, there really wasn't much worth looking at Out There.

Still, you have to make the effort. Those are the rules of the game, the only one in town. If you don't obey the rules they won't call you a sensitive soul, a man with esthetic of such high order that you can't take the vulgarities and obscenities out there on the street—no, they'll pin the label of psychotic on you and lock you up.

They pinned the label on my old man not without reason, though I must say if they wanted to get a full picture of his sickness they would have had to look into the sickness of American capitalism too. They took him away and locked him up in Yale's Institute of Human Relations where they had a psychiatric division devoted to the study of interesting cases. They judged my old man to be an interesting case. You don't get many factory workers who are devoted to the violin.

He entered Yale's Institute not long after I entered Yale. That gave my academic career a certain focus.

I'd been at a loss as to what field to do my honors work in. I definitely didn't want to major in literature in an English Department that did not recognize the existence of James Joyce when he was knocking the whole literary world on its ear. Now, however, I saw a course of study that would make sense. I would concentrate on psychology, more specifically, abnormal psychology. At the same time I would fulfill all the pre-med requirements, and after graduation go on to medical school and become a psychiatrist, maybe a psychoanalyst.

If I couldn't find out in Yale's curricula what was wrong with the world or at least with literature, I could bone up on what was wrong with my old man. I could in fact make an occupation out of it.

The Psychology Department headquartered in the Institute of Human Relations, was, if I remember rightly, part of it. I visited there often to talk with this or that professor. On my side the conversation was often a little forced because I was aware of my father's presence in another wing of the building and discussions of the mind's gnarlings were therefore a lot less academic for me than the professor could guess. The professor, I mean, could speculate freely as to how the mind gets twisted one way or another—if he was wrong that was O.K.; he had no stakes in this. My stakes were high; if he didn't know what he was talking about my old man was going to be cooped up in that locked room with his violin for a long, long time.

One of my instructors was a first-rate fellow named Florian Heiser. I took to him because my Marxism didn't bother him, as a matter of fact he was something of a Marxist too, enough of one that after a while Yale told him to move on. I visited with him often. One day he packed up his briefcase and walked outside with me after our business was done with.

We went along Davenport Avenue toward the spot where he had his car parked. I happened to look up at the row of barred windows that marked the psychiatric wards. Behind one set of bars was my old man, just standing there testing, I suppose, if there was anything besides walls worth looking at. I don't know if my memory is writing additional dialogue for the facts here but as I recall the scene he had his violin tucked under his arm.

Florian Heiser didn't notice anything. He went on talking about some exciting experiments somebody was just then doing in conditioning aggression out of rats with electric shocks—socialization through traumatization, I think it was called. That was Florian's field, experimental psychology. It's the same snap-to treatment they've been using more recently on autistic children, who I suppose can be seen as rats for being so unsocial.

Florian was an instructor in why some people get things done and some get *un*done, and in general a right and sympathetic sort of guy, pretty much on my side, certainly not on the enemy's, but there was no

way to break into his impassioned talk about the new Pavlovian trau-
matizings of rats to say, "I don't mean to change the subject, I'm really
interested in all these things they're doing to rats, but that skinny old
geezer up there, he's my father, he's had some shocks recently too—
they didn't socialize him much—would have had more, in fact, they'd
decided to give him electric-shock therapy and were wheeling him into
the jolt room but at the last minute somebody thought to check his
blood pressure, it was way up and they found he had an advanced case of
arteriosclerosis, the voltage they'd been about to run through him might
have killed him." Nope, there was no way to work this information in,
which, it seemed to me, said just about everything there was to be said,
between clenched teeth and with gorge that wouldn't stay down, about
the discipline of psychology, the University, the country, the system,
and the human how of it all down the line, some (only some) of which,
to be sure the system's not responsible for.

Outside there on the avenue, I slowed down a bit. Then I did the
only thing I could think of under the circumstances, raised my hand in
a snappy military salute.

My old man made the effort to smile. He returned the salute with
the closest thing to jauntiness he could muster, like a man on his death-
bed trying to go through the motions of the Charleston or the Suzie-Q.
I got his message—carry on, trooper. He on his fronts would do his
level best to carry on. He was issuing orders to me to keep the battle
going on as many fronts as I could get to, and to make sure none of them
was anywhere around his.

Sometime after this the psychiatrists at the Institute decided they'd
exhausted all the interesting aspects of my old man's case and he was
accordingly transferred to the state mental hospital in Middletown.
You can see what's coming, you've watched enough television dramas
to know all the plot twists, the crazy crossings of paths, the O. Henry

surprises that life dishes out so much more ingeniously than do the television dramatists and the O. Henrys in general.

It was arranged for our class in abnormal psychology to make a field hip to Middletown to observe some of the more interesting cases they had up there. In anticipation of that outing, I suddenly recall after a lapse of 37 years, I sat down and wrote a short story, not exactly light-handed, about a college student whose class in abnormal psychology visits a mental hospital to have some of the weirder cases trotted out for their inspection, and one of them turns out to be his father.

It was a failure of my dreamery centers. Life is not that cliché-ridden. It simply has more imagination and far subtler turnings than television will ever have the good grace to acknowledge. When life decides to write a soap opera, as it does over and over, the thing may turn into grand opera, and not a posy, swoony one either.

My father was not one of the shells of human beings dragged into that amphitheater for the edification of Yale students in between weekends at Vassar. My father made no appearance in that vaudeville at all. But after the show, as we were walking back to our cars, I spotted him on a bench on the grounds, with his violin case across his knees. I went over and sat down.

"How you doing, Pop. Get to play the violin much."

"Plenty, son. I keep busy here, don't you worry about me. I'm even giving lessons, I've got five patients signed up already. One's a very interesting man, he used to be an engineer and he has a plan to float icebergs down from the North Pole and melt them to make more water, he says the reason for the Depression is too damn many frozen assets and this is his scheme for straightening things out, unfreeze the water assets. He's got a real knack for the fiddle, he's already playing Schubert's *Serenade*."

"It sounds like he's got talent, you teach them good, Pop."

Pretty soon I caught up with our party in the parking lot. One of my classmates—his first name was Clay, he was from Grosse Point and his father was something big in the diplomatic service—was curious about my going off like that.

He said, "Who was that you were talking to?"

I said, "He's my father."

He said, "Come on, I don't think that's funny, you've got a warped sense of humor."

Life is a very good writer. I'd give anything to be able to write dialogue like that. What an imagination.

Irving Fisher! Ever hear of him? The name doesn't mean much nowadays but it was once to be reckoned with. He was for many years Yale's most eminent economist. One study he put a lot of time into was ways and means to control the economic cycle, an undertaking at which, as revealed in the newspapers if not the history books, he was not conspicuously successful.

He did something to straighten out my personal economic cycle, though—my one-man economic cycle. It was Prof. Irving Fisher who created a job for me on my last visit to New Haven.

It's very hard to figure out what you're doing hanging around a college town when you're no longer in college. The place where they catered to your head is best left far behind when you step into the world to do some paid-for work, otherwise all our categories, compartments for thinking over here, ones for doing over there, melt together, and you know what that can lead to—thoughtful action, activist thought, town-gown merger, the sort of thing that can get Mr. Agnew to seeing red in many more places than are so colored. There could even come out of the blending, the mind-body reconciliation, some worker-student joint ventures. Those aloof spires might eventually flop sideways and drop their frozen frills and inch into the spurned ghettos, metamorphosing into mobile libraries and medical checkup vans and consumer armories and strike headquarters and community action centers. Brain and brawn might get to belong to the same union and in fact talk face to face, exchange notes, listen hard. Finally, finally, people in the University might stop going on with their nonstop wind about alienation, and making it their field of expertise, and writing their doctoral dissertations on it, and moving on to other universities to teach it to other candidate-scholars of alienation, a thing more to be dodged than majored and lectured in. . . . Well.

Where was I. The next best thing to going to the college that rules the municipal roost is to work for it, especially since it hands out most of the jobs in the area. So I went to see one of the officials of the Sterling Library who'd been helpful to me when I was a student, Donald Wing. (I'd always had the utopian hope that one day they might build an annex to the Library and name it after him so it could be called the Wing Wing.) Donald said there was a parttime job open on the staff, that somebody was needed to come in and make order out of and catalogue all the Irving Fisher papers and memorabilia. Five mornings a week, 60 cents an hour, 12 bucks a week.

I took it. Next to nothing was in those days a lot better than nothing. On that kind of pay you could cough up three bucks for a furnished room and have enough left over for the 35¢ breaded veal cutlets at the Greek's or the pork-chop sandwiches in the Dixwell Avenue greasy spoons.

Irving Fisher was an expert on tax structuring, fiduciary policy, how to keep inflation and deflation in line, interest rates, cash flows, balance of trade, what the Federal Reserve should reserve, and the like. He was forever going down to Washington to testify before Senate committees or act as consultant to government agencies, and often his services were called upon by foreign governments too. Then he began to be consulted less and less, and after a while not at all, and you could understand why.

The Great Crash and Panic of 1929 happened. For all his scholarly investigations into the reasons why boom economies go bust with such regularity, Fisher had never suggested to anybody that anything remotely like 1929 could or would happen. He had, in fact, ruled out any such possibility. After all, the Hoover people down in Washington were handling the system pretty much as he'd advised them to. His policies were specifically designed to keep us from going into decline.

Irving Fisher all his life considered himself the architect of prosperity, though it turned out he was more its wistful camp follower. It followed that any nation that used his blueprints would stay rattlingly prosperous. That's the kind of thing that happens when gown gets such a swelled head as to imagine that it doesn't have to go into town, just look it over from the highest University tower and through a bullhorn inform it what's what.

Fisher wanted very much to know what had brought about the catastrophe all his ideas had been designed to prevent. He began to look about for etiological variables he might have neglected or underestimated. He found some dillies. Sunspots. It appeared that just before the Stock Market Crash there'd been significantly increased activity on the sun, where there had been spots were larger ones and where there hadn't been any some showed up.

Looking over the terrestrial canvas more broadly, Fisher found other matters that seemed to rise and fall with the waxing and waning of solar spots, among them pregnancy rates, the incidence of coronary thrombosis, the number of highschool dropouts, crimes of violence, abortions, strikes, small-business failures, automobile purchases, gang wars, home foreclosures, divorces, any number of things. Prof. Fisher had hit late in life on the cosmic-cyclical theory of history and the cycles he suddenly turned up everywhere in human affairs he traced directly to the periodic variations in the sun's acne. Again, that's the sort of thing you see when you climb so far up those Gothic towers as to lose sight of the clutter of facts all about on the ground.

You can imagine with what mixed feelings the Hoover people down in Washington listened to Prof. Fisher's strong new thoughts. In their innermost beings they must have felt a warm glow from top to bottom, an impulse to embrace the Professor and kiss him all over. After all, a theory that traced this economic avalanche to extra-terrestrial sources, sunspots or Halley's Comet or the furthermost red stars or whatever, automatically absolved the Hoover Administration of all responsibility for the collapse, as well as the free-enterprise system it was constantly embracing and kissing. But they were just enough in touch with the pulse of the public to know that, however much they themselves cottoned to Fisher's proposal to make economics a branch of astronomy, the American people wouldn't buy it.

I'm not saying that overnight the nation had turned Marxist in its approach to economics, nothing like that. But with the pinch of very hard times, with all the belt-tightening, the scramble to eat, rudiments of a materialist interpretation of history had been planted in many heads, enough at least to make them look to the workings of the profit system for the culprit rather than to the sun's sporadic discolorations.

Prof. Fisher, finding himself accorded the treatment a prophet usually gets in his own country, with all the other countries following suit, retired from his role as economist, in fact, retired from public life and teaching altogether. And he donated all the papers from his busy life to the Yale Library, thereby making work for me.

I was impressed by the reverse logic here. It was the Depression that finally divorced Prof. Fisher, the excommunicator of depression, from his function in the world, in short, eliminated his job, excommunicated him. It was the Depression that had eliminated all sorts of jobs for all sorts of people, including me. But it was in response to the Depression that the Professor gave all his papers to the Library, creating, finally, a job for me. Unless you're a dialectician you're just not going to understand much of what goes on in this dizzy, dippy, turnabout world.

This was early 1940. If you want to know what it was really like in those days let me sum it up by saying that I was making $12, a week and banking $3 out of it, and I wanted for nothing—nothing I wanted, outside of a job, a real one.

CHAPTER 3

CHEW 32 TIMES

My room was on Dixwell Avenue, two blocks west of the University, two blocks south of my mother's place on Ashmun Street. My life developed a certain rhythm, get drunk at night, make faces at Prof. Fisher's spill of print matter in the morning.

I had to get drunk (when somebody had a bottle, and somebody always did) to face the prospect of those crates of papers in the morning. Then a spell with those less than memorable memorabilia would drive me to drink again. It was what the psychologists call a motivated life, though a circular one, exhibiting cycles that had more to do with the spots before my eyes than those on the sun.

Fisher had been a man of varied interests, the result perhaps of finding that his discoveries about sunspots aroused no other human the way they did him. He'd gotten into all kinds of things that took his mind off the solar measles the whole world insisted on overlooking. Eating your way to health and vitality, for one.

Decades before the general public turned to dietary fads, there was Irving Fisher amassing all sorts of literature on the wildest of them. I waded through hundreds of pamphlets and brochures on vegetarianism and fruitarianism. Fisher had been preaching, and pushing broadsides on, the restorative powers of wheat germ a third of a century before people became aware that wheat had germs.

There was a lot of stuff, too, on Yoga. I was struck by its eloquent arguments for assuming the lotus position and doing hyperventilation to get a new slant on things. As a result, in the huge basement storage room where I worked on Fisher's cartons of papers I spent hours sitting on a desk with my legs interwoven, breathing deep. Being pretty supple in those days, I could tie all sorts of knots in my lower members to correspond with the knots in which I was tied upstairs. I don't know how *new* a slant I developed on things, but slant I came to have in abundance— the whole damn room would begin to pitch and yaw, and once there was such a radical tilt I fell off the desk.

Prof. Fisher also championed—long before such thing became battle cries and marching songs—roughage, yogurt, cod liver oil, regular doses of the benign lactobacillus known as acidophilus to line the intestines and speed up digestion, papaya juice, sauerkraut juice, pomegranate juice, lots of nuts, pushups, five-mile walks. The man had campaigned for so many transparently healthy things that were no least part of my life that his papers were making me feel, at age 24, like a terminal case.

I worked up a theory as to why he developed these systemless enthusiasms late in life. He'd found it so hard to develop a therapy for the body politic and social that in order to feel useful in some way he'd turned to therapies for the body somatic.

The Depression caused queer swerves like that in many formerly sober and mainstream heads. They recoiled from the social centralities that were suddenly running off their tracks and going hogwild, making hash of all their neat systems and savvies; sprinted as well from inner cities of the mind that were exploding in riot toward little side-pockets in the mental suburbs; and headed where they could make a show of being in control of something, however small. So the soberest of citizens could turn quirky, the most rational thinkers show up bizarre, if not downright off their rockers.

If you can't find some last-ditch tonic for the economy, which is supposed to be your business, what you're paid for, what gives you a role and an identity, you can at the very least claim to have come upon this or that snake (or cod) oil very good for the human liver. A man has got to feel he can help somewhere, some way.

One thing Prof. Fisher was unreservedly sold on was Fletcherism. You wouldn't know about Fletcherism but it was all the craze back there just after World War I.

Dr. Fletcher had come up with a sure-fire formula to make the human digestive tract work as it had been intended to. In the hurly-burly of modern urban life, Dr. Fletcher came to see, we simply bolt our food instead of masticating it as Nature meant us to. He promulgated a procedure to counter this—take small bites and chew each mouthful 32 times, after which thorough pulverization and salivation the stomach and small intestine will have very little further work except as traffic cops for the nutrients ready and eager to do their duty and down the tissues.

Moreover, Dr. Fletcher guaranteed that if you chewed each morsel 32 times you'd get so much more food value out of it that your intake would go way down. It was in the happy-go-lucky and prosperous Twenties when the doctor presented his theory, but the hungry Thirties when the Professor latched onto it. No doubt Fisher was hoping that America's depressed stomachs would feel fewer hunger pangs if American mouths did more pulping and enzyming of the sparse foods that did trickle their way.

I've found a scrap of paper containing a notation I made during my Irving Fisher phase; it may have some bearing here:

"This Fletcherizing really works. Lately I've been so nervous I've been chewing my nails a lot. Now that I chew each sliver 32 times my nails get broken down into their components and absorbed into the bloodstream much faster, and therefore get delivered back to the fingers in a fraction of the former time, feeding the nails in formation there and encouraging them to grow back on the double. The only part of the theory that doesn't seem to work out in my case is having to consume less when you digest better. I find myself chewing my nails *more* than ever, my intake way up. I think this is because I'm more nervous. But why? The fact is I get all tensed up thinking of those nails pushing out and pushing out, I sit for hours watching them, and I swear there are times I can actually see them forming and extruding. What really terrifies me is to picture them growing across the room and into the far wall; that makes me chew them all the more, which, of course, thanks to the Fletcherizing, makes them grow like wildfire. I think in spite of the dramatic proof of Fletcher's theories, I'll have to give up the 32 jaw-stokes, at this rate be doing nothing but chewing, and nail-forming, and chewing some more, and Irving's papers will never get catalogued. . . ."

If it wasn't one thing it was another in those plaguey Depression years.

My father thought he might like to leave the hospital and look around a bit. He didn't expect to find much to inspire him but with his inherent sense of fair play he thought he ought to give the world another chance.

I installed a cot in the alcove in my room, dropped a curtain in front of it to give the illusion of a suite, and got the old man down from Middletown, violin case and all, I mean, violin case and that was just about all. He traveled light. Of course, he packed his dentures, he was always ready to chomp 32 times on any food nice enough to detour through his jaws.

A man really doesn't need much stuff to get him through life—not if he's a smart and efficient wayfarer—just a box to contain a useful amount of the available cultural baggage but no more, and a set of store-bought teeth to process the body foods you need before you can open up to the more luxurious mind stuffs. My old man was as much of a Manichee as conditions required; with his dentures he was ready for the body front and with his violin for the mind front, but he allowed for the possibility of a hyphen somewhere along the way, a joining of the fronts, and maybe to symbolize this openness to a healing, a holism, a total nutrition, he packed his dentures in the violin case.

He wasn't encouraged by what he found in the big city.

It's a piece of sentimental soupiness, all too current in our fiction, that mental institutions are arbitrarily set off because the insanity inside their walls only echoes the insanity outside. The fact is that Sammy found the insanity all over the place much less to his liking than that he'd become used to in the Middletown hospital.

Pretty soon he was spending his entire days in that alcove, sitting on a chair with his eyes fixed on the wall. In his scheme of things the walls I had to offer him on Dixwell Avenue were less interesting and eventful than the ones they had up in Middletown. He asked to go back, and I put the dentures inside the violin case and saw him off on the bus.

He was to spend a lot of years in Middletown and other hospitals, with time off when he ran away to convince himself that he was after all missing nothing in the big cities, and finally, in 1962, at age 87 or 88, nobody was quite sure, he died in Middletown, in a senile ward, blind now, but with eyes still turned to the wall, trying to say something about his dentures, the male nurse couldn't make it out. The violin case was by his side but the violin was long gone, he'd hocked it on one of his flights from the nut farm to buy some hamburgers to keep his dentures busy (body feeding off mind again), and I think the knowledge that the instrument was gone for good was one thing that drove him into his final depression and drained his will to live, maybe even shuttered his eyes for good, he was finally convinced there was nothing worth looking at out there, nothing at all, no hyphens available in a world where you dine on your own musical instruments. He needn't have worried about his dentures, though. They were found intact in the otherwise empty violin case.

We had him cremated. His ashes are resting on my brother's mantel today, up in Hamden, Connecticut. I think those dentures are around somewhere, too. I've had the thought at times, late at night, of putting those ashes between those two rows of false teeth (they'd almost fit, there wasn't much left of that little old bird once he'd been reduced to the least common, most common, denominator) and saying, try chewing *that* 32, times, Pop, and see where it gets you.

If you opt for the psychotic's posture in this world you'd better pick and choose your psychosis carefully. Some brands of nuttiness work better than others. Certain ones truly insulate you from the insanities outside and others make you more vulnerable to them.

My old man picked the worst possible variety of mental disorder for himself, in view of the way in which the world about him was disordered. The outside disorders simply fanned and sped up the inside ones. My old man had the bad judgment to become a very extreme, very quickchange sort of manic-depressive, in a world that was spectacularly manic-depressive.

If he'd been smart enough to be a full-fledged schizo, a hebephrenic, say, or a catatonic, he'd have cut himself off from the nonsense out there very effectively, he'd have been immune to the demented ups and downs of the scene, nicely sealed off, but as it was he was on the dramatic cycle kick and he found himself forever spurred on and then outdone by the leaps and prat falls of the world. When the society got hyperthyroid he did too, and when the society tripped and fell on its face and got the clammy terminal-case blues he did the same, and on both the jumps and flops he found himself a rank amateur, an awkward, fledging bumbler compared to the world, and a man just can't stand being forever in competition with the world and forever finding himself hopelessly outclassed, it can throw him into a depression there's no manicking out of.

The country did shake itself out of its depression, finally, by finding another world war to rally its energies and ambitions and hopes. It wasn't easy, but FDR, a man in tune with the national interests, managed it, in the end. My old man never found any war to rally around. He got tired even of the walls and went blind and confused.

Very confused, in those last years. At times we had him at home with my mother. He'd get to thinking the Boss, that was our nickname for my mother, was trying to put roach powder in his maple walnut ice cream. Sometimes at night he'd go to use the bathroom and manage to shit in the bathtub, which the Boss, probably without real grounds, took for malice.

I direct your attention to the old man's confusion, in those last years, on his trips to the bathroom, to how the distinction between what you do with a bathtub and what you do with a toilet got clouded in his mind, and I ask you this question, whether you still are dedicated to the proposition that art imposes order on the chaos of life. My father was an artist, yet he managed to shit in the bathtub and, for all I know, wash his face in the toilet. He was an artist, all right. When he played Schubert's *Serenade* on the violin, even with his factory-roughened fingers, people sat up and listened—even visionary engineers determined to melt the polar icebergs to shore up the shaky world and make it solvent again.

Work on the Irving Fisher papers went slowly. I was doing much more reading than sorting and cataloguing.

In those cartons I'd made a real find, some old copies of a French literary and philosophical magazine that over a period of months carried a lot of long excerpts from a little-known work of Thomas Mann's called *The Reflections of a Non-Political Man*. There was a reason, I discovered, why this book was so little known.

Mann had written it, during the four years of World War I, from the vantage point of a loyal German given body and soul to the values of Prussian militarism; it was an out-and-out defense, more in psycho-philosophical than political terms, of Germany's role in the war. But after the war, Mann had done a turnabout in his politics, finally embracing the Weimar Republic after making caustic pronouncements about it, and I guess he didn't want his followers around the world, most of whom were sold on his new appreciation of democracy, to know the kinds of things he'd been saying a few years before—this was the one work he'd never allowed to get translated and reprinted.

For two years, during my stay in Mexico and afterwards as I shuffled between New York and New Haven, my head had been full of two writers, Thomas Mann and André Gide. I ate up their books, seldom stopping to chew anywhere near 32 times, I was too hungry for that. At one point I was so caught up in these two, the ways in which they overlapped, the ways in which they were worlds apart, that I played with the idea of doing a book-length study of them, putting all their efforts side by side. In fact, I think that somewhere along the way I talked to the people at the Yale Press about such a project. I seem to recall they saw as much value in it as in my other suggestion for a study of the Thermidorean tendencies in modern revolutions, and were just as sure that it would be a most worthwhile study for someone with the proper scholarly credentials to do some day. But I'd never in all my explorations of Mann's work come across the eyeopening *Reflections*, because he hadn't wanted me to. Now I saw why, and just how wrong he'd been, and how unfair to me.

Reflections is a gorgeous book. Not for its defense of Prussianism. That was just plain silly, and one more proof that intellectuals, especially artists, are just too tipsy with ideas to fool around with the politics of day-to-day social struggle, in which ideas are never allowed to interfere with interests. Mann's enthusiasm for the Prussian bulletheads was just as haphazardly and cavalierly thought out as his later veneration of the Stalinist wardens, and therefore, I guess we can say by inference, as his intervening salute, significantly belated, to Weimar's clutch at republicanism. (In fact, if you want to see his progress dialectically, look at his late Stalinism as a retrieval of more than a little of his early Prussianism—to be sure, on a "higher" plane.) But the running attack he unfolded against the Western democracies, and against those German intellectuals, including his own brother Heinrich, who'd exiled themselves from their homeland to support the Allied cause—that was a thing of beauty, a literary savagery that stunned me, it rang so true.

Mann saw the Western democracies as playgrounds for lawyers, loudmouths, the merely eloquent, the wordmongers, the conscious mind, the new brain, a culture of spouting and empty rhetoric, as against a Teutonic world stoutly folk, non-verbal, highly musical, rooted in the unconscious, the old brain, way-back sources, the passions that precede and underlie mere words. He concluded that his country had a strong mission in World War I, to stand between West and East, the lands of the over-touted cerebrum and the lands of the enduring hypothalamus, so to speak, of chatter on the one hand and the harmonic sounds of the under-mind on the other—a mission to keep West from invading East and taking over altogether, which would mean a triumph of the fast-talking lawyers over the folk singers. The political conclusion was, to make no bones about it, birdbrained, but the cultural analysis on which it rested, at least its negative side, had enough plain good sense about it to shake me profoundly.

Remember the living context in which I was reading these words so scrupulously withdrawn from circulation. I was sitting on a desk in the basement of the Sterling Memorial Library, surrounded by great piles of all the eloquence the West could summon up in times of mortal crisis, the chatter of the West pertinent to its deep troubles, and all these torrents of words did was to reflect the troubles in the air without in any way explaining them or indicating how they might be coped with. Everywhere in and out of the asylums, people were babbling, it seemed to me, about sunspots, melting the icebergs, eating more wheat germ, trying hyperventilation, doing more knee bends, while the country continued to ride to hell in capitalism's express hand-basket.

The words were coming faster and faster, and sounding more and more demented. Of all the sounds in the cultural air, indeed, the only ones that truly related, that made some sense, were those of jazz, especially the blues. All the blabbermouth lawyers were talking a mile a minute but all I could stand to listen to were the relevant noises made by Bessie Smith and Lady Day, Louis Armstrong and Little Jimmy Rushing all up and down Dixwell Avenue in the non-library night hours.

I tried many times in the next years to get some offbeat publisher to bring the *Reflections* out, in a pirated edition if Mann wouldn't consent to an official one. The main reason was to make this devastating analysis of Western culture available to Western readers, whether or not Mann had in the interim reconsidered his judgments. There was another less pressing, more literary reason.

Some aspects of *The Magic Mountain* had always puzzled me, especially the marathon forensics between the ex-Jewish Jesuit Naphta (ancient times, repressed origins, the unconscious, music, anti-rationality, etc.) and Settembrini (revolutionary democrat, rationalist, optimist, cerebrator, humanist, onward-and-upwarder, etc.). It seemed to me that for the major part of the ongoing debate Naphta gets all the best of it, though in a sudden twist at the end it's Settembrini who wins by provoking Naphta into blowing his brains out. *Reflections* explains a lot in *Magic Mountain* that the novel's own text leaves a mystery, or at least an enigma, and the one is therefore a necessary companion volume to the other.

Mann, I discovered, started *Magic Mountain* in 1912, when he was still very much in his Prussia-forever stage. He found he couldn't work on it during the years of the war, and put it aside to do the essays that ultimately made up *Reflections. Reflections*, then, continues the intellectual state in which he'd begun *Magic Mountain*. When he returned to the novel after the war, though, Prussianism was finished and Weimar was announcing itself, and before too long he had to declare his allegiance to the new, democratic order. This final ideological shift is reflected in the later pages of *Magic Mountain*, most specifically, I suspect, in the winding down of the Naphta-Settembrini contest through the modern politico's triumph over the anti-progress mystically-minded medievalist.

What I'm saying, in short, is that Mann must have started the novel with the intention of having Naphta survive Settembrini, but reversed his logic when the political winds in Europe shifted. So my argument is that in keeping *Reflections* from us Mann did, in a very real sense, withhold a central portion of the text of *Magic Mountain*, a portion that holds the key to many puzzles in the novel.

I don't think we're going to ward off the flood of chatter in our world through a music-folk revival, though a lot of young people today are acting as though this can be the antidote to our runaway eloquence as it goes more and more crackers. In fact, I think young people are barking up the wrong tree if they look for revolution to come from and through music, pleasant though it is to have lively music around. I also worry that in reducing themselves to a monosyllabic kind of verbal communication they are in important ways disarming themselves in the face of the enemy. The way to deal with the glut of words isn't to drop out of words. The great thing would be to say some right and forceful things for a change, not stop talking and leave the field to the doubletalkers. . . . The only reason I mention how I embarked on the cataloguing of Prof. Fisher's papers and wound up struggling through the French translations of Thomas Mann's incredible book is to establish how that book swamped me, and has haunted me ever since.

It doesn't matter one way or the other that I've never published a novel that doesn't reverberate with Mann's suspicions of elaborate talk and his insistence that the important human matters are to be looked for under the cloakings of words, in the deep, soundless spaces. But this orientation, away from the new brain and back somewhat to the old, if you want it in the language of cerebral cyto-architectonics, was what inspired me all through my efforts at pornography, was, in fact, the leitmotiv of all my porn writings, and very possibly accounts for the enthusiastic reception I got from my employers in that field, once I got going and could show my stuff.

That's not my point either. I only want to say that if I hadn't come across Mann's masterful tract downgrading and lowrating words, I could never have produced such simpy words in such abundance for the porn people, and made a career in that field. You have to have developed a considerable irony about the linguistic function to be able to manufacture and dispense pages in wholesale lots, as I did in my porn year. I won't say I made any countering music in my life to keep going, but I did make quantities of money, which helps you to keep going, not necessarily to any destination, of course.

I moved in with my friends Mike and Doris Sviridoff. Mike was a very bright young fellow and a shoe clerk in a men's shop called Chipp's, on Chapel Street just across from the Yale Art School. The three of us had many things in common, including a high regard for jazz of blues origins and an utter lack of interest in any aspect of our various jobs.

My life at this moment can be described in lacks.

I lacked a girl. We can't count Mildred. Mildred was the daughter of a geology professor and had the femininity of pumice. Mildred was a Klee-ey water colorist whose paintings were all in shades of mouse, which she insisted be taken for germane political comment. When drunk, which was whenever her swallow reflex was working, Mildred would play leapfrog over Chapel Street hydrants or perch wamper-jawed before her easel to lecture on the theme that all who did not sob over a novel titled *Jews Without Money* by the folksy *Daily Worker* columnist

Mike Gold were proto-crypto-psycho Storm Troopers. Her acrobatics discouraged outdoor ventures with Mildred, her logorrhea, indoor ones. Besides, she cut off communication with me when I suggested to her that Mike Gold would not be seeing the world and seeing it whole until he gave us a companion volume entitled *Money Without Jews*.

Back to my lacks. These included any prospect of work. I couldn't indefinitely go on pretending to sift Fisher's papers, and there wasn't any other work to go after. I could have gone back to the merchant marine, yes. (I forgot to establish that a few times in 1938–1939, when there was absolutely no alternative, I went down to the Sailors Union of the Pacific headquarters in New York; wangled what they called a trip card from them; hung around the hiring hall until jobs were posted that were so vile none of the people who outranked me, the full members and the probationary members, would take them; and signed on for this and that single trip.) I just didn't want to do that again. Our freighters were now dropping away from their convoys to head for the bottom of the North Atlantic with shivery regularity, and those that did get through often wound up in Murmansk, a port too far north for my tropical tastes and much too far east for my vaguely Trotskyite heresies.

What's more, my living quarters lacked a certain something. Mike and Doris had offered their living-room sofa to me but their attic apartment was much too small to accommodate a third person, nobody would have had any privacy. It turned out, though, that if you opened their rear door you found yourself in a *real* attic: bare rafters and laths, a couple of storage rooms. By luck I was able to arrange with the landlord to sleep on a cot in one of those storage compartments, using my friends' bathroom and kitchen when I had to.

The landlord was the third vice-president of the local union of clerical and warehouse workers, something like that. This unjocular man, who wore celluloid collars that looked like neck braces for a bad whiplash, who expelled his words as though they were phlegm and had the social graces of a sickle, was a rabid admirer of all things Soviet. He took bulky and voluble satisfaction in collecting five dollars a month from a former housemate of Leon Trotsky (whom he rated the chief demented mastiff among Russia's mad dogs) for the privilege of resting his wrecker's bones in a forest of outmoded picket signs from Nazi-Soviet Pact days demanding that the grabby paws of the hireling jackals of yowling Yankee imperialism be kept off the Workers' State. (After Hitler and Stalin had carved up Poland between them, of course, Hitler had turned on Stalin, and the latter was now making loud sounds of anti-fascist alliance in Washington's direction, which put a lot of picket signs out of action.)

The landlord only snapped his ruby sleeve garters in loud undupa-bility when I told him my paws were nowhere near anybody's State. He remained firm in his conviction that I'd been one of the chief schem-ers in the plot to sell the Soviet Republic down the river to Hitler. I couldn't get it to register on his brain that when Russia had finally been deposited in Hitler's hands it had been done by the Kremlin itself, presided over by Stalin, against the protests of people like me. This man took my five bucks every first of the month as though they were partial payment for my years in the Gestapo's employ, a mea culpa from an old social fascist.

So 1940 was developing into a rinderpest of a year. If 1936, 1937, 1938, and 1939, to name a few others, hadn't been beds of roses, 1940 was promising to be impetigo in the winter and erysipilas in the sum-mer, with a spew of herpes at the equinox and sprouts of glanders at solstice time. Less dermatologically, 1940, if it kept going this way, was bound to be 365 slow days of the hyena at the heels, making soft, sly sounds of slobber.

I'll elaborate on that. 1940 looked like a long stretch of pox with my name on it. I was foreigner to assets. My one abundance was in the shorts. All I was holding was my breath. You could chart the economy's slump by the sag in my belt. I couldn't see the clouds for the locusts. My fixed address was between a rock and a hard place.

Considering that I had background in no area of human endeavor except inhaling and exhaling, plus a fund of sympathy for my over-looked self—that I had only to survey my life circumstances to bring tears to my eyes—it might be asked: why didn't I become a writer there and then?

Admittedly, total innocence about the human condition along with unstinting compassion toward oneself have never deterred those with the literary itch; they inspire flaming careers at the typewriter. And, as I've hinted, I had the itch. All the same, the incipient proser in me was stopped cold. Not that I wanted to *live* before I took to emitting words professionally. Nothing that Byronesque. I wanted to *eat*, and the world was routing its nutriments elsewhere.

I mean, that was the answer I gave in those days when people asked why, if I was so hipped on writing, why, for Christ's sake, didn't I write? It was very close to a total lie, of course. I didn't write because I was abso-lutely terrified of writing. Even more terrified than I was of not writing.

To make things blacker still, my draft board was beginning to wonder what sort of figure I'd cut in O.D.'s.

That really pissed me. I didn't get their interest in my name at all. I failed to see why, after encouraging Hitler's boardinghouse reach for years, through Neville Chamberlain's solicitudes, through letting him and his pals romp unmolested through Spain, through sundry other services, the Western Nations and the Soviets now felt free to fish for my help in slapping the fellow's wrist to teach him table manners.

It was a matter of record that the Spotless Powers hadn't consulted me in the businesses of Spain, the Rhineland, Finland, Czechoslovakia, Munich, or even Addis Ababa. I thought it fucking presumptuous of them suddenly to face about and call on me to set right the Polish grab and Hitler's turning on his fellow grabber to the East. I wasn't in the mood to drop everything and hurry over to start a second front for Stalin, in view of all the Polish grabbing he'd done himself. I was still unenthusiastic about starting a first one for Franklin D., I was beginning to sense in him a tendency to get more upset over Berlin grabs than Moscow ones. Also, you know, he wasn't really that concerned about the poor Jews being gassed by the millions. First of all, his concern got started late. Second, he wasn't so concerned that he couldn't turn down boatloads of refugee Jews when in their naïveté they came sailing toward U.S. shores for asylum.

My impression of all Sovereign States, right, left, or center, was negative. By definition, I'd concluded, government of any location or hue was a steamrollering instrument that would up you from Field Worker to Project Supervisor without giving you the proper salary hike from $18 to $21. (That's exactly what they'd done to me on the WPA Writers Project.) You had to expect bilking from that source. Governments always stockpiled more field packs than pogo sticks. The thing to do when a government reached down for you was to move rapidly sideways.

Many afternoons I sat around Chipp's with Mike. Sometimes I tried on shoes, sometimes we talked. One day Mike said to me, "No matter how I look at it I don't see any future in shoes."

I said, "I don't see any future in stockinged feet, and the way things are going that's what I'll be in soon. What do you suggest?"

He said, "Defense jobs are opening up all over the place. Some of those plants with military contracts, you know, lend-lease supplies and all that, are working on three shifts. We could investigate."

I said, "I'm not against turning honest if that's the only way to get a living wage."

You have to understand the background against which this conversation took place. The idea of going to work in a factory had a very different connotation in 1940 from what it has now.

The Thirties had been overrun with blue-denim cosmotheisms and that in itself was strange. It seems that prolonged unemployment will move some men to theorize sweepingly about the significances of the thing they know the least about, work. The Depression had in fact produced a bumper crop of philosophers of labor who'd never known any labor but philosophy.

For a time I too had been partial to hammering proletarian ideologies, while abstaining from all forms of manual exertion. But no ideology was behind my positive response to Mike's suggestion that we go knocking on factory doors. There was one thought in my mind, that the military was showing signs of interest in me. If I could make myself an unideological proletarian there was always the chance that I could get myself seen by the authorities as an indispensable civilian, a role for which I felt a genuine calling, my first.

Defense industry was really clanking away in Connecticut. In 1940 our nation's posture was that of a fellow who doesn't care to muss his nice clothes by getting into a dirty fight but is more than happy to hold his less fastidious friends' coats while they go at it, and even supply them with the requisite brass knuckles. A defense job, I reasoned, would improve my situation in several ways: finance my eating; ward off or at least delay my merger with the armed forces; keep me too busy to lie around the attic, surrounded by moldering League for Peace and Democracy posters (on which Uncle Sam was forever shining J. P. Morgan's pearl-buttoned boots with a bloody rag labeled "Monopoly Profits") and staring ambiguously at my Royale portable.

I said to Mike, "I went around to a lot of factories when I was in New York last year, I never had any luck."

Mike said, "Things are different now, they're really short of help. Besides, they've set up procedures, they've got centers in the public schools where you can go to get tested for your manual skills. If they give you a paper saying you rate high in manual skills you can take it around to the employment offices, it carries a lot of weight."

I said, "Do you think we have any manual skills?"

He said, "You type with the best of them, and I slip shoes off and on very deftly, I've had many compliments on it. I wouldn't be surprised if we turned out to be manual geniuses."

We did just that. We took all the tests at the George Street school, we put together three-dimensional jigsaw puzzles, sorted odd geometric shapes, dropped the right curvy objects into the right curvy holes. Our hands won, if not hands down, at least handsomely. We both had genius mitts. Mike's, it turned out, were somewhat more genius than mine, which was understandable, they were more trained up, they'd been doing a lot more slipping off and on of shoes than mine had been doing typing. We both got certificates from the vocational-testing people saying that Connecticut manufactures would not come into their own until we two were running the machines.

Bridgeport, Mike pointed out, had most of the heavy industry. Bridgeport, he thought, was where we ought to look around. He left his shoe boxes, I left my Irving Fisher boxes, we headed for Bridgeport.

You chew. Sometimes even in the scratchiest of times, just by the law of averages, your teeth, if you keep them in motion, may connect with something not air.

CHAPTER 4

GRINDER DAYS

The first place we hit was Sikorsky's, where they made helicopters. That was the end of the line for Mike, they grabbed him and put him right in their apprentice school to learn spotwelding.

He learned it, all right, but I don't know that he ever did much of it. Just as he was taking his place on the assembly line the UAW started its organizing drive at the plant and Mike, a fellow with a level head and sharp instinct for human dealings, found himself leading it. When he did finally come onto the premises it was as shop steward for the newly recognized union rather than as a welder on the line.

He didn't stop there. Over the next years Mike was regional director for the UAW, then head of the Connecticut CIO, a power behind the election of governors and senators, as well as the labor representative on the Connecticut Arbitration Board, then a State Department official (under Kennedy, by special presidential appointment) developing contacts with organized labor in Latin America, then New Haven's Urban Redevelopment Director under Dick Lee, then New York's Commissioner of Human Resources under John Lindsay, finally, vice-president of the Ford Foundation in charge of its Division of National Affairs.

I don't know what the moral of Mike's story is—I *can* say that when you had the canniness and drive to get yourself moving in the

Depression, a time of general stall, you got to be quite a mover, practically a speed demon, and kept on going. I don't recommend finding yourself a depression from which to launch yourself into a career, that's doing it the hard way. All the same, if you're alert enough to make an inventory of your buried talents at a time when nothing's happening and there's mighty little call for talent, if you sweat to get yourself high on your toes when the world about you is stretched out flat and dozing, it can when life quickens again, when human affairs start to hum, pay off in unexpected ways—what you got mobilized in yourself is suddenly in demand on all sides, a lot of doors swing open wide, you're recognized as a doer and mover, you can just about write your own ticket.

Come to think of it, pornography did for me, a bit later that same year, just what the UAW drive at Sikorsky's did for Mike—gave me a focus, a thing to jump all the way in, an escalator I could ride on, a way to go.

Sikorsky's wanted no part of me, deft hands or no. I think they were suspicious of hands like that attached to a frame that had gotten itself a college degree. They couldn't imagine why a college graduate would want to put his hands to spotwelding unless it was to mess up their spots. Mike was all set but I had to make the rounds.

Each day I got out on the Boston Post Road and hitched a ride to Bridgeport, that hive of forges and mills. Though the lunchbox under my arm was empty I hoped soon to have the wherewithal to fill it. (It was built with several compartments for wherewithals.) I hadn't had the wherewithal to buy the box outright, I'd wheedled it, plus some dungarees and work shirts, from the manager of the five-and-dime in our neighborhood, leaving my Royale portable as security. That churlish hawker of ribbons and hair curlers, who wore a clip-on leather bow tie and an expression of goatish gloom, and who was never without bicycler's clips around his ankles though he owned no bike, was an addict of Mike Gold's stories about the estrangement between Jews and money.

Before I had the wherewithal to ransom my machine he'd almost finished typing a novel about the colonialist impulses behind some old Pope's Albigensian Crusades. Literature will rear its fitful head anywhere.

Heavy industry along the Eastern Seaboard had come to a major policy decision, to try to make its way without me. Sikorsky's had shown me the door despite the many vocational aptitude tests that said I had a knack for assembling copters, was devoted to the copter industry, and would likely come up with design innovations to revolutionize the engineering of rotary-blade aircraft. G.E. turned me down. G.M. had no openings. Westinghouse was suddenly full up. Baldwin Brass wanted neither hide nor hair of my person.

Considering how eager I was to speed up the flow of guns and how determined the gunmakers of the region were to keep me from their gates, you have to ask just how devoted those firms really were to the defense of the Free West. But subversion of this topside order went unnoticed by the FBI. Its shoulder tappers were too busy screening "premature anti-fascists" out of sensitive areas.

It's a fact, our security officers had taken to classifying political hotheads according to the "maturity" or "prematurity" of their hot flashes. (This might have had something to do with my trouble in locating a defense job.) Anybody who'd jumped the gun by getting more than oratorically riled up about Hitler before our government did was deemed worth keeping a dossier on, and maybe frisking from time to time for small bombs.

Right, the degree of pollution in a dissenter's politics was now to be measured in the fourth dimension, by the clock. The new horologers of our security bureaus were seldom sophisticated enough to appreciate that some who had been so skittery as to become early-bird opponents of the Hitler grabs had been for the same reasons, and with the same precocity, opposed to the Stalin grabs—much more singlemindedly than, say, Franklin Delano Roosevelt.

One day, maybe, our history books will be asking pointed questions about the *tardy* anti-fascists. The latecomers to the ranks of folks who don't take to grabs of any color, will, in other words, stop pointing fingers at the prematurists in the fight against the power players and turn them finally in the direction of the Roosevelts and other loudmouths, the ones who thunder that peace is indivisible until they see a chance to do some profitable dividing, and then, at last, we'll be boning up on our true history instead of our chatter of yesteryear.

Eventually I got lucky. In Bridgeport I came upon a small metal-working shop with a manpower shortage so acute that it asked nothing of job applicants except a standard number of hands and feet and enough sense of balance not to keel over during working hours.

My extremities were counted. My perpendicularity was established. I was led to a grinding machine where, after a 20-minute on-the-job training course, I was left to shape minute steel cylinders into high-speed drills to be used by the Picatinny Arsenal in Western Pennsylvania for boring certain crucial holes in hand grenades.

Holes were essential to grenades, I was suddenly essential to the holes. As a key figure in the production of these strategic cavities I was bound to be pretty strategic too, even in the eyes of my draft board.

I was ready to further the hole industry every way I could.

A grinding machine looks simple enough. You lock the metal element to be worked on in a heavy steel chuck. You position this chuck on the work table and flip a switch which magnetizes the table to hold the chuck in place. Suspended over the table is a belt-run wheel covered with a carborundum abrasive strip—by turning hand cranks on either side of the machine you maneuver the wheel up and down and back and forth, to bite into the element from various angles and to various depths.

A fluid of the color and consistency of condensed milk is fed from a nozzle onto the surface being ground, to keep it cool. A backlash of this fluid sprays over your face and hair, to keep you hot. The job sheet for each grinding batch specifies the tolerance you're allowed.

Let's talk about tolerance. The term refers to the measure by which the dimensions of the finished element can be off, how much departure from the specifications the foreman will tolerate before throwing you out on your ear. I found out that foremen are fantastically intolerant in this matter of tolerances, real bigots.

Sometimes the tolerance is 1/1,000th of an inch, sometimes 1/10,000th. You check the accuracy of your cuts with a hand instrument called a micrometer.

Some people, I know, would say that in my new career of shaving inch-long slivers of steel into sharp-tipped drills I was making more trouble for Adolph Hitler than I had with all my clarion speeches and articles over the years. It's possible. But I never felt more cut off from the mainstreams of human striving than when I stood at that machine 10 and 12 hours a day, going through Chaplin routines with my arms as condensed milk slid down my face. Nor so set upon. I felt vastly set upon.

It wasn't a case of paranoia. Though the grinding machine stands there meekly and modestly, as though with no thought but to serve, it's really a contrivance designed to abrade its operator's sanity. Here's the whole source of the trouble. As the wheel bites, it in turn gets bitten— grinding, it's ground. Because the wheel wastes steadily away, the calibrations on the cranks controlling its movements become less and less reliable guides to the depths of its cuts.

Let's say the wheel gets 1/1,000th of an inch scraped off it. Plainly, the cut it now makes is going to be 1/1,000th of an inch shallower than it's been set for. This is a circumstance that can, and does, make strong men weep.

What do you do about it? Well, there's one thing you *try* to do. As you set the hand cranks you do your best to make allowances for the wheel's wear and tear, you correct the calibration readings by the amount you judge the incision would otherwise fall short. You *try* to compensate for the wheel's own abrasion.

Ah, but you can never estimate the degree of the wheel's wear at a given moment and stop there. Its erosion is an ongoing process. No sooner have you figured out, by the most delicate testing, how far down the wheel's been worn than your calculations are ancient history.

After 20 years devoted to outguessing his wheel a master grinder gets to be pretty good at reckoning allowances on a progressive scale. I'll remind the reader that my own indoctrination in the mystique of carborundum had lasted for 20 minutes, and that prior to this my experience in abrasive activity had been limited to scratching my head.

When I discovered that the calibrations on my hand cranks couldn't be taken as fixed guides but were relative to the wheel's shrinkage at a particular moment, I had to guess at the corrections. Invariably, with the impatience of the hotspur anti-fascist, I over-compensated.

On the analyst's couch over-compensation can be dealt with. In the grinding of high-speed drills for Picatinny's hand grenades it's a disaster. Let's say you're working as I was, to a tolerance of 1/10,000th of an inch. If your first cut is too shallow, what you come out with is a fat drill, which isn't too bad—you've got another try. But suppose, in your effort to compensate for the wasted wheel, you bite too deep. Say 3/10,000ths of an inch too deep.

Suddenly you're out of business. What you've got on your hands is a very, very skinny drill. Over-slenderized tools are not in demand in the American armaments industry and you can understand this prejudice. If Picatinny used skinny drills, its grenades would have skinny holes, and you wouldn't be able to pull the pins out of such holes.

There's no way, of course, to paste the removed steel back on the cylinder and try again. The thing is unsalvageable, a reject. So you sneak it into your lunchbox when the foreman isn't looking and start on a new cylinder, mopping the condensed milk from your brow, wondering why, when they invented the wheel, our forebears didn't have the get-up-and-go to invent a wear-proof one.

My particular grinding wheel was one of the ranking saboteurs in our defense effort. The match between me and it was rigged from the start. Try though I might to figure its sly wearage, I invariably, after many small sly maneuvers, allowed myself a disastrous sprint, the result of which was a drill too slim for anything but picking the teeth. At the end of each workday my lunchbox was crammed with steel toothpicks.

I still have a supply of them among my war souvenirs. I can recommend them to those dedicated toothworriers who shy away from the flashy gold tools of their trade but will not settle for gimcrack wooden or plastic ones. The price is right.

I ground those drills. I ground my teeth. I wasn't suited for the life of a grinder, it rubbed me the wrong way, I found it as galling as it did me. Standing there at the machine day after day, making drills both over-fat and over-skinny, I got a picture of all of humanity hunched over buffing machines, leaders and government heads in particular, all the kings and all their counselors, trying to smooth the world into the right shape, polishing away at the rough surfaces, most often making too timid cuts that evened an inconsequential patch here and there but changed the basic shape of things in no essential way, now and then in fits of temper leaping at the bullheaded elements, scouring, scraping, filing, scuffing like mad, attacking all surfaces within reach, and overdoing it, of course, forgetting the specifications on the job sheet, the tolerances, ruining the job so it has to be thrown away—and with no lunchbox to hide the botched work in.

CHAPTER 5

SUMMONED, SAVED

Deliverance. Letter in the mails one fine day from Bettina Tokay.

Bettina was a colt-cute Mormon girl from Provo, Utah. The year before, when I'd been hanging around the SUP hiring hall on the Manhattan waterfront trying to wangle another shipping job, I'd met her in the Village, where she frequented bars and spaghetti houses favored by Trotskyites.

I won't call Bettina a Trotskyite fellow traveler because you can't travel with a thing unless it's in transit and the Trotskyites we knew in those days were seldom going anywhere but to the movies.

It would be stretching a point to call the Trots of that time a movement—the motion they most often engendered communally was one for adjournment.

No, the Trots, in those profoundly Stalinized days, were a sodality, a debating society, an anvil chorus, a constituency of the outermost outskirts, an onmium-gatherum of those extremists so anti as to be against all the other antis. Bettina Tokay was a sometime socializer on the fringes of this Trot bunch, which, since it was not often called upon to unseat governments or so much as the men's-room attendant in a wardheeler's office, had a lot of spare time for socializing.

Don't ask me what a prancy-legged Mormon girl from Provo, Utah, was doing on the feather edges of this microscopic coterie. The fact is that there was a sizable contingent of Utah Mormons in and around the Trotskyite ranks and nobody knew what any of them were doing there. I asked about this. One fellow, a sailor we called Irish, offered the thought that Trotsky's beard was reminiscent in its patriarchal charisma of Joseph Smith's—I think he was being facetious. Somebody else suggested that Trotskyism might have stirred up archaic departurist sediments deep in the Mormon racial unconscious; the Mormons, after all, had been the leftmost wing of 19th-century Protestantism, oppositionists in a church that had itself started as an underground opposition, the Trotskyites of the Frontier. I saw a further possibility, once a Mormon takes up smoking and drinking there's a big chance he'll lose *all* control.

In any case, Bettina Tokay was only a hanger-on. Trotskyism was for her less a political credo than a place to go and people to see. By profession Bettina was a comparison shopper for Macy's and a shoplifter (not necessarily in that order), two conveniently linked occupations.

Bettina wrote:

"Big news! Things are happening that may change your whole life! This Argentinian beauty, a real knockout, has blown into town. Her name sounds like Zoma Borracha de la Ciudad (but don't hold me to that, I don't know much Spanish) and take it from me, she's the living end, speaks nine languages, plays concert harpsichord, old friend of Henry Miller and all the Paris artists and writers, this one's gone and she's having too much of a ball to come back. She's settled in the Village and I can tell you, it's having an unsettling effect on the Village. The impact she's had on our stodgy (compared with her) crowd is nothing short of a revolution. Thing of it is, Zoma happens to have connections with a big-money literary outfit that needs all the good writers they can get, and they pay well, a dollar a manuscript page, and a lot of our friends through Zoma are getting rich working for these people, and I told Zoma what a gorgeous writer you are and she said fine, by all means get the boy down here and we'll make him a capitalist. So you quit fooling around with those grenades or whatever they are and get your butt down here fast, O.K.? There's no future in hand grenades for a type like you, for God's sake. Besides, suppose you got to be the best little old grenade maker in the Western Hemisphere and then the war's over and there's no more call for those hard apples, where's that leave you? War's war but you've got your future to think of, Bern. Get to grinding out some words, I say, the market for them is steadier. You were always mooning around about how nice it would be to sit down somewhere and be a writer, well, here's your chance to sit, buddy. This is the boat with your name on the prow so if you miss it it means all that big talk was just talk. Some destinies are manifest. *Do not take this summons lightly.*"

Bettina had lost her Latter-day Saintliness but she couldn't quite get rid of the messianic ferment behind it. During her Mormon indoctrination she'd spent two years as a missionary in some place like Tanganyika and her air of tooting-the-flock-to-hallelujah-land had never altogether dissipated.

I didn't mind the salvatory klaxon note in her letter. Whatever it was she was scheming to get me into, I knew I'd be doing it seated, with no milky fluids cascading over my cheekbones.

My removal to the World of Letters was not accomplished without a hitch. Down to the Post Road again. Thumb a petitioner again.

Hours later I was sitting in a skylit studio parlor on West 11th Street, surrounded by Hindustani silk screens decorated with the lush horizontal pageantry of the *Kamasutra*, blinking at the beauteous, gazelle-necked Zoma Borracha de la Ciudad, known to her intimates as Zo-Zo though zo-zo she visibly was not in any aspect or dimension.

"You are familiar with the Lady Chatterley?" this dazzler said for openers.

"Uh, you could say we have a nodding acquaintance," I said. (It was true. Each time I'd tried to read Lawrence's book it had put me to sleep.)

"Sum and substance of this entire whole enterprise," she said, "is precisely that we are trying to go beyond the Lady Chatterley."

"I believe we should always make an effort to progress, and not rest on our laurels at any one place," I said.

"Mr. Lawrence but opened up the door," she said. "We subsequents, if we are to carry on forward his pioneer's work, must pass now through. Beyond of those portals sleep new and unfingered continents but hungry for our shovels."

We were drinking green crème de menthe on shaved ice, a refreshment the WPA had neglected to serve during coffee breaks, maybe because they tended to run from 9:00 A.M. to 5:00 P.M.; I was not in the mood to argue.

"I'm ready to dig," I said. "Just what is it we're looking for? How far down will we have to go?"

"Until the fundaments and the ultimate bottoms!" she clarified. "Unto the nucleus of the heart of the core of all surge, where reside the First Whys and Wherefores, there, precisely! Down amongst the veriest deeps, to the hatchery of sizzles, where rock is moltened and the essential steams hiss backward and forth! Finally, to the source of the bubble and the scorch! We are overdued for some centrality!"

This was the overall program. At my urging Zo-Zo filled me in on the specifics.

Seemed there was this man whose name, when uttered under water, would sound something like Barneybill Roster. Barneybill Roster was of the view that current creative writing fell short of potential. In particular, that branch of it billed as science fiction. Science fiction was constructioned on a premise of the wedding of science to fiction, no? Well, which science has in our hurtling times been most revolutionized, most overhauled with new insightments, if not the up-and-comer science of Sexology? Now, where was being written a science fiction based on the new science of the sex activities, eh? Where was the literature to dramatize our new laboratory knowledge of Eros, now that the sly and snaky Señorita was being examined from nostril to haunch through microscopes?

We were not speaking of the trash scribblings, comic-strip titillations, the junky thrill tales for masturbators, understand. Such a bilge literature has always been in existence, giving out more heat than light. But where was the *serious* fiction incorporating within itself the new sexological informations in re orgasm through all its gradations, the breaking forth from the muscular armoring of the impotents and the frigids, the liberational homecoming to the state of natural polymorpher perversing, climax as the neurologic technique for the oceanic alterationing of consciousness, the dialectical subtleties of the clitoral-vaginal interactions, premature ejaculateness and aspermia as merely differing signs of the regression into orality, the enthronement of matriarchical over patriarchical and its many consequences in positional varieting, the female castrator with her consuming penis enviouses as the latest reincarnation of the icy White Goddess with her many phallicky snakes, the aphrodisiacal aspects of hasheesh and similar stimulates, all these recent approaches? No, no, as regarded the science of sex behaviors science fiction was still in the Glacier Ages, the time of mud burrows. Well, this Barneybill Roster, he understood that the time was arriving for fiction to open this door too. Rather, he understood that D. H. Lawrence, Freud, Reich, Bergler, not to mention the Marquis de Sade, Herr Leopold von Sacher-Masoch, Kraft-Ebbing, Havelock Ellis, and Fatty Arbuckle, *had* opened this ultimate door, and fiction makers were now only called upon to proceed through. Barneybill Roster wished to make his contribution to the expanding of man's consciousness in this final area by bringing into being belatedly such an up-to-date true fiction of the genitals and their logics and logistics.

For one reason or other—*for one reason or other!*—Barneybill Roster had urgent need of numerous good and serious writers to create the after-Lawrence and after-Freud sex-science fiction, conceived with depth and caliber and also, to be sure, though without descent to junkiness, a certain spirit, a dash, even some verve. Not to tickle people, but to enlighten them and encourage proper energy concentrations to their various erogenous zones, bringing to pass an increased vibration and glow in all vital parts and with a further bonus of hygienic, therapeutic enhancements in the fields of family and social dealings, politics, all interpersonal transactions—which, of course, *could* entail some incidental sensations of tickle along the way, but as side blossoms, not main fruits—some agitational heats in such undertakings are unavoidable but let them be accompanied at all times by intense educational light. Man must be made to function in orgonizational grandness again, with overall energetics, with unabashment, below the neck as above, to correct finally the cerebral over-emphases. Barneybill Roster was ready to pay for such a healing new literature of the sex functions, provided it was not conceived in the low spirit of peepingtomistic trash, which was a hangover from the old emotional plague of those frozen in muscles and orgasmical centers. Barneybill Roster was ready to pay well. At the rate of one crisp dollar per manuscript page, more than Dostoevsky got in his best week. . . .

"Do not steer yourself bum," Zo-Zo concluded. "Naturally, Barneybill Roster requires of his writers a certain élan and dramatic vividness. He is not interested in the textbook dryness. We must present sex as actual, not actuarial. So—you are ready to assist in the efforts to pull away this larky contessa Miss Ursula Eros from the hands of the academics and make her loose in the foots again?"

"He knows that in a free society individuals should be free to go where they want," Bettina observed. "Sure he'll assist."

"I know that in a free society individuals should be free to go some place that's not Bridgeport, Connecticut," I said. "Sure I'll assist."

"Bravo, bravo!" Zo-Zo said. "Splendidly phrased! I sense in you the vocation! I have the most high of hopes! Two weeks from hence I meet with Barneybill to present my new work and also the work of my increasing protégés. Bring to me on the Wednesday after Wednesday next your first Eros-ive novel, please, Eros-ive, you understand, this is my phrase for the New Fictioneerers of the Sexualistic Enlightenment, and assemble your creation with such cunning, please, that without being scabby and garbage it is nevertheless of a decided lushness and unstinting in the warm detail, do this, my lad, and pretty damn quick I make you to become enrolled in the honors list of Barneybill's Blooming Boys! The length of the opus is utterly up to you, provided it has spice in the breadth and depth. Merely determine the arithmetic of your wants and write from this sum accordingly. Otherwise to say, be as long in the pages as you wish to be fat in the pocketbook. Remember only, we are devising here a literature to enflesh what through all previous history of the written words has been scamped over by the blue-nose asteriskers! Elaborate and make to do the tarantella those thin-lipping asterisks! Compose of those cold anti-genital asterisks a turmoiled landscape! Away all Puritan killjoyous draperies! Write! Write!"

CHAPTER 6

I Write! I Write!

I took a furnished room—one more—on West 13th Street near the corner of Seventh Avenue. I borrowed Bettina's typewriter. My assignment, as I saw it, was to produce a spicy novel that proceeded fleetly from the Marquis de Sade and Herr Leopold von Sacher-Masoch to a point somewhere beyond Fatty Arbuckle; and mine was a sheltered head which to this moment had produced nothing but Kremlinological book reviews, war correspondence from a safe distance, analyses of the ethnic components of Connecticut's population, tributes to flaking ceilings, and an occasional laundry list.

I needed a minimum of $300 to get my belongings out of hock, establish myself in a modest apartment, buy some clothes, and have a fast month's sense of solvency, so my first piece of fiction had to be at least 300 pages long. I had 15 days to complete it, which meant that, if I began that evening and worked seven days a week, I'd have to write 20 pages daily.

The question was—about what?

I hadn't the least idea. The flesh was more than willing, but the spirit had had no training in a prosody of post-Lady bent. Nowhere at Yale, not even in the English Department of the Graduate School, had I noticed a course in Advanced Lit, Eros-ive Subdivision. A college education, it appeared, was not always a Preparation for Life, not the sort of life you ran into south of Union Square, anyhow.

First, I needed people to write about. I asked myself if I'd come across any notable sepia souls lately.

My thoughts padded to that cabinet in my memory bank marked WPA WRITERS PROJECT (AND OTHER FEDERALLY FINANCED NARCOLEPSIES) then slid open a drawer and extracted the punchcard labeled WALDO GROSSCUP STIGGLEE III AND FAMILY (WHO THROW EMPTY CIDER JUGS AT OWLS)—on seeing it, I went into shock that was partly of recognition, partly of miasm revisited.

On our WPA staff had been a contingent of old-stock Connecticut Yankees from the less stylish backwoods stretches outside of New Haven, the rural-delivery districts of Cheshire, Branford, Hamden, Guilford, Bethany, Wallingford, and the clusters of weather-clawed cabins in the clam-digging communities you found up and down the shoreline of Long Island Sound going east. These people had been assigned to the guide-making project not because of an aptitude for words but because of a total ineptitude in handling tangible tools. They were not helpful on road gangs: their hands shook too much to hold a shovel. They were a hazard on wood-clearing squads: with their tendency toward inertial labor they might after sawing through a tree go on to saw through any legs in the neighborhood, including their own.

The Writers Project was a logical dumping ground for these viscous-eyed, slack-jawed last gasps of the flakier First Families of Connecticut; at our typewriters they would inflict damage on neither their fellow workers nor themselves, though the mayhem they visited on the English language might be irreparable. Before the WPA they'd lazed around on their front porches without, I judged, even whittling—they had no fingers missing.

Waldo Grosscup Stigglee III was of this leaden-lidded breed. As a member of our graphics task force he had the specialized job of going over our maps to color paved roads red and unpaved ones blue—on a lively day, when he could make his eyes focus, he got them right almost half the time.

Waldo's only gainful employment before Washington pre-empted him for the Arts had been as attendant in a rural gas station. He lost that job the ill-starred day he went to service a plumber's truck and, hazed by hangover, inserted the gas pump feed into the first hole he saw, the unplugged end of a fat pipe protruding from the half-ton's rear. The other end of the pipe, it turned out, was about two inches from the cowlick of the plumber's assistant, who was in the driver's seat; it, too, was unplugged. The plumber's assistant, a bucolic type, was smoking a corncob pipe. Ten gallons of high-octane suddenly cascaded on him and his cowlick and his corncob, with results which would have awed Prometheus. Waldo went home with his severance pay and the conviction that plumbers' assistants are a bunch of soreheads. It didn't occur to him that this particular plumber's assistant had cause for some soreness in the head. There was no hair on it, and only an occasional relic of skin.

I'd visited Waldo Stigglee and his kin in their shingled lean-to on dazy weekends. The blood of Puritan divines was alleged to run in their veins but I found no Cotton Mathers among them. What intensity existed in their lives came less from piety than from homebrew. Though their forefathers had established a state famed as the "Land of Steady Habits," the one habit surviving in them with some degree of steadiness was that of lofting the elbow.

Their gin, unlike that of another eminent Yankee, Eli Whitney, was developed exclusively in the bathtub. Indeed, their blurry faces suggested that in their view gin-mixing was what *bathtubs* had been developed for.

Days, Waldo mapped country lanes for the WPA; nights, he tore along them—blue lanes or red lanes, it made no difference—in his rachitic, early-model Reo, surrounded by an assortment of sisters and cousins and aunts, all of them heaving empty applejack jugs at the owls. I'd been with the Stigglees on some of their nocturnal joy-rides. I'd heaved a few jugs myself, without being clear as to just what we had against owls. Nevertheless, with enough applejack in you, you can get enormously incensed at owls.

The Stigglees were a more tightly knit tribe than most. Knit? Say, rather, interwoven, blended, fused, homogenized.

At one point, when Waldo was holding forth in graphic artist's detail about the amative talents of a woman I assumed to be his wife, it was suddenly borne home to me, by the direction his hands as well as his words were taking, that he wasn't talking about his wife at all, but his youngest sister. His thesis seemed to be that, cohabitatively speaking, this bobby-socked sister was notably more gifted than the two older ones. Other members of the family were present. They voiced their opinions pro and con.

It was a long and complicated forum, full of technical jargon and conducted in gross violation of all rules of parliamentary procedure. The heated diatribes from the floor were interrupted frequently by lengthy draws from the hard-cider jug. As the debate's intramural referents became clear I made more and more visits to the jug myself, so the reader will perhaps forgive me if my minutes of the proceedings are somewhat jumbled.

What follows in no way pretends to be a verbatim transcript, which would only land us in jail anyhow. I'm trying to do no more than recapture the sense and mood of the demented thing. Though aural memory falters, gamy aura hangs on.

It seems to me that Waldo's youngest sister accepted his high commendations but offered some critical remarks about *Waldo's* prowess.

It seems to me that the two older sisters hotly disputed Waldo's rating of the females in the family, and reminded him of their own merits.

It seems to me that Waldo's father then took issue with Waldo's assessment of skills on the family's distaff side, it being his own contention that the *middle* sister was far and away the frontrunner.

The impression persists that Waldo's wife then spoke up to say that her father-in-law's evaluations had to be more accurate than her husband's because the older man had established for all present that he was the more competent to judge in these matters.

The suspicion lingers, as I wish it wouldn't, that Waldo's mother then disputed Waldo's wife's valorization of Waldo and Waldo's father.

I have the bothersome notion in my head that there was also a brother present who argued with a knowledgeable air that none of the ladies in the family could hold a candle to Waldo's wife in these delicate caliperings.

So it went at the Stigglee get-together. More or less like that: as I say, my report is unavoidably fuzzed.

In any case, when I remembered this family that seemed to stay together so remarkably through the scrupulous avoidance of prayer, I saw that they would be promising folk to follow down the primrose path from Leopold and the Marquis to the exuberant Fatty and beyond. It would be no hardship to portray the reeling Stigglees in their full state of polymorph-perverse pottiness. It required no act of imagination, only a re-creation of their ingroup recreations.

Stigglees of assorted sizes, shapes, and laxities were *what* I'd write about. But *how*—what was to be the approach, the tone, the flavor, the style?

I'd never been able to read the classic works of erotica—all they aroused in me was my sleep center, not the kind of arousal I was now called upon to write from and about; the masters could furnish me no models. Though I was partial to the fine frenzies of Dostoevsky, his head-long manner, it seemed to me, would work more satisfactorily with characters bound for Siberia than with those bound for bed. Louis-Ferdinand Céline, too, had caught my fancy, but an eroticism conveyed in his vomitous argot would, I feared, come out rather like a hymn composed by B. S. Pully.

Inspiration: I would present the Stigglees in the fashion of Henry Miller, an old hand at presenting Stigglees!

Why Miller? For one thing, his first books had dazzled me when I was in college, and his crackling, muscled, high-energy style was well suited for the groinier projects. But there were other considerations.

Zo-Zo was not only a friend of Brooklyn's ranking expatriate, she considered him *the* fecundative seer of our time, a man who battered open balky emotional doors when they were there and blasted holes in spiritual walls that were doorless. Zo-Zo screened this Sexualist-Revolutionary prose for Barneybill Roster. She was the door I had to pass through, or the wall through which I must blast passage, to reach Barneybill, from whom came negotiable dollars. A Milleresque novel, I sensed, would give me a passport through Zo-Zo's magic portals and safe conduct to Barneybill Roster and solvency.

Ask not why I went looking for literary models when all I had to do was write like myself. I was 24, and who this self was that I might write like was a total mystery to me, nor was there any Washington Square Rorschach I might petition for quick defining.

True, I had done a bit of writing, but not in fields which encouraged the raising of an independent voice for the utterance of strong personal statements: in Marxist polemics you do a lot of quoting, often without quotation marks, and in ethnic sociology you spend most of your time counting heads without having the slightest idea what's inside them or, for that matter, your own.

Besides, even if I had evolved a personal style in those highly routinized fields, it wouldn't have worked too well in a dramatization of post-Lady tendencies.

My furnished room was too small to get a desk in. I sat on the bed, typewriter on knees, and began to bring the many versatile Stigglees together in all the permutations and combinations the human anatomy, if not the law, allows.

The human anatomy, I discovered, unlike the law, sets very few limits on the whims of sexual athletes. The human anatomy, with its smiling, rubbery laissez faire, permits the erotist's imagination to go completely double-jointed.

I diddled Stigglees. I Waring-Blended Stigglees. I interwove Stigglees. I tossed Stigglees back and forth. I invented all manner of exotic flying trapezes and attached to them many lusting young Stigglees, and some not so young. But invent is the wrong word. I simply thought myself back to that upcountry frowst littered with empty cider jugs and owl corpses and set down my noisome recollections, uncottened by mather.

On the 15th day of my labors—at the exact bottom of the page exactly numbered 300—all permutations and combinations exhausted, all Stigglees neatly laid away, no loose ends left after such a post-Lady looseness of ends—I typed that magical word, FINIS, and lapsed into a self-congratulatory coma. Thinking, $300 I needed, and 300 pages I wrote.

Had I been capable of working to such fine tolerances in the machine shop, I would have been a master grinder. If words were grenades, as Carl Sandburg and Archibald MacLeish were beginning unconvincingly to argue, my contribution to the war effort might have been immense, immense.

. . .

There was nothing to do but wait. It would be days before we knew how my first literary effort had been received. To pass the time, Bettina Tokay briefed me on the background of the Zo-Zo-Barneybill partnership.

Zo-Zo Borracha de la Ciudad (her name would sound something like that if spoken under water) was the wife of a Rumanian wheat and coffee trader. She lived for some years in Paris, playing her harpsichord, a good knife and fork, and the field. Fiercely vanish in her tastes, she'd hung out with the advanced poets and painters, among them Henry Miller. An incorrigible patroness at heart, determined to further the more flamboyant arts, she'd distributed moneys to these poets and painters with a glad, even exulting, hand.

Zo-Zo's husband, being both Rumanian and economy-minded, if one can be permitted that redundancy, questioned her acting Horn of Plenty to the Left Bank. His argument was that she had a perfect right to stake all the scrounging esthetes she wished, *if* the capital came from her pocket. Zo-Zo saw his point. She granted that it would be unethical for her to go on distributing her husband's profits if he reckoned her lavishments a loss. She began to look around for ways to earn her own moneys, which she could dispense without qualms.

This was when she remembered Barneybill Roster.

Barneybill Roster, a Manhattan book dealer, had long doted on the works of Henry Miller. Barneybill had made the long trip over to Paris expressly to seek Henry out, announce his adoration, and inquire as to whether Henry might have the least interest in writing Sexualist-Revolutionary fiction at the rate of two dollars a page, twice what its less eminent practitioners received.

Henry had replied that he wouldn't write any such garbage for *$200* a page. He was ready, however, to make a concession to the entrepreneur of erotica. He would make carbons of the pages he wrote for himself, for his own books, and sell these *carbons* to Barneybill, regardless of content, at the rate of two dollars per page.

Not precisely what Barneybill had in mind, but he wasn't rejecting any proposal from the avantgarde's new stormy petrel. In Barneybill's glandular pantheon Henry Miller was rated the foremost New-Sexologer of them all, the shackle-breaker of our times. How refuse carbons from this man's typewriter? It would have been like turning down an offer from the Essenes' chief rabbi of Xeroxed copies of the Dead Sea Scrolls as they came hot from the scribe's table.

Barneybill expressed his gratitude for any and all crumbs. As he boarded the boat-train to head back to New York he told Henry and Zo-Zo that if they ever did hear of some lively new talents who *would* write genitalizing fiction for him at the prevailing rates, he'd love to be put in touch.

Barneybill Roster was the answer to Zo-Zo's fiscal problems. She would go to New York, join the Sexualist-Revolutionary word mill, compose tome after tome of royally purple prose out of the richness of her own explorations in this area, make oodles of money, support oodles of poets and painters.

"So here she is," Bettina told me. "Thanks to his wife's impeccable ethics, which he called into being, the Rumanian wheat dealer's wifeless. Zo-Zo's on her seventh post-Lady novel now, and going strong. She's big-hearted, Zo-Zo is. Here in the Village she's found lots more deserving artist types. She can't very well finance *them*. She's working around the clock as it is to keep her Paris friends eating. The best she can do for her new disciples, the literary ones anyhow, is to get *them* writing this New-Sexology for Barneybill Roster. At last count she's got 20 Village writers pouring out this stuff for Barneybill. It's caused a revolution around here. All up and down Bleecker Street you'll find writer types eating who never ate before, some in French restaurants, even ones where you have to wear a tie and look clean-shaven. The sweatshirt is disappearing from our streets, some actually starch their collars. It's a whole new way of life. If you pass muster, you'll be Number 21 among Barneybill's Publicists for the Privates. You may wind up buying a suit in Brooks Brothers, if they like your stuff. You might even take me to dinner at Pavillon, should you turn out to have a dirty enough mind and not too many Trotskyite scruples against white tablecloths."

I hoped against hope I'd turn out to have any sort of mind needed to establish me in this magic inner and under circle of Barneybill Roster's. First and foremost because I didn't want to let Zo-Zo down. I hadn't before had a mentor of any description, let alone one with a gazelle neck. I wanted to please that stylish lady in every way. Next to her Nora, the blond English teacher of my high school wet dreams, was a pepless pimple in too large tennis sneakers. I was ready to take harpsichord lessons, if Zo-Zo was so minded.

CHAPTER 7

I MEET MY MAKER

I was made! I'd be paid! I was in! Zo-Zo found my chronicle of the Stigglees of the randoming pelvises to be inspired, a revelatory unpeeling of the squirmy Yank psyche.

Better still—Barneybill Roster, from whom all blessings flowed, considered me a find. If Trotsky could say that Céline had strolled into Literature as other men do into their parlors, it was Barneybill Roster's joyous opinion that I cakewalked into Pornography as a Capone into the federal pen.

I was launched on a meteoric career chasing the post-Lady. Barneybill Roster had decided to pay me *two* dollars a page for my grand offering. He wanted to meet me. He'd deem it an honor and a privilege to hand me my $600 in person and salute me for the New-Sexological portals I was dynamiting open.

Triumph, yes. But I didn't feel triumphant.

The man was praising me to the skies, showering the wildest compliments on my first literary try, and what it stirred in me, unexpectedly, was annoyance, even resentment. Somewhere in his accolades I sensed an insult that made me want to belt him one though I'd never laid eyes on him.

I suppose the only kind of acceptance I could have taken from this man with some grace would have been a grudging acknowledgment that I was just barely competent for the job but that I'd have to do. There are some professions you'd prefer to just barely squeak through, some employers from whom faint praise might be endurable. But all-out acclaim? An outrage.

Maybe if I'd previously won a few Nobel Prizes for my contributions to the deciphering of the Rosetta Stone or the molecular analysis of dioxyribonucleic acid I could have taken these heaped congratulations with some equanimity. As things stood it elevated my hackles to hear myself hailed as "a fellow called to Genital Fiction as few have been since the invention of the written word."

Barneybill Roster actually said that. The intemperate man. I found myself chafing under his adoration. Of course, the bonus of double pay was going to cushion the heavy blow of this rollicking success.

I set out for my appointment with mixed feelings. I perked up immediately when I discovered that the office I was going to was in the Time-Life skyscraper in Rockefeller Center. It was in this very building that the personnel people of Time-Life, Inc. had informed me over and over that for a Yale grad I showed a distressing deficiency in vocational concentration.

Time-Life, Sikorsky, and even Lev Davidovitch Trotsky had found the same lack of career focus in my personality inventory. Now I was going to meet with Barneybill Roster, who was convinced that I had not only the focus for Pornography but a positive genius for it. There was an indication here that the personality canvassing of helicopter manufacturers, Luce editors, and Bolshevik-Leninist firebrands alike was spotty enough to leave certain of the rarer talents unexplored.

Barneybill Roster's place of business was indeed a book center. Barneybill Roster was a dealer in literary Americana of the loftiest order. His establishment was low-key lavish, featuring mahogany-paneled walls, Chippendale love seats, renovated cobblers' benches for end tables, a colonial spinning wheel made into a lamp base. Behind the protective glass of the hand-carved wooden bookcases placed here and there were locked all but priceless first editions of Thomas Paine, Thomas Jefferson, Benjamin Franklin, Herman Melville, many of them in mint condition. Nowhere in view was there a work of erotica, not even Frank Harris' hyperthyroid autobiography.

I took it that Barneybill Roster pushed founding-fatherly classics over the counter and the New Fiction of the Sexualist Enlightenment under it. His two occupations of Patriotism and Pornography did not seem to me so clearly linked as were Bettina Tokay's comparison shopping and shoplifting. Bettina simply made a note of an article's price and then stole it. I saw no way in which you could sell a first edition of the *Federalist Papers* and slip in a copy of the *Stigglee Chronicles* as book dividend.

Barneybill Roster was a disconcertingly ugly man. He was unprepossessing to a degree that made you wonder how he had the nerve to leave the house. His mere presence was an affront. Taken one by one, his features were not particularly obnoxious, but they had been put together with such slapdash indifference to elementary design principles as to make you cringe.

His large head would have worked all right on a large man but he was small, small and meagerly fleshed; so he appeared almost hydrocephalic. His long arms too were all right of and by themselves, but they were attached to the wrong frame: his hands were almost lateral to his kneecaps, giving him the appearance of being perpetually crouched. The bulbous nose could have had some majesty in another setting, but it was not balanced by the kewpie-doll mouth. The beetling black brows were in themselves dramatic, but when you added to them the equally fat wads of hair projecting from nostrils and ears there was too much of a muchness, this seemed a Lhasa apso face that had been shaved haphazardly.

This man sweated. He seemed to make it his career to sweat. His cheeks were sheened with damp, his hand, when you shook it, was clammy with the oils of unease, you had the impression that he was oozing moisture all over and that as a result his smartly tailored Union League suit was somewhat waterlogged.

His eyes I liked least of all. They were the darting, pillaging eyes of an undernourished ferret. They seemed to be making meals out of you and your thoughts while his polysaturated voice laved out with the well-oiled amenities of greeting.

"Well," he said with routine geniality. "Well, well, well. So you're our boy wonder. What a way you have with the word-weaving. You don't just turn a phrase, you make it bump and grind. You'd better install a cooling system in your typewriter, young fellow, or it'll go up in smoke. You drop into our midst like a bombshell, a veritable bombshell. Tell me, where've you been hiding till now?"

"I was in the grenade business until recently," I said guardedly. "If I'm now a full-fledged bomb it's a step up for me."

"Ho, ho, ha, ha, oh, hee, hee."

He went through the motions of being overcome with zany gaiety. He exploded for some time. His eyes remained perfectly dry but he mopped them anyhow, in imitation of a man carried away. He was totally in the grip of artificial merriment.

"Oh, ho, ha, hee. You've got quite a sense of humor too, yes, indeed. Droll, and impish besides. I like that. I expect great things from you, young fellow. You have a real future with us, I want to assure you of that. I look forward to a long and fruitful association. A talent like yours doesn't come along every day in the week. Those Stigglees, what a zestful gang. Old Ned's in them, no doubt of it. Hee, ho, hm, hm. A nest of rascals, absolutely. Thoroughly uninhibited, where they itch, they scratch. Well, you're a breath of fresh air around here. We'll be wanting lots and lots of books from you. We'll do extensive business, you and I. I want you to know the whole nature of our operation. Though I must say, with the flying start you're off to, you've obviously gotten a rich orientation from Zo-Zo and caught on fast, your instinct's perfect. Zo-Zo has explained what we're up to, hasn't she?"

"I think she gave me the main outlines. You feel that Lawrence and Freud opened up certain revolutionary legs which shouldn't be allowed to shut. I mean doors."

"Hee, hoo, hee, hoo, haw," he said. "Legs, I mean doors. Oh, you put things smartly, you do. Never lose sight of the comedic element. We'll get along, you and I. Yes, that's essentially it. Take up where the pioneers left off. Carry on the trail-blazing work. They let Eros out of the box, if you don't mind my phrasing it that way, out of the *box*, you know, hee, hm, haw, and now, well, now it's up to us to strip her down and dissect her lusty insides, take a real close look, that's about what it amounts to. Let's put it this way. It's a matter of statistics. Do you know where you spend one-third of your life? In bed. That's right. In bed. Eight hours out of every 24, you're horizontal. Now. In the whole range of Literature, considering all the classic works of fiction, and all the serious modems too, how many novels will you find which devote one-third of their words, one page out of three, to the events of the bedroom? The answer is, none. Which is ample proof right there that Fiction is untrue to Life. Fiction concentrates on the events of the dining room, the living room, the office, the auditorium, the council chamber, and practically ignores what goes on in the bedroom, which is one-third of our lives in bulk and nine-tenths of it in essence. Literature will be out of touch with Life until it goes into the bedroom, dawdles there a good long time, takes a careful look around, and tenders a full report on the germinal and groundwork things that transpire there, and that's precisely the kind of literature we're trying to encourage, to correct the anti-genital emphasis, and this is where you're going to be a big help to us, breaking new ground, getting Eros all the way out of that *box*, out of all *boxes*, hig, hig, with liberating results all around. Lawrence and Freud gave us the passageway. Now we march through. That's the general idea, lad. I think that about sums it up. How do you like the approach?"

"While we're on statistics, can I ask a question?" I said. "We spend eight hours out of every 24 in the bedroom, yes. But most of those eight hours are spent sleeping. On an average night about 460 of the 480 minutes spent in the bedroom are spent sleeping. If you want your new literature to be a perfect echo of the human truth, it follows that 460 of each 480 bedroom pages should describe your characters asleep. Or wouldn't you care to make your new realism *that* realistic?"

Again he guffawed. Once more he went into mirthless gales. Yet another time he wiped his perfectly dry eyes.

"You're a joker, sir. You do see the lighter side. Hig, hig, hoog. No, you're right, we don't want quite *that* degree of realism. Not just yet, anyhow. Let the pendulum swing back to the other extreme for a time, to get a balance. At the moment we'd better spend a bit *more* than one-third of our pages in the neglected chamber, and *quite* a bit more than 20 of the 480 bedroom pages on waking activities, a very great *deal* more, in fact, under present circumstances we'd better not dwell on the sleeping hours at all, if we hang around between the sheets for say nine-tenths of the time, eyes wide open, that's all right too, it's a corrective, help to establish a better balance. But I do like the humor in your suggestion, I can say that without qualification. There's a slyness to it, it's very original. I appreciate a good joke as well as the next fellow, I really do. But for the present, better devote 460 of the 480 bedroom pages to activities *other* than sleeping, make your characters severe insomniacs, it's a more dramatic situation. We'll explore the fiction of sleep when there's a more substantial market for it. Oh my, you are a kidder.

That's an unexpected bonus. I've got a very sensitive funnybone, it's been remarked on many times."

He noticed how my eyes were exploring the rows of volumes by our founding fathers and sobered immediately.

"I want you to be perfectly clear about one thing," he said. "You must have no false notions about the set-up here, it's important. I am *not* in the pornography business. I despise Pornography in any shape, manner or form, and I abominate those who trade in its sleazy precincts. I deal in rare books. The writings of those who shaped this Republic, in their original issuances, are *all* I deal in. Through Zo-Zo and others I have encouraged certain young and aspiring talents to write along Sexology lines, true, but let me point out two vital aspects of that, one, that I'm after a *serious* literature of the genital flourishing, not dirt, and two, that I'm not encouraging the production of such works to make a profit, I don't distribute them to the public, I don't do *business* with them. Then what, you may well ask, *do* I do with these manuscripts I solicit and pay for? It's a fitting question, and I want you to pay close attention to the answer. I have a client, a collector of the very best Americana, an Oklahoma multi-millionaire oil man, a power in the West, a figure of national stature. Tulsa, that's right, he's based out in Tulsa. This man has spent many hours with me in this office, talking. He's told me all about his wretched sex life, it's been a ghastly parade of defeats, no track record there at all. Over and over he's said to me, Barneybill, here I am past 50, and struck out with every woman I ever took up with, just couldn't carry it off with any of the ladies, and at my advanced age, with all my millions, I don't have the slightest idea why. There's plenty wrong with me I know, but what exactly? I've read all the books I could get my hands on but they don't tell me much, they're full of fancy theories and terms but skimp on the practical, minute-to-minute details. In particular, I've made a careful study of Freud and D. H. Lawrence.

Those two lads got hold of something, I thought, but they just didn't go far enough. Just when they were getting down to cases, about to give it to me straight and head-on, why, they quit on me. What I need is a shelf of books that take up where these fellows left off. I'd pay damn near anything for a literature like that, spelling things out and dramatic, but it just doesn't exist. Americana's fine, I've got my house loaded with the stuff, as you well know, but Americana, while it tells me a lot about how our country got started, isn't going to tell me a thing about how I, one single genitally backward contemporary American, got stopped. You're well acquainted in the World of Letters, Barneybill. You know the good writers of today. Couldn't you persuade some of them to stop niggling themselves and their public and get down to brass tacks in their books, continue the work Lawrence and Freud started? I'd be more than happy to finance a project like that. I'd consider it a privilege. It'd be putting my millions to good use, bringing into existence a whole library of Sexual Science Fiction in keeping with our revolutionary times, books that could help a lot of people outside of myself. This was how the oil mogul put it to me, my boy. He's been a good customer and a good friend, I wanted to do what I could for him. That's why I've got these crews of writers mobilized, through Zo-Zo and others. I don't *sell* their works, for heaven's sake. I'm just sort of an unpaid volunteer middleman, I get the things written, and pay for them with this oil man's money, and pass them along to him for his belated education. I must say he professes to be more than pleased with the results so far. He tells me he's received much pleasure and also edification from the manuscripts prepared to date. He's made ample sums available to continue the good work and recruit new talents into it. My only interest in this project is to help an old friend and good client out. Of course I take some satisfaction from the knowledge that Letters is the first benefactor here. Worthy writers who otherwise would be sleeping on park benches are living comfortably and paying the rent, and a long overdue New-Sexualist Literature is coming into being, one which is finally bringing the fiction craft into the Twentieth Century. But I don't make a penny out of this. I'm just the financial and esthetic go-between, that's about it. It's a labor of love, on, with, and about, hig, hig, love. I hope this clarifies things for you, young fellow. I don't want you thinking you've been caught up in some sort of shady enterprise. We're entirely on the up-and-up around here. All I do is bank and dispense the funds, and mail the scripts as they come in to Oklahoma in plain manila envelopes. Tulsa. Tulsa, Oklahoma, to be exact."

I did some rapid multiplication in my head. Zo-Zo appeared to have 20 writers hard at work for Barneybill. Assuming that each turned out five novels a year, a quota he'd certainly have to meet to earn even a marginal living wage, and assuming each novel ran about 400 pages, this meant that through Zo-Zo alone Barneybill was getting 40,000 pages of New-Sexualism per annum. If these writers were being paid the standard rate, they were collecting $400,000 annually. But Barneybill had spoken of "Zo-Zo and *others*." There were *other* subcontractor mills turning out this stuff, how many, it was impossible to say.

Conceivably Barneybill was shelling out hundreds of thousands a year for New-Sexualism. This was a nut an Oklahoma oil man *might* be able to carry. But he'd have to have a *lot* of hangups, and a *lot* of wells. In and around Oklahoma, that's right. Tulsa, Tulsa, Oklahoma, to be exact.

"Well, now, lad," Barneybill said toward the end of our first meeting, "I suppose you'd like to have your palm greased with a little cash. Glad to oblige, only too. I don't keep that kind of money in the office, though. What say we walk over to the bank and I'll draw the requisite amount of filthy lucre for you, that suit you? Though I don't consider this lucre in any degree or manner besmirched, and I trust *you* don't fall into that wrong mode of thinking. When you make a major contribution to Literature like the *Stigglee Chronicles*, all lucre happily derived from it's clean as a whistle, and well-earned. Come on, laddy, let's go make you rich."

As we walked down Fifth Avenue, Barneybill's thoughts switched from Literature to Politics. It may have been because, as we passed a newspaper stand, his eye was caught by the chilling headlines, more lend-lease ships blasted out of their Atlantic convoys by German subs, Hitler rattling his sabre again, Maginot Line being reinforced, all of that. Without looking directly at him, I sensed that Barneybill was suddenly a bundle of nerves. His voice had lost its oily drip and developed a second-string growl.

"Bastard," he ground out. "Rotten dirty slime. Get hands on his scabby hyena throat for one full minute."

"Who, John Steinbeck?" I said. A moment before he'd been explaining how *Grapes of Wrath* could have been made a modern classic by the addition of a couple hundred pages of New-Sexualism to balance and round out the social documentation. "What'd Steinbeck ever do to you?"

"Not Steinbeck, Hitler," Barneybill barked. "The swine, the scum. Terrorizing the good people of the world like that. Making a mess for everybody. I'd like to get into this scrap myself and help settle his hash, once and for all. If there were some place I'd fit in, I'd sign up in a minute. We've got to get that second front open and take some of the pressure off the Russians. We should have stepped in three, four years ago, in Spain, and stopped him cold there, before he began steamrollering all of Europe. I wanted to go to Spain. Lots of our best youngsters went over there to fight, and I wished I could have been with them, giving the paperhanger and his minions their due, but I was too tied up, I couldn't just drop everything. I tell you, my fingers were itching for a gun and some stinking Falangists to point it at. That, Spain, was the last chance we had to let that beast and his stooges have it right between the eyes, but we didn't take it, we dragged our feet, we stalled, Wall Street wasn't interested in giving a hand to any progressive People's Revolution, but I would have given anything to go, I couldn't."

We were now on a corner. We had to cross over east to get to Barneybill's bank. The light changed and we started across, Barneybill saying, "We could have cooked his goose on the Madrid front, we could have torn him into little pieces, I was figuring every angle as to how I might drop my various involvements and get over there to do some shooting for a change instead of impotent talking—"

If I'd been listening to his blood-and-thunder talk I might have noticed sooner that it was terminated in mid-sentence. As it was, I was so full of slobbering anticipation of the $600 I was about to get my hands on, I was so busy mentally counting those nice noisy bills, and in addition pondering the fact that if Wall Street had stamped out the People's Revolution in Spain it had had expert assistance from the Kremlin, pondering it and trying to shut up about it in view of how rich I was about to get—I reached the middle of Fifth Avenue before it occurred to me that Barneybill's newly savage voice was no longer in my ear and its freshly militarized owner no longer at my side.

I looked back. Barneybill had retreated to the curb. He was standing there stock-still, looking south with agony on his revolting face.

I went back to the corner. I looked in the direction he was looking. There was one car heading in our direction. It was still almost a block away.

I looked at Barneybill. He was shaking. His whole body was in motion though his feet remained rooted to the spot. He was sweating so much, his hair was wet.

"Is something wrong?" I said. I almost added, but managed not to, "Spain's east of Fifth Avenue, so's Hitler."

"Damn miserable fiends," he mumbled, eyes still on the approaching car and saucered with terror. "You don't stand a chance on the streets. They'll mow you down and never look back."

"He's some distance away," I said. "Besides, the light's with us."

"Pedestrian's a sitting duck for them," he whispered. "They'll run you over and not even slow down. Bunch of fascist berserkers in Buicks."

He literally couldn't get his legs to carry him off the curb. He'd scurried back there in panic and was paralyzed.

The car did stop for the light. I had to get firm grips under his arm socket and at the wrist and half lift him off the pavement to put him in motion. That was all right with me. If necessary I'd have carried him piggyback, I'd have hired a dog sled and 20 huskies and gotten into harness with the huskies, to haul him to that bank.

"Careful!" he cried out. "Watch it, will you! You'll get us both killed, for God's sake!"

But there was only one car anywhere close, the Buick waiting meekly for the light to change.

I was beginning to know my Chief. He yearned to open second fronts, get his hands on Hitlers, he'd have come to glory slaying fascist dragons in Spain; too, he had the mighty urge to blast through all genital barricades in the manner of a Robert Jordan blowing Franco bridges, though for the benefit of the under-orgasmed poor oil Millionaire of Tulsa, Oklahoma, never a thought for himself; and he'd somehow equated these two belligerencies so that he saw his progressivist political scrappiness and his drive to smithereen all orgasmic straightjackets, all Falanges of the groin, as two faces of the same derring-do. But he couldn't bring himself to buck traffic on Fifth Avenue when it consisted of one lazing Buick a block away with the light against it; if Hitler's downfall depended on Barneybill's crossing this all but empty thoroughfare, too bad—Barneybill couldn't do it.

A lesson in the inner workings of the horizon-staving mind, the avantgarde tough, the bold barker against walls and obstructions, I wouldn't soon forget.

CHAPTER 8

INTO THE HAYSTACK

I wrote five novels for Barneybill without a day off, hardly taking time out to change my typewriter ribbon. I was working at such a clip that I didn't have time to move into better quarters. There in the furnished room on 13th Street I stayed, typing on the bed, until I had to do exercises to *un*lotus my legs. But I had money in the bank, more and more of the lovely, larrupy stuff.

I bought myself that Brooks suit. I took Bettina to dinner at Pavillon and discovered, not entirely to my satisfaction, that my ideological spine was flexible enough to accommodate to an occasional tablecloth. There were days when I wrote as much as 60 or even 70 pages of these pelvic histrionics, others when I lay flat on my back, maybe not in capital condition but nicely capitalized, sexless, nerveless, wantless, counting flies on the ceiling, wondering, though not intently, if they were counting me.

I had finally come across a ceiling—still another in an advanced state of decay—I didn't want to write a word about. As I gazed at it, I traced only one fantasy, a life that didn't call on me to trade my words for a ceiling over my head.

Thomas Mann had established that the old brain, in which such primitive matters as sex presumably reside, lies deep beneath the

verbalizing surface and has no need for words, indeed escapes words—
here I was hauling all its contents into the new brain and making them
conversation pieces, subjects for chatter, and if I stopped my income
would stop. No wonder I'd gone sexless. I was too damn busy making
words about sex.

At Bettina's urging, I took a breather. She and I went up to New Haven
for the Yale-Princeton football game to watch this season's Albie Booth
run a pigskin up and down some striated grass as though life were a
business to be conducted outdoors, in the full sun, with no brain but the
animal old brain calling the shots.

It was a mistake. The autumn air was clean and bracing, it was good
to suck in, but I looked around the Yale Bowl at those 70,000 rosy-
cheeked Ivy League respectables huddled in stadium jackets and lap
rugs and I thought—Maybe one of them has read something of mine,
Stigglee Chronicles, say? Maybe *all* of them have read something I wrote?
How would I know? How will I ever know?

I have to explain my thinking here. As it had been laid out to me I
wasn't writing for the general public, I wasn't writing for a public at all,
my entire word output was being funneled into Tulsa, Oklahoma, into
the bulging eyes of one chopfallen oil millionaire. Sure. That was the
official word. So it was said and so it must be. All the same, we know
that even oil millionaires have friends and relatives. We know people
lend their most cherished books to their loved ones. There are also book
thieves all over the place, our libraries are depleted from year to year.
And it's not a rarity for people to get their hands on hoarded works and
bring them out in pirated editions. There were, in short, all sorts of
ways in which the Oklahoma oil millionaire's private copies of my private words might spill over from Tulsa into the world. It has also to be
allowed for that these United States contain any number of Tulsas, they
dot the scene from one coast to the other. This country is a spreading

Tulsa. The name of a Tulsa oil millionaire can be Legion. I could be writing for this single, solitary, mopish oilman and be addressing the whole American people in hushed national assembly.

Faced with this mass of people in the Bowl, I was reminded that somewhere Out There, or, to put it with more geographic and emotional accuracy, somewhere *Up* There, above ground, in the sunny open, among the law-abiders, the nine-to-fivers, I could have an audience of undetermined size, and I'd never know about them, and they'd never know about me—Barneybill insisted, as did I, that there be no hint of a byline on my scripts when they got mailed unostentatiously, in the world's plainest wrappers, to some Tulsa.

It was depressing to have it brought to my attention how incorrigibly anonymous must be any success I might have in the field of New-Sexualism. Any words of mine that brimmed over from Tulsa would be as nameless as a newborn babe deposited on a suburban doorstep in the dead of night. The Plight of the Artist in the U.S.A., I think it's called.

I decided to avoid crowds. The urge was too great to search the faces of passersby for some gleam of recognition, by the nature of the case a highly romantic quest. Every cop, every receptionist, every proctologist, every steeplejack, every pole vaulter might be a fan of mine, thanks to this or that link-up with this or that Tulsa, but their names would be forever held out. Better to skirt the wide, wide world of the Up-Out people and forget about who might be consuming my words.

I went back to my cubicle on 13th Street with a sense, if not of joy, certainly of relief. My followers, who were doomed never to glimpse my face, would be forever faceless to me too.

At Bettina's urging again, I stirred myself at last to find a decent apartment in a decent neighborhood, a two-room basement floor-through in a nice old brownstone on West 88th Street, half a block from Riverside Drive.

Decent is a badly overworked word in this context. It's supposed to mean, cleaner, fancier, bigger, more expensive than what you've been used to. Its inner connotation, though, often comes down to this—elsewhere. That which has up to now been out of reach, the unattainable attained. Well, listen to what the unattainable did to me when I moved in on it, made it my address.

This was the first time in all my years of moving around that I'd had more than one room, let alone a kitchen, a private bath, and that luxury of luxuries a separate entrance with my very own mailbox nailed to the wall nearby. There was no view from my basement hideout, of course, but if I stood on the street and looked west I could see the unhurried Hudson and the bulking Jersey Palisades to the far side; and there was the fine riverfront park to walk in.

It was a wild surge into respectability for me. I felt, as I sat at my typewriter, piling up the pages of my sixth novel, that all the ingratiating assets of the neighborhood, the river, the park, the hills, were my personal property, registered in my name. I had the idea that I was batting out this new book to make money for monthly payments on this most excellent real estate, an added incentive to juggle more and better Stigglees.

I reveled in my new-found status as lord of an imaginary manor built by pornographer's jack; for exactly two weeks.

One night it began to blow, then to drizzle, then the skies opened up. It was a wild storm that flooded streets and whipped down power lines. In the middle of it, my ceiling, loosened by seepages of water, fell in. The whole ceiling fell in. On me.

I was fast asleep, exhausted from 12 hours at the typewriter. I bolted awake with the impression that several dozen booming tigers had pounced simultaneously on me; found myself powdered, drifted over, inundated, with ancient, sour-smelling plaster. I had, you will understand, more than a tickle of déja vu—that damn disintegrating ceiling that I'd first begun to study during my cold guard-duty nights in

Coyoacán had finally fulfilled its promise, or its threat, and come down. On me. Its student. Its superintendent. Its maker.

I took this for an omen and a monition: people who live by peripheral labors ought not to occupy centrally located quarters—downtown mentalities reach for uptown addresses at their own risk. I remembered that Virginia Woolf, that remarkable and frail lady, had written about the delights of adequate housing in *A Room of One's Own* and then, though blessed with an amplitude of rooms and views, had walked into the ocean to a watery grave where open space was at a premium and the ceiling perpetually zero.

The Hudson was a hop and a skip from my place, but I was not going to let the mere descent of a ceiling drive me to a similar liquid end. I decided to get the hell out of there, back to where I belonged, to the saloons and pizza parlors below 14th Street, my home away from home-owners and home-makers. That was the one and only time, in my more than 20 years in Manhattan, that I made the mistake of taking my downtown pursuits uptown. . . .

I was in solid with Barneybill Roster. Each of my books left him more aglow than the one before. Over and over he assured me that in the Garden of Erotica I had the greenest thumb yet. I wanted to stick that happily-hued digit right in his febrile, suctioning, iguana-intent eye, but didn't.

Prolonged porn output, while it can make you rich, has startling side effects. Two of them should be mentioned.

First, remember that our pages were fabricated on a piecework basis. Literary piecework will inevitably turn you into a word-counter. It makes you very miserly with your units of merchandise—you want to part with fewer and fewer of them for the page fee. So you begin to devise ways of distributing two words over a page in such tricky arrangements that they will do the work of three.

You became a graphic artist with words, a typographer, a layout man. The space they occupy becomes more important than the jewels of wisdom they contain.

To begin with, your chapters get shorter and shorter, giving the narrative a somewhat joggly, staccato effect. There's a good reason for writing skimpy chapters and lots of them: a chapter begins on a new page, even if the concluding page of the previous chapter contains only a few lines. More than that, you can drop the opening of a new chapter several lines, down almost to the middle of the page, on the grounds that such spacing is good layout, pleasing to the eye.

Next, you begin to chop each chapter into short sections, adding to the fitful quality of the prose. That is to say, you use a liberal number of section breaks within your chapters, because these breaks are heart-warmingly blank spaces—and you make the spacings fatter and fatter, up to 10 or even 12 lines in depth, again on the grounds of visual esthetics.

Then you write shorter and shorter paragraphs. Then you begin to widen margins, first the side ones, then the top and bottom ones. The ideal you have in mind throughout is a perfectly white, a virginally alabaster, page, unsoiled by type. You compromise this millennial vision as little as possible.

Each piecework porn-worker works out his own word-doling techniques, finds his own way from de Sade to McLuhan. Mine became quite effective. On a normally typed page I get something better than 300 words. On the pages I prepared for Barneybill Roster I was finally able, after many slide-rule calculations, to get a finished look with 200 words or less. You can see that through such strategies of shrinkage I gave myself a raise of exactly 33 $^{1/3}$ percent.

This brings us to an interesting question in esthetics.

You may have heard from some Advanced Lit professor that content generates form, it's a phrase that gets around, especially in Advanced

Lit circles, as much as the one about art pounding some order into chaos. Well, yes and no. Sometimes it does and sometimes it doesn't. It all depends. In the porn I wrote it was clearly a case of total war between content and form. It wouldn't be an exaggeration, in fact, to say that every time content tried to suggest some kind of form, form went right out to do the precise opposite.

There was a reason for this battle to the death between materials and wrappings. The source of the trouble was that the content was not generated by me, it flowed from Barneybill Roster, he laid down the law as to what I was to write and my job was simply to write it nicely, properly, interestingly. It was Barneybill Roster who proposed and my function was no more than to dispose, he expounded, I expanded. Forbidden to generate any of the substance at all, I was driven, in my need to create something I could call my own, to generate the package.

You see now where the war between matter and manner originated, it was just an echo of the undeclared war between Barneybill Roster and me. I imposed my frame on his wadding, violating it, chopping it up, to make him pay me one-third more than I was meant to be paid, to squeeze more money out of him, money in lieu of satisfaction, control, artistic autonomy, as they say in Hollywood, where the art is minimal and the autonomy non-existent. It may be, as Samuel Beckett said of the later James Joyce, that form is content, content form—but only when the two are working the same side of the street.

Barneybill never complained. You don't cavil when the greenest thumb in the blue business decides to purple up one-third more pages with no increase in the total amount of coloring matter. One thing about the consumers of porn, they don't have quantitative minds. You can make a little go a long way with them so long as that little is, by voyeur's standards, too much.

But stretch though you may, you finally must run out of raw materials. You get to be the most ingenious chopper of content through various formalistic tricks but in the end there's nothing left to chop. Your supply of Stigglees peters out, if you'll forgive the porn jargon, and the day arrives when you simply have nothing left to write about.

There's one iron rule for the steady worker who wants to carve a career for himself in porn—take your Stigglees where you find them. Even if the place where you find them is a book written and published by somebody else.

As a matter of fact, that's the best place of all to find them, in a book, provided the book is obscure, long since forgotten, and delightfully out of print. It speeds up the assembly line like nobody's business, certainly not Barneybill Roster's.

The sixth work I was composing for Barneybill, I will confess, was not my creation from scratch.

I had been struck, more, shaken to the very insteps, by Barneybill's remarks at our first meeting about what an infinitely better and more lasting work of art *Grapes of Wrath* would have been if expertly pornographized. The concept of the *pornographization* of *existing literary properties* had been seared into my brain never to be erased. When the last of my Stigglees heaved the last of his applejack jugs at the last remaining owl in the Connecticut countryside and collapsed in the drainage ditch for good, never to rise again, and never again to be gotten a rise out of, a condition which automatically excluded him from further pornographer's consideration, I remembered Barneybill's comments about John Steinbeck and I said to myself—*When inspiration flies, pornographize!*

All I had to do was find a little-known novel by a little-known author in a little-known edition and double its length by making fully explicit the eroticism which, because it's always lurking in human affairs, is similarly always lurking between the lines of even the nicest, sweetest, gooiest, fluffiest bit of fiction. It was, as Barneybill himself had put it, simply a matter of helping a standard work of fiction to fulfill itself by guiding it into that much-neglected chamber, the bedroom, fount of tomorrow's freer, brisker prose, and plumping it up with some of that free, brisk, saltatory prose in a series of enthusiastic mating scenes.

I'd been an insatiable reader of minor French and German novels during my college days, and I remembered them. I began to browse in the stalls of the second-hand bookstores along Third Avenue, looking for some of these out-of-print things.

I found the perfect one for my purposes. It had been published in a minuscule New York edition way back in the early Twenties. At the outside, a few hundred Americans had read it. It was, as nearly as I can recall, by a German named Bruno Franck. Its title had two first names in it, linked in the idyllic manner, something like *Thomas and Hannah*. It cried out for erotizing, the heat treatment. It was all about two healthy, sprightly, clean-limbed youngsters who meet and fall in love in the Black Forest, a fine locale for dramatic couplings. They met a great deal. They were forever sneaking off to a meeting. The job was simply to make their meetings longer, fuller, richer, juicier, definitive, dramatic, and very, very graphic.

I was now deep into a New-Sexualist version of *Thomas and Hannah*. The two glandular tikes were constantly tiptoeing off to the haystack, where their originator had discreetly left them behind a sedate screen of asterisks and ellipses. All I was doing was ripping away the asterisks and ellipses. I followed them to the haystack, then in, through, over, and around the haystack, my Zoomar lens trained unwaveringly on them, my microphone boom picking up each quavery sigh, each oceanic groan, each rapturous outburst

All these interposed haystack close-ups produced 500 pages where only 250 had been before. Which meant 1,000 hard dollars for me, far more, I'm sure, than poor Bruno Franck, my unwitting collaborator, had ever received from the American edition of his tenderly romantic work.

Once more I'd given myself a raise. In point of strict fact, a 100 percent raise, because I got my collaborator's fee as well as my own. The literary game is overrun with inequities.

Barneybill Roster was riven. My tragic idyll of teenage passions brought to the boil and then thwarted in the mysterious recesses of the Black Forest—it moved him to tears, real ones. For several minutes after he finished reading the last pages, he couldn't speak.

"You're incredible," he said at last. "It's a whole new vision and a whole new flavor. You change styles like other men change their underwear."

"And for the same reasons," I said.

"Hig, hig. Don't treat this lightly, boy. The relationship you've spun out here, in words fresh and green as the woodlands, is a sacred thing. It's haunting, haunting. Where'd you ever get the glorious idea of having Hannah go off with the circus at the end, after Thomas's terrible hunting accident?"

"That part of it comes from a very old Lithuanian folk tale my mother used to tell me as a child," I said. "They had a lot of hunting accidents in Lithuania, and all kinds of circuses."

"You're truly a genius," Barneybill said in a low, awed voice. "You use everything in your writing, everything, it scares me."

"Everything," I agreed. "Sometimes I get a little scared too."

CHAPTER 9

VILLAGE NIGHTS

Nights when the weather was good, Bettina and I would get on the marrowbone stage (as they used to say in 1887, a good year for walking) and bat around the Village. Not exploring. You don't explore your own backyard. Sniffing, sipping, rolling the good commonplace allaying tastes of home on the tongue. Checking to see all things were in their right places.

I can't stand a playground where careless kids from other neighborhoods drop the borrowed toys any old place instead of putting them back where they found them. Show some respect for the grounds where they let you romp and kick your heels unmolested. Leave them to their home-grown servo-controlled messes instead of imposing your own personalized ones—that's uncouth and uncool.

The Village was still looked on as the country's playground, psychic drainage ditch, id-siphon, zone of anything-goes. It hadn't yet become one more of Manhattan's frilly upper-class domains of overpriced high-rise apartments and insultingly expensive shops and restaurants, that sad facelift was to come in the years after the Big War. Back there in those last fading months before Pearl Harbor the shambling sprawl of blocks below 14th Street was still an ingratiatingly seedy spot you could run to to escape the States without the trouble and expense of leaving the States, a bit of unamerica within our continental borders. You could take a deep, slowing breath, much like the con who's made it over the walls and has been tearing through the wood and now hears the trustees' dogs baying off on the wrong scent, you could slow down and watch the States recede toward Central Park and across the Palisades.

It was, in other words, a hole to drop into to drop out of the national scramble, about the only trace left of the open road given too many hard-sell commercials by Walt Whitman, that PR man for our early highway system—a rope ladder going straight down.

It wasn't totally a bohemian hangout, it was never that despite the rosy, racy lore they've built up about it. But it did have a friendly bohemian flavor in the way it announced to people—Everywhere else in the city hands are laid on you all hours of the day, kneading you, hopping you here and there, frisking you, here it's strictly hands-off no matter what you do provided you keep your hands off others.

Only minor and tucked-away pockets of the place worked up the extremist ferment to go all the way polymorphous-perverse, but the whole dingy expanse, from 14th to Bleecker, from Third to the Hudson, was as a matter of principle as well as taste permissivist and what's more, inhospitable to snoopers. A place so free of spies will invite voyeurs and to be sure the voyeurs came; there were the ogling tourists from Des Moines and Wichita even then. But you can put up with Saturday-night invasions of the starers, they aren't making sneaky notes on their cuffs and taking pictures with palmed Minoxes. If you stuck to the side-streets you didn't even see these walking delegates from America, that distant and exotic land.

The first thing the Village insisted on was that nobody be defined in terms of where he came from, or of what he did, either. This was in good part because so many of its residents had reason to shut up about where they originated and, aside from that, were up to little or nothing they cared to have brought to light and discussed.

All the same, you did get to be known as this rather than that. You took on an identity from the stride you showed as you walked down the main drags, the laxness with which you occupied a space on a Washington Square bench, the angle at which you tipped your beer mug, the frankness or sneakiness with which you eyed the passing girls.

You were, I mean to say, what you added up to in your day-to-day stances and gestures, your style at a bar, your bearing on the street-corner, sum total, in short, of your impacts on eyes and ears, and you weren't to be questioned about what you did, or did not do, by way of vocation or hobby or horseplay or penance in the privacy of your own paid-for quarters—no matter who paid for them, that was between you and the landlord, or you and your sponsor, or you and whoever it was whose wallet you'd lifted last Friday on the IRT subway.

I was comfortable in the Village. In the tensest and taintedest of times, as during my porn year, if not comfortable, at least left alone, momentarily undogged.

Just then I wouldn't have stood for being tagged by what I did because in those terms I was somewhere to the left of the rapists and muggers, the kidnappers, assaulters of grandmothers, robbers of blind newsies. I was satisfied that nobody inquired as to where I got the dollars to pay my rent because each time I settled with the landlord I had the tachycardiac feeling that I'd just snatched a purse from some old pretzel-vending lady on the IRT, lifted her entire week's proceeds and her tattered skirt with them.

During that year I didn't do much sitting on Washington Square Park benches. It would have been hard for me to look lazy and cozy on a public bench. Every minute I worried the cops would be coming for me any minute.

It may have been that in the strict language of the statute books the criminal in our porn operation was Barneybill Roster, not me. Just shows you how meticulously the superego does not go by the book.

The Village was host to many prime movers but itself could never be moved.

Many who lived there were centrally involved in the stirrings that developed elsewhere, political events in the streets and auditoriums, art events in the galleries and theaters and book world, but the Village was not the scene of their activisms, it was the place they came back to for shelter after the fusses and the shows were over. The place to recuperate from these exertions, to breathe easy, regroup the energies, plan further provocations when they were ready again to invade the hostile territories all about.

The Village could not be moved, and not just because its inhabitants were oriented to making waves outside its borders. It went on idling, going nowhere, because, finally, its wheels could never be coordinated to hum at the same time and in the same direction.

Think of it that way, if you will, as a conveyance of some sort, an old stagecoach, say, or a weathered hay wagon. It had two wheels, rather, two hubs onto which wheels might be fitted. One was called Union Square, the other, Washington Square, and those two supports couldn't be made to roll together, a condition without which no motion was possible.

Union Square, there just above 14th Street, was the focus of our political life; that's where the rallies and outdoor demonstrations took place or started from. Ringing this park, always reverberant with the hot rhetoric of oddsing sects, were the headquarters and bookstores and publishing facilities of the various radical parties, from the mighty CP, which owned a whole multi-storied building and other institutions, to the SWP, which occupied a small loft and owned very little beyond an address and a mimeo machine.

Due south just a handful of blocks was Washington Square, focal point of the non-politicos, the painters, the sculptors, the poets, the novelists, the NYU students, the schemers, the carpet knights, the easy strollers, the mere shadow-show hangarounds. Fifth Avenue was the shaft linking the two Squares. Consider these two open patches of scrawny green to be the community wheels, or hubs, mounted on the axle of Fifth Avenue, that slow-paced arthritic dowager of boulevards, a lady with a torn parasol.

I'm well aware that axles are seldom dowagers and just about never develop arthritis in their joints. But don't blame me for the mixing of metaphors, it was the daily life of the Village that did the mixing, I'm just reporting the facts—sometimes Fifth Avenue in that extraordinary stretch *was* a full-fledged axle and sometimes, I swear, an old society lady with rundown heels.

That, in fact, was a big part of the trouble. When you wanted a functional rod of steel there, to get things moving, what you found was a fading lady with a thread-bare umbrella. You needed machine parts that would fit together and set things in motion; what you found were eccentric humans one by one, who simply wouldn't dove tail and link gears but would, when thrown together any old way, elbows digging into each other's sides, generate animated talk, some of it inspired, some of it just hot air.

The world-changers tended to hang around Union Square; the art and scholarship people, the idea-jugglers, the speculators, the conceptualizers, the free-form headworkers, the kidders, the gab artists, the clowns, around Washington Square, and there wasn't much traffic between them. When they did mingle, in the taverns and cafeterias and bowling alleys all around, you had a lot of lively exchanges but no true meetings of minds.

There were no real barricades between Polis and Bohemia in those days, at least in the Village. Most of the artists and intellectuals, remember, had been politicalized —and very much toward the left. But the Union Square politicos looked down their noses at the Washington Square esthetes of any political stripe, and the esthetes backed off from the politicos, even those to whom they gave ideological support or at least lip-service, out of uneasiness over the activists' ultimate plans for intellectuals, a certain intuition that activism, if it ever made the much-needed new social order, might come down hard on those not inclined by temperament to be constantly and demonstratively and copycattishly active.

So the Village stayed in one place, chugging away slow and easy, while one of its contingents kept busy planning political disturbances elsewhere, another, art and idea commotions for the export trade. The place itself could never be mobilized for intensities of either order.

When Union Square wanted to get organized for a fuss, Washington Square lagged behind. When Washington Square bestirred itself for some high-energy ploy, Union Square dragged its feet.

It was a blessing in disguise for both parties. It meant that no matter how much commoting these or those Villagers got done, it was confined to other neighborhoods, and the Village they came home to after their sweaty labors was the same sleepy, slouching, project-lacking Village they'd left. Politicos and bohemians alike could count on a good night's sleep.

I didn't get much rest in the Village during my porn year, though I made out better than when I'd tried to live on respectable 88th Street. I was so sure a knock was going to come at my door in the dead of night, and in would march several hundred cops.

Bettina and I had a fair number of things in common. For example, a lack of vocation for politics.

She'd tied mightily to carve out a place for herself in the shadow of the Jim Cannons but by taste and tendency she gravitated into the world of the Zo-Zo's. Same with me. I made a big effort to keep one big toe in the UnionSquare swim but every anarchic fiber in me urged toward the full dive into the Washington Square wading pool.

I'd done my level best to siphon all my words into politics, into the Trotskyite press, into Trotsky's heroic battles way down in Coyoacán to clear his name and cleanse the revolutionary cause, but here I was, funneling all my phrases into the Barneybill Roster hopper. Barneybill himself liked to imagine that his heart was in Union Square but it was clear that his instincts and genitals were rooted in, or at least circled wistfully around, Washington Square.

We were, I think it's no exaggeration to say, all of us split one way or another, some up and down, some sideways, some between new brain and old, some, I guess, between gut and groin. As I suggested before, you try to live with your separate parts, juggle them, keep them spinning, or you sit in a dark corner with your face to the wall. Staring contests with walls, shut-in solutions in general, didn't seem to us the way to go.

Bettina and I were not yet ready for a life all Washington and in no socially redeeming small way Union, just as Barneybill had his head full of pulsating cunt and had to talk loud and fast about Popular Front— worried (if I read him right) about a failure at individual erection, he held forth about the world's need for uprising. But he couldn't Unionize his Washingtonianism, get sociology to infiltrate his sexology, and no more could we get Lower Fifth Avenue to double back on itself so its upstart and upheaval ends were in line.

More and more often, we'd take off from Union Square of an evening—Bettina for a time was living with three other girls in a loft on 14th Street—and start our march downtown, south from the political commoting, down right past the art commoting, till we were finally at Vincent's on Mott Street just above Houston, filling ourselves with those sensational fried shrimp with the spectacular hot sauce that the mouth would not tolerate without repeated washings of icy lager. Sometimes we'd go on to Pell Street in Chinatown to get glassy-eyed on shew muy, pork bits with cassia lily, hot-sour melon soup served in the melon half, and sizzling sesame balls, and crisped lobster chunks in sweet-sour sauce, and Chinese peapods spread with a cheesy melt of fermented soybean curds.

We dropped to mindless and ate. We ate as if there was no tomorrow (a message the headlines were beginning to carry), as if it was going out of style, as in fact for a very long time, except in a few high-hogger enclaves like Park Avenue and Sutton Place, it had.

That was the big lesson of those days for such as us. If the war between Union and Washington in your head showed no tendency to abate, no progress toward even uneasy truce, you were moved to bypass both of them on the map and continue on to Little Italy and Chinatown, to feed the one part of you that seemed to stay intact, and know its own mind—your stomach. Some of the most severely split people we knew were, in their drive toward holism, toward some unitary purpose in life, turning up very fat and with their livers shot.

Well, there was a war coming, war was already the order of the day, and it's common knowledge that when there's a chance of dying tomorrow you go after the eat and the drink, though merriment stays a fugitive.

One split in Bettina interested me greatly, that between her comparison-shopper and shoplifter sides.

The Bettina that held down a responsible job for a department store, checking out the prices in its competitors, was a socialized sort, ready to take part in the world's affairs, falling in with the widespread transactional precept that you have to trade your time for other people's money, accepting the nine-to-five routine, punching the clock. The Bettina that after jotting down the price of an article went on to slip the article into her wide-mouthed totebag was the nay-sayer, the nihilist, the balker, who announced in effect, the world owes me a living and if I have to work my *ass* off, I mean to make sure it *pays* off.

There was a terrible irony in all this, as I was forced to observe— the work-dodger in her had to work a hell of a lot harder than the clock-puncher.

When she came home at the end of the day with her tail between her legs, drained, barely able to move, it was the thief in Bettina that had reached the end of the line, not the wage slave. It took a fierce lot out of her to steal, incomparably more than her lackadaisical price-checking duties ever did. Not because the work was so hard; after all it's not exacting manual labor to slide a pair of earrings or a bottle of French perfume into a waiting handbag. Rather, because the wage slave in her was approved on all sides, and the sneak thief held low, and Bettina was a girl who, much as she denied it, needed approval, acceptance, applause for her efforts.

The thing was, the thief in her couldn't elicit any applause from the inside, where it was needed most. Bettina heartily disdained her law-breaking component, much as she tried to give it a carefree bohemian gloss, and so, the more she got away with on the lightfingering end, the worse she felt. The judge had to have the miscreant before the bar daily as proof he was needed. So the miscreant was outstandingly needed.

If Bettina was addicted to anything, I'd say it was to her own super-ego's renunciation of her hobby, not the hobby itself. She was perpetually hungry for the self-contempt she managed to feed herself through her petty breaking of petty law. Certainly she had no use for the earrings and perfumes, as often as not she gave away the bent goods, showing that the bending was the important thing here, not the goods.

I was interested in this ongoing tug of war in her head and for a good reason, it echoed mine. The clock-puncher and the sneak thief in me weren't operating separately, that was the only difference. I had these two sides too, only they were working for the same boss and sharing in the weekly paycheck.

The worker in me had never worked harder, I was really slaving away at my job, paying my dues as I'd never paid them at that fucking grinding machine up in Bridgeport. But the one who did the toughest work, met the schedules, followed all the job sheets, stuck to the specified tolerances, was the thief in me, the mugger, the second-story man, and when the wage-earner stepped up to collect the paycheck a voice kept booming inside my ear, it's the bum who's getting paid off here, the snatcher, the pickpocket, the breaker and enterer, and it made no difference that I'd worked my fingers to the bone for this loot, that I'd earned it by the sweat of my brow, it was an underworld operation and the cops would have to be on my tail sooner or later.

Even though technically I was breaking no laws. I *was* breaking the Law of Laws—one you'll never find in any legal text—just as dear, thin, tense-faced Bettina was. The Law of Laws says, in letters of flame that lick at your ceiling every night—Do your own work in the world, and make it count in ways apart from money, and have something to show for it besides money, in particular, your name stamped on each and every item, your brand, your mark, your signature, proof that you passed this way.

That rule comes least of all from the Puritan work ethic—fuck all Puritanism and all ethics of work for work's sake. That rule got written by your own head out of its need to grow and realize all its promise, come up from potential to an impactful all-thereness. It's the rule of all protoplasm that wants to spend its total energies, pump to the fullest.

It's the rule that says, it's not the paycheck you get that determines the value of the work you do, it's the inspired and organized energy you put into the project, the invention, inner direction, personal thrust; no matter what payroll you're on, the best payrolls are your own, the best jobs are free-lance. That says, the difference between those who do and those who get done to and in is what's hungered for, the life on your feet or the life flat on your back. That says, there are the active ones, the makers; then there are the passive ones, the made. That says, work ethic be damned, what we're talking about is the nature and direction of hunger, whether your need is to stiff the world a little or be steamrollered.

The criminal in Bettina and the criminal in me were very passive people, that was the whole damn problem. The criminal in Bettina was moved not by her, in her own true interest, but by an image of her progenitors turned on their heads, which meant she wasn't in control of herself, her buttons were being pushed. The criminal in me was shaping my words to Barneybill Roster's forms instead of my own, and that was the nature of *its* crime—it was serving a head not mine. We were both soft and malleable, moved from the outside, and we paid heavily for it in the fiery messages we read on the ceiling late at night—and this perhaps is the source of all the interest passive people have in ceilings, the hot reading matter there, warnings, alarms, bills of particulars.

About Bettina's old man. . . .

On one side of her family, never mind which, Bettina had descended in a straight line from Brigham Young. That would have been no cause for worry except that around Provo, and up around Salt Lake City too, the lineal descendants of Brigham Young counted themselves in the many hundreds.

Even that circumstance would not have been troublesome if the U.S. Congress had not gone and passed a law wiping out polygamy among the Mormons of the Western States. In that peculiarly savage piece of legislation originated many of the tensions that played across Bettina Tokay's face whether or not she'd lifted any baubles or beads that day.

Mormonism's founding fathers, though in general they frowned on fun, had managed to arrange for themselves in their home and kinship institutions a very considerable amount of sexual fun. (For the men, anyway.)

I imagine it was this spurt of indulgence in a human landscape of hard work and no fooling around that our national legislators found intolerable.

Puritanism elsewhere seemed to mean what it said in all departments, cut out the light stuff, keep your mind on business. Mormonism, though it insisted on carrying a heavy baggage of Puritanism, seemed to be making light of it, even mocking it, in the way it insisted it was quite all right for one man to have access to several women, in fact, encouraged this profligacy of the bed chamber. The elders said it was a crime and a shame to smoke a coffin nail, a crime and a rotten dirty practice to take a shot of corn whisky, but perfectly in order, in fact a damn fine thing, a bolstering of the home values, a service to the community, to take unto yourself several wives and get them all, and repeatedly, with child.

You don't have to be a chowder-headed robot Marxist to observe that in the early frontier days the Mormon community suffered from a severe manpower shortage, especially after the massacres and plagues they'd experienced in their trek westward, and maybe the need for many more hands on the plow had as much to do with their turn to polygamy as a runaway, orgone-popping genitality. They had to get from their fund of sperm first of all a maximum return.

But it couldn't have been all economic. It's true that the cultural superstructure grows up from the mode of production and continues to rest on it and feed from it, but as Claude Levi-Strauss has made it plain for all to see, once the cultural leaf systems come out they tend to develop a very considerable interplay, and to shape one another more than the underlying economy shapes them all from afar.

I see the shortage of strong hands as one powerful impetus for the polygamous family but I continue to believe that the Mormons, whether they put it in so many words or not, were feeling their way toward just the thing that all of America had lost in the split from the tight human concentrations of Europe and had been yearning for ever since, the extended family, the reactivated tribe. What a few venturesome souls are trying to experiment themselves into right now through group marriage arrangements, a commonality of nuclear family units, an overlap of kinships, a familial nuclear fusion, so to speak, not to mention McLuhan's instant electronic globe-wide tribalism, the Mormons a hundred years ago and more had gotten to (male-chauvinistically) as a way of home life through setting up a brigade of mothers, a shove of mothers, a thicket of mothers, a medley of mothers under one roof. If nothing else, such a personnel policy is bound to improve the cooking around the house.

They're crying out now for the augmented family to give the kids a feeling of belongingness, of being plugged in again. The early Mormons augmented themselves patristically around the hearth to the point where each tike most certainly felt many folds of connective tissue binding him to a teeming tribe on all sides. They made a true contribution to their country, and a jealous Congress, determined not to let them get away with that which was forever denied to themselves by their own joyless fiat, took it away, crushed it out.

That left the many hundreds of Youngs and Smiths in a tough spot. The law read that these descendants of polygamous matings did not have equal claim to legitimacy, only those derived from the elders' first wives could count themselves in the legal strain. (Again a morality measured by the calendar.) There began a mad scramble among all the latter-day Youngs and Smiths to establish that each one was of the legitimate line and all the others, sorry bastard droppings along the way.

With one stroke of the Congressional pen, in other words, an originally proud and lusty institution was thrown into the moral limbo, sooted with the pall of sinfulness, made to look reprehensible and dirty. Guilt came to the forefront of the Mormon psyche, shame stepped in for pride. Only those whose lines traced back to the first-wives were pure; all others, that is, almost all of the offspring of the awesome old ones, were tarred to the marrow.

It was a cultural trauma such as few peoples have experienced in human history. All that was revered was suddenly tainted, this whole world was turned upside down. It's no wonder that as the Mormons of the time slowly began to come out of this federally administered shock and pick up the pieces of their lives, they veered into the most stiff-necked and rigid-spined conformity, they tried to outdo their Puritan forebears of the Eastern Seaboard in uprightness, sternness, thin-lippedness, a hewing to the line, a whipping of all into line.

They became the Puritans' Puritans. To the list of cardinal sins, above smoking and drinking, they added the worst one of all, the coveting of more than one mate. The prohibition, as is true of all efforts of lawmakers who come late to the law, especially when the law has come late to them, was over-emphatic and tended to spill over, its pinpointed target broadened to the whole area in question—thus, the coveting of even one mate was, though not in so many words, called into the deepest question.

Sexuality freely and fulsomely expressed had gotten the Mormon community in a hell of a lot of trouble. It was only natural that after such a fierce Congressional slap, such an avalanche of retribution right from the home office, the community in rebound should become very leary of all sex, all man-woman coveting, however carefully channeled.

The Mormons became very timorous about the genital life. They began to encourage a rerouting of energies away from the genitals, those wrongdoers whose wrong deeds can invite a culture-wide flogging. It was in this straight and narrow climate, this scramble for on-the-double respectability through staunchest denial, that Bettina's father and mother grew up. Her legacy from her parents was—don't, hold it, quit it, tell it to go away, say you don't want any, keep your hands in your pockets, freeze.

Maybe her case was somewhat atypical. Her family claimed derivation from the one legitimate strain of Youngs. The legitimates can be fiercer in their moral thunderings than anybody. They were, after all, the only clean Youngs in a swarm of smirched Youngs. They had to set an example for the befouled. Under these genealogical circumstances, it's no surprise I suppose, that Bettina became a compulsive, career befouler, a Trotskyite to all rules, especially those she couldn't get out of her system, the ones that followed her across continents and oceans, on her missionary trips to Tanganyika, her prison breaks to Greenwich Village.

She didn't come up with major moral breakthroughs. No outsize scandals or commotions. She built no new Sodoms or Gomorrahs down there by Washington Square. Just heisted a necklace or a vial of Joie de Nuit here and there, and felt bad afterward, and gave the swag away.

The day we first met was one of incomplete merger, in fact nothing got merged but our respective housing shortages.

I was hanging around the SUP hiring hall on the Battery waterfront, hoping a shipping job would come up of such vileness that the sailors who had seniority over me, the full and probationary members, wouldn't touch it. At night, having no room of my own, I joined the men who slept on the wooden benches there—I wasn't going to invite Bettina to such a dormitory. She was actually sleeping in a bed, in a place that had a roof on it and her name on the door, but she couldn't make way for me.

She was, as I've said, sharing this loft on the top floor of a commercial building just off Union Square. There were four girls in the loft, and one bed, so the bed was already filled to capacity without an interloper like me. I wouldn't have joined them even if the roommates had offered to make room for me, which they didn't. In a mass meeting like that about all you can make is conversation, which in those days Bettina and I were getting our fill of in other, more public, mass meetings.

We walked the city most of that night. Having seen all there was to see up and down the Bowery, then back and forth in the Village, we unaccountably headed uptown, found ourselves finally in Central Park.

We were dogtired. We stretched out on the grass near the corner of 59th and Fifth, across from the Plaza, not far south of the Zoo. We huddled together against the knifing cold.

I had a copy of that day's *Times* that I'd fished out of a trash container, having learned from veterans of the outdoor life that sheets of newspaper slipped under your clothes make a pretty good insulation. It was a hell of a cold night. I guess the Sunday *Times* would have worked better than our weekday edition. Still, it wasn't so bad. When we began to shake too much we'd cross Fifth Avenue to an all-night snack place and have steaming hot coffee and sometimes a doughnut.

We sat at the counter, reviving ourselves and looking across at the sparkling fountain that faces the Plaza. Short years before, Scott Fitzgerald and his elegant friends used to gather at this famous landmark in their best evening clothes, after a night of partying at the Plaza, and throw themselves into the fountain's pool, having the impression that this sort of dunking was great and uninhibited fun, which showed how free the American people had become. We sipped our black coffee, chewed our sugar-dusted doughnuts, and discussed how ideas about the pursuit of happiness change with the times. We weren't particularly interested in the subject but the more we talked the longer we postponed our return to our grassy bed in the Park.

The next day things took a turn for the better. We'd gone to Bettina's loft to wash up and have an hour indoors. One of the roommates had a bright idea.

A painter had been evicted from his loft on the floor below. The landlord had left the key to this vacant loft at Bettina's, in case prospective tenants came around to look at the place. There was a mattress on the floor, nothing else, the floor had a month's accumulation of dust on it but there was this mattress and it didn't look too impossible. Bettina and I could let ourselves in with the key and spend the night there and nobody would be the wiser. Definitely we would be the warmer. Another night in Central Park would eliminate our housing crisis by eliminating us, a drastic solution and one which according to some humanist schools of thought attacked the problem at the wrong end.

We took the suggestion. The night began to shape up fine. The mattress seemed to us not altogether impossible, though by that time our standards may not have been too high. We didn't mind the fact that you had to put your shoes on to navigate that beshat floor, it was our intention to keep our floor-walking to a minimum.

At the worst possible moment, the very worst, there came an emphatic knocking on the door.

There was no reason for anybody to be at that door, that was the trouble. Nobody knew we were there, nobody could. But somebody was hammering away as though he knew beyond all questioning that we were inside and any number of lives depended on his seeing us without delay.

I wasn't exactly happy about this interruption but I wasn't thrown into a mortal panic, either. It was highly unlikely that whoever it was out there would have a key, but in any case I knew for sure the door was heavily bolted from the inside.

This was the comforting logic of the situation but it seemed to be escaping Bettina entirely. She froze. Every muscle in her body was in maximum contraction, she was suddenly all alert steel. Then she began to shake. The pounding stopped eventually, but she went on shaking, worse than she had on the grass in Central Park.

I said, "There's nothing to be afraid of, Bett. It couldn't have been for us, besides, whoever it was is gone."

She said, "Maybe he's not gone, maybe it's a trick, he could be hiding in the hall to jump on us when we come out."

"Well, we're not coming out, Bett. He's not going to hide in the hall all night if he's hiding at all, which I very much doubt."

She said something which absolutely floored me then. She said, "You don't know him, he could hide for years, ready to jump out any minute."

I said, "Come on, who do you know who's a marathon hider like that?" I was trying to talk her out of it, her teeth were actually rattling.

She said, "He could have lunch in Provo and by midnight be pounding on this door on 14th Street, that's how much he gets around, and take it from me, if he comes this far, if it's this much of a program with him, he's not going to get discouraged and evaporate from the hall in five minutes, what'm I going to do, Bern, my God."

I said, "I take it you're talking about your father. Why the hell would he be coming all the way from Provo to be knocking on your door at this ungodly hour?"

"You know what we're doing—"

"Were doing."

"You can't imagine what lengths that man'll go to to stop me doing anything like that. Stymie me in each and every thing I try, God, I just can't make a move."

"You certainly can't now, we can consider that established, but all right. I think you're exaggerating, Bett, I really do. Maybe he would like to keep an eye on you but be reasonable, he's not sitting on a mountaintop out there in Utah with a high-power spyglass trained on you in New York every minute of your waking and sleeping life, we don't have the technology for that kind of surveillance yet. I can't yet prove his eye has wandered from you at sexual moments, I don't know you well enough yet to have weighty data on that end of things, but look at the shoplifting side of it, Jesus, if he takes a dim view of your fucking he's got to be less than enchanted with your stealing, and just add it up, will you, how many times have you stolen things in the last year and how many times has he suddenly parachuted down on your head in the middle of the act and caught your itchy fingers in midair and tied the totebag shut?"

I thought I had her there, I really did. It turned out I'd badly under-estimated that little girl.

She said, "Each and every time. I've never once done it without his dropping on my head and practically cracking my skull open."

I said, "I see two pieces of evidence to contradict that statement. One, I've never noticed even a minor bruise on your scalp. Two, each and every time you *do* manage to come away with the boodle, so we have to say that if he did drop on your head he never stilled your fleet hand."

She said, "Well, it's a battle every time. I start to reach for things and there he is, coming down on me hard, grabbing at my hand to hold it back. Naturally, he can't stop me altogether. I'm small but you know I'm not a weakling, I keep in shape, I've got muscles, I put up a fight. He generally wins when I go for the big articles that would need the use of both hands and a lot of muscle coordination, anything major, but after all he can't pin my arms to my sides altogether, I can make short and quick moves with my fingers, the fingers of one hand, enough to lift the small objects, you know, costume jewelry and bottles of perfume. Haven't you noticed how I keep coming home with all these small-scale things and never anything big? Huh? Hasn't it ever occurred to you that there has to be some explanation for that? I'm in bad, bad trouble, Bern. I can't make a true move. I can't fucking *breathe*."

I saw that I'd been taking the wrong tack with her. When you confront a true case of paranoia suddenly 10 feet tall in somebody not much more than half that size you don't try to talk them out of it, it's a waste of breath.

I knew that because I'd had some experience with this order of stubbornness. I'd had all that coaching from my old man. The thing about the paranoiac is that he *knows* the enemy is there, against all the evidence to the contrary you can bring in, and he knows his knowl-edge is broader and deeper and truer than yours because all you see is the evidence but with his eagle eye he's spotted the enemy when they were manufacturing and planting this fake evidence, so he's not going to listen to you, at best he'll pretend to lend an ear to the blind and the deaf, to humor them.

There'd been the time my old man had called me up in a panic because he'd found out my old lady was systematically slipping arsenate roach powder into his maple walnut ice cream. I'd gone down to their place to handle the problem. My old man had what he thought was clinching evidence, there was maple walnut ice cream in the refrigerator, and the can of roach powder that had been in the cabinet under the sink was gone, and when you put these two irreducible facts together you got an irrefutable attempt by wifey dear to poison her long-suffering mate.

You don't try to bust into the iron circle of such logic. The best you can do is turn your back on it and try to come up with a stronger iron circle of your own. What I did was go to the refrigerator, take out the carton of maple walnut, get a spoon, and begin to shovel the stuff into my mouth, and keep on going until I'd downed a pint of it. The old boy had backed off to the wall. He stood pressed against it in mortal terror, hands to his cheeks. He pleaded with me not to kill myself to make some quixotic point, he urged me to remember that I had my whole life ahead of me, it didn't make sense to cut it short like this, who would come out ahead but the witch over there? I kept on eating, he kept on holding his head and moaning. When the carton was empty I sat down on a chair and made as though preparing to meet my maker. I sat there for some time with the attitude of patient waiting. Minutes passed. I didn't die. Finally I looked at my old man with a mild and polite questioning. I'd been a fool to imagine I could knock a mile-high reinforced concrete structure like that out of his head. What he did, after the minutes of anxious observation of his favorite son now so clearly and tragically moribund, was to heave a mile-deep sigh of relief. He came over and embraced me, intoning his thanks to the powers for sparing me. He undertook to explain to me how my life had been saved. I had to understand about witches. They knew how to slip any roach powder they cared to into any maple walnut they wanted, I was to believe that. They had their black talents. Well, if they could get the stuff *in* so nobody saw them, it stood to reason they could get it *out* again, fast, in the last split second, and they moved so expertly you couldn't see them then either, that stood up tall to reason, didn't it? We should both be thankful the old witch didn't harbor the same homicidal feelings toward me, her fine, lovely son, as she did toward her husband. At least she wasn't going to do in her own flesh and blood, that was something. He didn't mind getting poisoned so much now, he could go with an easy mind, even fold up singing, now that he knew the old witch wasn't going to feed on the bones of her own son. . . .

No, sir, I wasn't going to argue the unlikeliness of Bettina's old man's instant presence in New York, gather up the many pieces of evidence against this reading of the knock on the door. I wasn't going to remind her that by the rule of Occam's Razor, which suggests you ought to look into the explanations close to hand before reaching for those a million miles away, by that sensible guideline, when you heard a knock on a door like ours, it was wise to think of local plumbers, panhandlers, drunks who've lost their way, friends of the recently evicted tenant, Girl Scouts selling boxes of stale peanut brittle, trick-and-treaters, Christmas carolers, drivers with flat tires, all sorts of close-by citizens, before your mind got to your old man 3,000 miles away in Provo and most likely not giving two seconds' worth of thought to his fallen-away Trotskyite bad excuse for a daughter genitalizing her worthless life away in Greenwich Village, that ultimate Sodom of a Gomorrah. . . .

I said, "Suppose it was your old man, suppose he's still out there, what's the problem?"

She said, "Don't you see, can't you feel it, what'm I to do if he just won't fucking let me alone?"

"You're over 21. You have legal rights. If he won't let you alone you can call the cops and they'll protect your legally guaranteed privacy and make him let you fucking alone. No, I mean, fucking let you alone. Throw him in the clink to do it, if they have to."

"I can't spend the night here, Bern."

"Listen, is there the thought somewhere in your head that you're breaking some law by being in bed with me? If so, I should remind you that you also break several laws every time you steal something in the stores. You really ought to stop and give some thought to the two kinds of crimes, I mean, try to assess how large the crime of fucking looms as against the crime of stealing. Here's my view on that, fucking is by any enlightened standard a lot less serious a crime than stealing and for a very good reason, consider, Bett, when you steal you always damage another party, the person you steal from, I mean, any gain you make is somebody's loss, so the procedure is inherently anti-social, now fucking, on the other hand, in fuckinig you don't harm anybody, there's no vic-tim, really, any gain the one party makes is automatically a gain for the other, so really, when you take the social perspective you've got to rate stealing more serious than fucking in every way. Be sensible about this, Bett, if you let yourself break the laws about stealing I don't see why you can't make a small effort and—"

"I've got to get out of here, Bern. I can't stay here another minute, it makes my flesh crawl when I'm in a place where I know I'm being watched. Maybe if we're real quiet we can sneak down the stairs without being seen. . . ."

So we got dressed and got out. I don't argue with a girl who sees a roach powder of a father in a maple walnut of a hallway. We weren't seen, even though to Bettina's horror I whistled a few notes from "The Internationale" going down the stairs. The notes were the ones accom-panying the line, "No more tradition's chains shall bind us." Just then I was hearing the clank of many chains, all in Bettina's pretty head.

I wasn't going back to Central Park, it was fucking too cold, it was too fucking cold. I thought and thought and came up with an inspiration, even though it was the dead of night we would go knock on Irish's door and see if we could sleep on the floor or something.

Irish was around the Trotskyite movement, he'd been a sailor and was now working in a sheet-metal plant and living with a girl named Fanny. He'd come from Mormon country and would therefore be sympathetic to Bettina's shakiness. He was Irish, and that was why, in a moment of utter collapse of the imaginative faculty, we called him Irish. He was also a good and easy-going guy, so there was a chance that he wouldn't go for the meat cleaver when we busted in on him this much past midnight.

He did let us in. We didn't have to sleep on the floor, there was a foldout sofa in the living room that he said we were free to fold out if we wanted, though its insides weren't in good working order and tended to collapse when bodies were lowered onto it.

I have a vivid picture of how Irish looked when he came to the door with a towel wrapped around his middle, half asleep. The one thing I remember is how incredibly black his ankles were. He was very light-complexioned, really fair-skinned, but those ankles were dark as pitch.

I had no explanation at the time for the color of his ankles, and don't now. It couldn't have had anything to do with his occupation, whatever he did in that sheet-metal plant it wasn't with his ankles. Well, he'd come from the Land of the Latter-day Saints too. Maybe letting his ankles get dingy was his form of shoplifting. Everybody finds his own way to nose-thumb.

Irish wasn't exaggerating about the insides of that couch. The second we laid ourselves down it collapsed, forming a deep "V" with us in the precise dropped center.

The letter "V" was soon to take on the signification of Victory, thanks to its dramatization by Winston Churchill's two extended fingers and the accompanying proud notes from Beethoven. But the "V" we tried to sleep in that night meant Vexation—plus, for a bonus, Valediction to all forms of man-woman coveting.

Bett's old man was indeed squatting on her head. Every time she made a move of some promise, he was right there snatching her hand back. On each occasion she went after some major article, there he was barring the way. Maybe his presence made it impossible for her to breathe but it had the opposite effect on me, I was breathing like a winded Malemute.

To round out this picture I should note that things got better in the next weeks. Bettina got a letter from her father. Postmarked Tokyo. It announced that he'd gone there on business and would be traveling for months through the Far East. After a time this information drilled sufficiently into her head to make her see that, ubiquitous as he might be, the man was not likely to pop up on the headboard every time she got into bed with another party. She did get to relax some. There were nights when she actually reached for articles of some dimension, totebag on the ready, and actually got her hands full on the bent goods. . . .

About the night of the loud knocking, I finally got the story. It hadn't been a man at the door at all. It was one of Bettina's roommates. The girl, suddenly remembering that Bettina owed her a dollar, needed the money back because she couldn't sleep and had decided to go to an all-night movie on 42nd Street and she had come downstairs hoping to collect. When she got no answer she gave up her plan and decided to stay at home and read the only book around, Michael Gold's *Jews Without Money*. It was a wise move. Mike cured her insomnia in 12 minutes. That was the whole story.

I rushed to Bettina to tell her what had really happened. She didn't say a word, just looked at me blankly, I never did know whether because she didn't quite hear or didn't believe a word I said.

During the porn months we lived together for a time, Bett and I, in a pleasant one-room studio apartment off University Place. One night while we were lying around, I dazed from a long day of porn-typing, she from a busy stint of shop-derricking, I blazed up with what I thought was an altogether gorgeous idea.

"It's wild!" I shouted. "Whole new slant! Old, old thing freshly seen! Sacred matters viewed from the backside! The star, the Star of Israel, yow!"

"Were you saying something about stars?" Bett said. "If you want to talk about astronomy, all right."

"The Jewish Star, you'd know something about that, wouldn't you? Don't the Mormons use the symbol, didn't they take it over from the Jews?"

"They'd say it wasn't a taking over so much as a continuing. Remember, the Mormons consider that they're one of the 12 lost tribes of Israel, so any star the original Jews used way back there belongs to the Mormons too, by right of inheritance."

"Well, I just got a beautiful, a hair-raising, idea about the origins of that star. What's the distinguishing feature of the Jewish Star, isn't it that the thing has six points instead of the usual five?"

"I've always admired the way you count, Bern."

"Well, how do you go about making a six-pointed star, what's the geometry of the thing? The one sure way to get such a shape is to take two triangles of equal size and place them one over the other, right? Position them so all the points are equally spaced around the edges?"

"Your geometry's as good as your arithmetic, I've always said that, Bern."

"Well! Well, well, well! Now I put it to you why would anybody have thought of lowering one triangle over the other in the first place? One more or less equilateral triangle over another roughly equilateral triangle, you don't imagine an idea like that comes up out of nowhere, do you?"

"No, you're right, an idea like that has to come up out of somewhere, Bern."

"You bet your sweet life it does! And it's just shot across my mind what the source of this thought must have been, the event in nature that triggered this event in the mind! I ask you, Bett, where do you find articles in nature that are more or less equilaterally triangular in shape?"

"About everywhere there are articles having three sides more or less straight and more or less of equal lengths, Bern."

"Make fun of this if you want, Bett, I think I'm onto something here. Triangles don't occur that often in nature—"

"How often do you mean?"

"Often enough to register on people's minds. They're rare enough by themselves, and the times you come across triangles that fit one over the other or suggest such fitting, they're still rarer. Well, it just occurred to me what triangles the old Jews must have had in mind when they made up their first six-pointed star. Think, focus on this now, aren't our masses of pubic hair roughly triangular in shape, equilaterally triangular? In men and women both?"

"Just a minute and I'll check. What do you know, you're right, how about that?" She was very relaxed, she'd just received a letter from her old man postmarked Casablanca. "Women's, and men's too, what'll they think of next?"

"And aren't *those* about the only triangles occurring in nature that get superimposed one on top of the other with some regularity? See what I'm getting at, Bett? That old Jewish Star is taken to be the symbol of some very high and even celestial kind of holiness, you know, Star of David, Star of Bethlehem, the stars that shone with extra special brightness on such unpubic occasions as personal appearances of the Divinity, including even, if you remember, the very down-to-earth extended-tour personal appearance of Jehovah's own offspring, the Mighty Tike Himself, I remind you how those old Hebrew stars were shining all over the place the night Mary had that Issue! Look at the implications! The star got to be the signal for very unpubic happenings, heavenly more than earthly, but all the while it was itself the living reminder of pubic fusions, and if stars were shooting off all over the place the night of the Immaculate Conception that throws the whole idea of immaculateness into doubt, stars being symbols of the most maculate conceptions! Isn't that great? Think of the implications, Bett! The Jews have all along paid homage to the merging of the two pubic patches! The Mormons, even the Mormons bow down to the image of one pubis making up to another pubis! I think what I've gotten to here is close to an epiphany!"

In 1941, thanks to Joyce, it was fashionable to talk about epiphanies, they'd largely taken the place of traumas. People who were too fuzzy to know the time of day, let alone the date, were suddenly claiming to be epiphanized every time they brushed their teeth, that is, once or twice a week.

Her answer to that took me by surprise. She said, "No you haven't, unless epiphany means when you come across what it says in all the grammar-school primers."

I said, "What?"

"It pleases you to think you've concocted some kind of blasphemy but you haven't—to quote from the official texts isn't blasphemy."

"What official texts?"

"I hate to break the news to you like this, Bern, but the truth is that the putting together of male and female pubises to make the Star of David is the official explanation of the symbol back where I come from, it's what I was taught when I was growing up and I took it for granted everybody understood the six-pointed star the way we did. You're bright, Bern, I won't take that away from you, but my God, your education is, well, a little spotty. You just can't go on discovering what's common knowledge to the human race and calling it a bomb-shell to our consciousness—"

There it was. Once again a revolutionary concept of mine had turned out to be ancient wisdom; the best products of my most advanced new brain, ongoing sediments from humanity's old. It was further evidence that there's nothing new under the sun, just more and more sunglasses of improved design.

I tell you this story because it has a direct bearing on my porn life. The next day I was hard at work at the typewriter, rather, my fingers flew over the keys while I sat back and watched. I had a brilliant idea for another porn novel about a girl out of Mormon country whose new brain is filled with commandments to void and avoid but whose old brain remains alive, under the surface, with the symbolism of the sacred old star and the multiple mergements it memorializes. The girl wants only to arrange her life in the currently moral way, to form one perfect six-pointed star that her peers, and the elders too, will applaud. So she takes a mate, and in secret composes the right six-pointed star to commemorate the arrangement. She sits and studies the star day after day. It seems somehow incomplete, meager, the barest preliminary, a trial run. So she takes a second lover, and adds a third triangle to the two already joined, adjusting the nine points so they're equidistant. After a while, she gets to thinking this is a pretty cut-rate star too. She takes a *third* lover, adjusts the four triangles so the spaces between the 12 points are the same. In her search for a Platonic perfection of form and moved by buried archetypes somewhat Wimlimberalized, she keeps adding lovers and triangles, always keeping the points evenly spaced. Her life becomes very busy, of course, what with more and more lovers to be taken care of daily, but it's not nymphomania that spurs her, she's not in any true sense promiscuous, in fact she's rather undersexed, it's just that she's a perfectionist, a Platonist, and the jagged edge of the star, no matter how rapidly the points keep multiplying, simply nags at her, pokes fun at her taste for an absolute nicety of form. The quest goes on. Lovers keep getting added, and the points that correspond to them. And the great day arrives when so many points have appeared on the star, so many evenly arranged points, that the spaces between them have become infinitesimal, they've dropped out of sight—the points have merged to form one continuous line, a perfect circle, the Platonic ideal. Of course, it's been fearfully hard work for this idealistic girl, having to cater to all the lovers needed to produce all those triangles. On the day the jagged star has fleshed out to a flawless circle, she dies, burned out at 22, but serene in the knowledge that through her unflagging labors she has achieved one brief glimpse of perfection, the Platonic form of grace. . . .

I wrote that book in less than two weeks. It was an absolute natural; as they say in the literary world, it practically wrote itself. I called it *A Star Is Born*.

I had never seen the Fredric March movie of the same title. You can imagine how unamused I was when some years later a movie by the same name, starring Judy Garland and James Mason, appeared. The title was wasted on some silly story about a Hollywood actress rising to stardom and a great Hollywood male star fading away; you can see that the important aspects of stardom, which had received careful attention in my book, had been completely slighted in that inconsequential, commercially conceived movie. That's typical of the way Hollywood deals with weighty literary efforts. You know yourself how often the book is lovable and the movie derived from it hateful.

By which bridge we come back to:

CHAPTER 10

Dry You-Know-Where

To celebrate my new masterwork, *Thomas and Hannah,* and my still newer one, *A Star Is Born*, Barneybill invited me to go out on the town. I'd turned down previous social overtures from him; it was the politic thing, for once, to accept.

Spain was the rallying point for his many obsessions. As he saw it, half the killjoys in the world were putting down the proletariat, the other half, the pubis, and all, for him, were currently summed up in the person of Generalissimo Franco, squelcher of Labor and Libido alike.

From his elegant offices in the Time-Life Building, from behind his barricade of first editions, he was carrying on two unremittent wars, one against the reactionaries who would brake the People's Revolution, the other against those who were trying to soft-pedal the healthy horniness of the human race, most particularly, of the vital lower classes, and on both fronts his best volleys were aimed at the Iberian peacock, though Hitler and Mussolini—never Stalin—were legitimate targets too.

With this turn of mind, he logically enough led me to a Spanish night-club for our festivities. It was a small but expensive flamenco supper club in a cellar on Eighth Street. In a setting of bullfight posters, matador capes draped everywhere, a mural depicting Toledo soaring and dauntless in the raw sun, he found he could brood more authentically over what was happening in this retrograde world to anti-capitalists and pro-carnalists, who, as he saw it, were blood brothers, members of the same life-espousing army, though temporarily in retreat and somewhat disarrayed.

The martinis were cheering. The champagne was warming. The paella was a fine poultice applied from within. The filetes de puerco adobado made an excellent base for the Bodegas Bilbainas, an excellent red. The floor show was stimulating because the girls in the chorus, if sloppy, were naked.

I was in the mood to be stimulated: I'd finally gotten those gonadal brats Thomas and Hannah out of my system, and in addition brought my Platonist Mormon lady full circle, and I was a cool two thousand the richer. I could look at the naked girls not as models for prurient works-in-progress but as girls, warm lavings, pneumatic promises.

I swilled more wine and looked. I had the distinct impression that one of the peeled dancers, the cute gypsy, second from the end, was looking back, eyes gearing to gypsy transactions, none of the seven forms of ambiguity there. Always the literateur, I began in my head to compose the note I would send to this gypsy backstage indicating my predilection for transacting with gypsies, even those of Hoboken origins.

From time to time comments straggled through from the moody presence to my left. They seemed uniformly irrelevant to the business at hand.

At one point Barneybill said, "The potent masculine ethos of the Spanish people is being ground down by the unholy affiance of the exploiting land-owners and the fatcat Catholic Church, a hangover from feudalism."

The remark, though it had some historical probity, seemed to cast no interesting light on the maneuvers the gypsy's belly was engaged in at the moment. I ignored it.

A little later Barneybill issued a still more lugubrious bulletin:

"When the International Brigade and all the brave Loyalist armies were drowned in blood because the imperialist powers of the West wouldn't lift a finger to help their progressive democratic cause, all our hopes for a more equitable and humane social order in our time were drowned with them; we abandoned the field to Hitler without a struggle because we feared the inexorable march to socialism more than we feared fascist reactionism."

It was my impression, from what I'd seen as well as from what I'd read, that Stalin had done his share of sitting on the Loyalists, along with Roosevelt, Leon Blum, and Neville Chamberlain, and I was about to say so—but just then that agile gypsy started a particularly animated series of undulations, and I lost my train of thought.

They all began to undulate, all the sloppy, naked girls. It wasn't very flamenco but it was fine, hearty, and worth study. The drummer banged his big base drum, the girls socked and socked, it sounded as if the percussions were coming from all those lovely agitated bellies, abdomens hammering out the tattoo of war to all the tribesmen, and I was a tribesman thirsty for mobilization, counting the arrows in my quiver, drinking my champagne.

Remember, please, that I was not used to such sybaritic scenes away from my Barneybill pages. All this three-dimensional lushness was making me lightheaded.

Came a discordant rhythm. Unrelated to the drums and the bellies. To my left, an unmotivated jiggling that shook the table.

I looked. It was Barneybill. He had his napkin tight over his face and his face was down to the table, down on his hands; he was sobbing.

No question about it, the man was really in the grips of deep and turbulent sorrow. His shoulders were heaving. His whole body was in jog, as though he were passenger in a springless buggy proceeding at a smart pace down a corduroy road. He was making minor whining noises, interspersed with wheezes.

It didn't seem the right, tuned-in thing to do, with drums orating and pretty bellies on the loft.

"What is it—asthma?" I said. "The place *is* kind of smoky."

"We sit here drinking champagne and the world's falling apart," he managed to get out chokingly. "Everything's a shambles, one catastrophe after another, and we sit here drinking champagne."

"What're we supposed to do, go out and get shambled too, how would that help?" I said with some irritation—I wanted to watch that girl shimmy, not Barneybill's unaligned, knobby shoulders. "It's not our sitting here drinking champagne that's chopping up the world. If everybody were sitting here with us, the world wouldn't get chopped up, there'd be nobody left outside to do the chopping. Use a little logic, will you? Wipe your eyes and catch this floor show. That girl with the black hair is practically double-jointed, you don't see that every day."

"Decadence, decadence, decadence," he chanted in quaky hopelessness. "We've no fiber. Spanish workers and peasants groaning under the yoke of the Falange, and we look to our paltry, greedy bellies."

"You might try looking to *those* bellies," I said. "Find a paltry one and I'll give you a dollar."

He raised his tear-stained face and began to weep unrestrainedly again.

"We're swine to think of food and girls," he whimpered. "We don't have the right to cater to ourselves. People sweating and starving and dying everywhere. It will haunt me all my days that I didn't go to Spain when there was a Spain to go to and a Spain to save. Others went and shouldered guns and I stayed home keeping my books in order."

Sure, I wanted to say: all your dirty books in order.

"I was a coward. I was a self-server. My head was full of yours truly. My whole philosophy and outlook was me first. The world was crying out for people to take a stand and all I took was tax deductions. The imperialists and last-ditch fascist defenders of finance capital were setting matches to humanity, and I kept my head buried in the sand of profit ledgers. The manly thing was to go to Spain at all costs. I did a cost breakdown and decided on my accountant's advice that the investment was too risky. I'm half a man as the result. My manhood's lying out there on the bloody fields of Aragon, but I'm safe at home. I haven't been good with women since. I tend to fail with women. I think of the corpse of my manhood, lying broken-boned and rotting in Aragon, and I don't perform well. I don't have the right to sit in a nightclub and enjoy myself. I feel like I'm cheating, having a good time."

I wanted to say: oh, no, you're not cheating, buddy, nobody can say you're having a good time, you'll never be slandered that way.

"I'm miserable here. I just can't stand it, all the noise. Do you mind if we leave? I'd like to take a good long walk. What do you say we walk up to Lindy's and have a hot pastrami sandwich? This Spanish food doesn't stick to your ribs, I'm hungry, I'd like a nice hot pastrami sandwich, pickled green tomatoes on the side, that'd be fine."

My eyes bid apologetic farewells to the gypsy lady from some Hoboken or other. None of the seven forms of ambiguity was discernible in her look of letdown, which let me doubly down.

We walked the long way from Eighth Street to Broadway and 50th, no traffic at this hour, Barneybill could brave the intersections.

I sat in Lindy's and watched this misshapen, misarranged, misbegotten, misbobbled mishap of a man as he downed two fat pastrami sandwiches, a platter of French fries, and a season's crop of green tomatoes. I was fascinated, if a little sick to the stomach. I saw him clearly now. I saw exactly how he'd gotten politics and genitals mixed up in his cesspool of a head.

His mood seemed to be expanding with his stomach. He finally put his knife and fork away. He licked dabs of mustard and ketchup from his fingers. He wiped the pastrami grease off his blobby nose, patted his doll-dainty lips, belched softly to indicate contentment regained.

"I had a moment of emotion back there, I'm the first one to say so. Guess I was just carried away. I hope you won't hold it against me."

"Certainly not."

He thought it took cojones to shoot at fascists, and he was dead sure that shooting at fascists gave you cojones. A neat phallo-Marxist package: great libidos lead people's insurrections; fighting leftist wars is bound to make you very venereal; potency will come charging your way on a white Bolshevik-Leninist charger; become a card-holding member of The Party and you'll bowl over the ladies. D. H. Lawrence needs the stout legs of Loyalist General El Campesino to get moving.

"I hope you won't take what I said too seriously. When I get in that mood I tend to see the dark side, run myself down. My life's really not so bad, not bad at all. I just wish I might have gotten closer to the vital doings of our times, being in the thick of it must be quite exhilarating. But I don't want you thinking I'm on the sidelines entirely. I do have my moments, hig, hig."

"Right"

Barneybill Roster, I thought, would not be half so People's-Frontish and Francophobe were he not so worried about his arrears as to rut. His own, not the sagging oil millionaire's in Tulsa, Oklahoma. Maybe there was an oil man in Tulsa, maybe. But Barneybill's heart was out there in Tulsa too, running down to the mailbox each morning to see if more of the packages in plain manila wrappers had arrived to perk him up. Whatever the case might be with the Tulsa oil man, if there *was* a Tulsa oil man, Barneybill was the bum who had no track record with the ladies and needed this sexological bilge to slobber over: it allowed him wistful, wispy dreams of one day joining the lusters' fray, in the best and most remote International Brigade of all, that of the assmen. Barneybill Roster was his own best customer. The ranking hot-eyed impotent for

whom our masterworks were tailored. Tulsa might be filled with consumers for our product, all the Tulsas across the land might be, but
Barneybill Roster was the iguana-eyed patron of Our post-Lady.

"You know, Wilhelm Reich says you should never be ashamed of
crying, tears shouldn't be held in, you just get bad armoring and cancer
and such. If you're able to cry without restraint, simply let go, it's a good
sign, shows your musculature's not frozen, it's the stopped-up non-
criers who're non-orgasmic, you know, dry in the eyes, dry you-know-
where. Hig, hoog, hig."

"Sure."

Scabrous, stenchy patronage, this.

CHAPTER 11

GREEN THUMB, BLACK LEG

Insurrection: I was invited to a rank-and-file rally of Zo-Zo's porn crew. I came expecting to hear labor grievances discussed, I found myself facing charges of starting World War II.

There was a newcomer to our porn ranks named Albie, who accused me of all sorts of things. For instance, he was convinced I had devastated the Loyalist armies and turned Spain over to Hitler and Mussolini. I did my best to indicate the many ways in which Hitler, Mussolini, Franklin Roosevelt, Neville Chamberlain, Leon Blum, Stalin, Franco, and many of the top officials of the Loyalist government and armies had had a hand in this development, but he had had this epiphany and facts are no match for epiphanies.

I will not describe this young fellow other than to mention that he had hair like a scouring pad and gaps between his teeth which seemed impressively larger than the teeth. Political animus may have clouded my vision, it's possible, distaste may have led me to build up the minuses in his structure and belittle the pluses. Still, I remember those spaces as being about two feet wide and the teeth themselves as no thicker than toothpicks. The unappetizing image stays in my mind as a datum, not a political judgment.

Albie was born and brought up on the Lower East Side. From the time he started at NYU he was never without a copy of *Jews Without*

Money in his briefcase, considering it to be the only honest writing about his neighborhood and a literary masterpiece. The book was less than accurate about the pocket of the Lower East Side Albie came from, though; his father owned a lot of tenements and other real estate in the area and was bulgingly well off. The Jews of Lower Manhattan who were without money, and there were a swarming lot of them, were in that deprived condition largely because Albie's father and those like him had corralled all the money around, there just wasn't any left over.

Himself a Jew and with all this money behind him, Albie felt guilty about it, and preferred to feature in his thoughts and discussions those other Jews whose pockets were empty. He tried to handle his guilt in various ways, none of which involved giving up his allowance. He was guilty enough to join the Young Communist League. He was guilty enough, eventually, to sign up for the Abraham Lincoln Brigade and go fight in Spain. When he made his way back to New York after that rout, he was guilty enough to try to earn a few dollars for himself so his father wouldn't have to give him an allowance quite so fat. That's how he drifted into porn.

He wasn't sure of me when we first met. He wanted to test me. He asked what I thought about the ecstatic final paragraph in Mike Gold's novel, in which the narrator, without any advance notice whatsoever, no least build-up, discovers the Revolution, joins the Communist Party, and so becomes a man and is healed, a Jew made whole without money.

I said I thought the conversion was a little contrived, arbitrary, too, too nice, too neat, too wrapped up, signed, sealed, delivered, because no true groundwork had been laid for it. Other people had grown up in the same squalid tenement world, lived the same street life, had the same distressed experiences, and wound up joining the Union League Club and the Republican Party, some the American Medical Association, some the Mafia. I said in my view a winning over was convincing when we saw it growing and took it as inevitable, not when the author told us, almost as an afterthought, in one skimpy paragraph, it had happened, and asked us to take it from him on faith.

I said there were other novels of conversion I found more believable. For example, Dostoevsky's *Crime and Punishment*; in that one the hero is converted from homicide to love but it takes him about 600 pages to get to that point and we're following him every inch of the way, we see it building. There's also the case of *The Magic Mountain*; Hans Castorp needs about 800 pages to get converted from giddy elevations to the lowlands again, and we're allowed to accompany him in the process step by step, so the recruitment doesn't come entirely as an O. Henry trick ending, we're pretty well prepared for it.

I said, without the progression, without the slow unfolding of a logic toward the desired end, there's not a feeling of inexorableness about the hero's outcome, if Gold had announced in the final paragraph that the guy wound up after that big dose of the tenement life pimping for Lucky Luciano or icepicking hits for Murder, Inc. I would have believed him just as much, or as little. I said that my attitude toward all writers, even Marxist ones, was, don't say it, prove it, and for me Mike Gold had proved nothing except that he didn't know how to end a novel except by flashing a membership card in something, which I considered was a contribution neither to the novel nor to politics, feeling as I did that people should come into politics with their eyes open. This hero of Gold's, I said, was a sleepwalker, and it worried me that if somebody had held before his nose a lifetime subscription to the *Saturday Evening Post* instead of a CP card he might just as heavy-liddedly have signed *that*.

Albie said, fair enough, I'd shown my true colors, I was a fascist, more exactly, a social fascist, since I spread a thin veneer of social conscience, socialism, over my cynical fascism.

I said I was prepared to believe that Gold's own conversion to the CP was as mindless as he portrayed it, his column in the *Daily Worker* gave daily evidence of the total absence of a mind behind his words and acts, but he ought to allow that other people coming into politics might come with some ideas and have spent some time working out those ideas and arrive thinking, not sleepwalking.

Albie said, fine, we'd settle this at the barricades.

I said, O.K., I'd meet him there if he didn't make it too early in the morning, I was a late riser, but he'd better put up better barricades than he and his pals had made in Spain, those were for show, to divert people's attention while Stalin and the rest sold the Spanish Revolution down the river, I was interested in barricades that were for more than show and I doubted that people who sleepwalked into politics were capable of building such.

He said, wait and see, he and his pals would build plenty, and they'd be solid, they'd be made out of the bones of social fascists like me, the only solid parts of us sellouts.

You see how much we talked in those days and how little we said. You haven't got many points to make when the total contents of your head are derived from the *Daily Worker*, that means you're emptyheaded, and a sleepwalker.

The protest meeting was in the back room of a bar below Sheridan Square. It appeared that just about all of Zo-Zo's Village protégés were dissatisfied with their wages hours, and general conditions of employment, and Albie, always the organization man, had called them together to talk over what might be done about Barneybill the Exploiter.

It made me dizzy to see this heavy two-way traffic across the class lines. The leader of the labor drive, Albie, was a veteran of the Spanish Civil War and a Jew with considerable concealed money. The capitalist blood-sucker he was trying to organize against, Barneybill Roster, was all for labor, particularly its leftist wings, wept into his celery tonic at Lindy's for not being a veteran of the Spanish Civil War like Albie, supported just about all the People's Fronts Albie's people were throwing up all over the place, and was, like Albie, a Jew with very considerable money. There was no way to make a Marxist analysis of the socio-economic forces at work as porn labor prepared to clash with porn capital. There was a real worker-owner conflict, I saw when the facts came out, but one and the same ideology was fermenting in both contending parties.

Things got more muddied still when I discovered, much later, that Barneybill had for a time been a card-carrying member of the CP. Simon Legree as a loyal cadre in the proletarian vanguard, *there* was an O. Henry twist. Here was that very same vanguard assembled in a Sheridan Square bar to discuss ways and means of storming the comrade-oppressor's stronghold. . . .

"I called this meeting because we're facing a war," Albie said to start things off.

"That's right, looks like we'll be in it any day now," I said.

I'd been reading the paper just before the meeting. The headlines were ominous, more and more of our convoys being torpedoed, all of that. It sounded like we'd be getting in any day now. I assumed all present had seen the papers, and were as worried as I was, and that Albie must have had reference to this shared concern.

"I'm talking about the coming war with Roster, not the war in Europe, there's no chance of our getting in that one with you and your friends lining up with Roosevelt to keep us out so we won't go to the aid of the Workers' State and Hitler can take over everywhere," Albie said factually.

"My influence in Washington is tapering off, you can relax," I said. "They're staying up nights down there, figuring ways to get us in. Of course, it takes time, when you have a president who got re-elected with slogans about no American boys being sent to die on foreign soil he can't start sending the boys 24 hours later. You'll get your second front.

It would have saved time and effort to have stopped Hitler in Spain, not to mention Germany, but Stalin didn't see it that way, neither did Roosevelt, but they have the same idea about stopping him now that he's outside Leningrad."

"Where you put him," Albie said.

"I put Hitler outside Leningrad?"

"Nobody but. You and your friends were working for years to dismantle the Soviet Union and turn it over to Hitler, weren't you? We learned about your schemes in the Moscow Dials, you got exposed there, all right. Well, now you see how it works out, you did such a fine job trying to bust up the Soviet Union for Hitler, he figured the groundwork was laid and all he had to do was walk in and take over."

"You're overlooking some facts. For example, a development that encouraged Hitler hugely was Stalin's chopping the heads off two-thirds of all his upper-level army officers. My friends didn't do the chopping, all the oppositionists by then had had their own heads lopped off. It was Stalin who did the hatchet work, so Hitler figured there was no general staff or real officer cadre left in Russia, and as you can see from recent events he was right."

"And why did those heads have to be cut off, huh? Because you and your people filled them with all those Hitlerite sabotage and sellout schemes!"

"How would you know the contents of those heads, Albie?"

"Read the verbatim transcripts of the Moscow Trials, it's all there, they all confessed to their mad-dog plots."

"Look at the statistics, Albie. At the most conservative estimate Stalin's sent eight to 10 million heads rolling. Only about 50 of them ever came to trial. It's those 50 you read about in the transcripts. They got confessions from 50 or so. And those confessions have been proved to be phony, read the documented report of the John Dewey Commission. At the very least you're guessing about the contents of 9,999,950 of those heads. And lying about the contents of the other 50."

"I was against asking you to come to this meeting, I said all you'd do was disrupt, and I was right," Albie said.

"I'm not disrupting, for Christ's sake, I'm just trying to defend myself against the charge of starting World War II, I don't want people to go around thinking I did that, I'm not going to be known as a warmonger when it's your gang that wants to make this war as big as possible and is trying to draw everybody in, now that it's Leningrad being threatened, not just Berlin or Madrid, now that it's Russia being carved up, not Poland," I said.

"You and I'll settle this one day on the barricades," Albie assured me. It was invariably his final, crushing argument.

"It's no match until you chalk up some kind of record with barricades," I said. "So far Albie at the barricades is strictly amateur night."

That's how a lot of union meetings went in those days, agendas were loose.

They got around to considering the Barneybill situation eventually. They wanted my thoughts; as a six-book man I was now a Porn Worker Senior Grade whose rich experience should be drawn upon. Besides, it was rumored that I was an intimate of Barneybill's, the only one in the Zo-Zo cell, and therefore must know the man's makeup, could judge which tactics might be effective with him.

I come from a strong union family, among us it was always held to be a cardinal sin for a worker to turn his back on the bonds that unite him with his fellows. Mutuality, fraternity, class loyalty were the banners under which I grew up. Damn right I was ready to sit down with my colleagues and talk over their grievances, I'd said.

Though the only squawk I myself had against our boss was his demagogic insistence on his constitutional right to go on breathing: I was certain that in drawing up the Bill of Rights our forefathers had not for a moment meant to allow for such a ludicrously loose interpretation of their text.

I was interested to meet my coworkers. There were first-rate brains among them; several have gone on to become eminent writers, editors, and professors, some of such stature as to be included in *Who's Who*, though the biographical notes never mention their humble beginnings in Porn. You'll have to take my word for it that American Literary Culture of the Forties and Fifties was well and ably represented, though embryonically, at that barroom protest meeting long ago.

Protest they did. With good reason. It seemed that, solicitous though he was with me, Friend Barneybill could be the ogre-taskmaster with employees whose image of the post-Lady did not quite coincide with his own.

"You know what that son of a bitch makes us do when he doesn't like a story we've handed in?" one porner said. "He insists that we write another draft, and often a third, and sometimes even a fourth, and if we balk, no pay, not a cent."

"And then if the final draft doesn't please him he doesn't settle with you and write it off as a loss," another put in. "The prick. The low miserable cocksucker. He tells you this one didn't work out and if he makes a payment it's got to be considered an advance on the *next* work, to be deducted from future earnings. He comes out ahead every time, the risk's all on our side."

"He'll dole out just enough to keep you somewhat eating and somewhat hungry, never sums that'll let you get ahead," a third man told us. "He's got to have you in the humble petitioner's role, begging for pennies, he gets a kick out of seeing you grovel for eating money."

"If you want to be of some help to the boys, answer one question, what's this snake paying you?" Albie said to me.

"Well, it varies," I said. "Sometimes it's more and sometimes it's less, there's no fixed fee. That more or less your experience, fellows?"

More or less. A few were getting the standard rate of one dollar per page, some got 75 cents, some no more than 50.

"And the shithead penalizes you for missing deadlines."

"And occasional typos."

"He's been known to dock you for a minor misspelling, the rat."

This passionate friend of the downtrodden who wept at stripteases and had to comfort himself with pickled tomatoes.

"This correspond with your own experiences?" Albie asked me.

He was beginning to crowd. He imagined that the boss-enemy here was some kind of fascist of my ilk, not his own comrade, and he wanted, I sensed, to establish the unity of the fascists.

"It hasn't been any one thing with me, the picture changes from day to day. It'll start off in one direction, and I'll think I've got the situation pinned down, then the winds shift, so to speak, and it veers off on another tack, often a tangent, so, no, I don't believe it would be accurate to say it's been any one single thing in my dealings with the man."

"I was listening to that, I was following word for word, and you know what, I got the distinct impression that the longer you talked the more you didn't say anything. Give us a couple hard facts to go on and we'll figure out the winds for ourselves, for instance, what pay level are you mostly on, 50-cent, 75-cent, or dollar?"

"The way it's worked out with me, I started with the understanding my rate would be a dollar a page but I can't claim I ever got it, it was over before it began, Roster's reaction to my first book was so strong, he changed the rate and I haven't hit the dollar fee since."

"We thought you were in solid with the guy, you were getting the red-carpet treatment."

"Well, Albie, you thought I put Hitler at Leningrad and started the war, too. Don't go around believing everything you hear, there are a lot of loose mouths in this town."

Barneybill's Blooming Boys had had all they could take. They were ready to take on this militant foe of the Profit System who was getting rich off their hides. What did they propose to do about their exploiter? A series of clenched-fist things, under Albie's goading.

First, they would organize, and make their organization known to Barneybill. Then, present a series of demands to redress the many inequities. And if Barneybill refused to sit down at the negotiating table, or at least the cobbler's bench? If he insisted on an open shop?

Work stoppage! Said Albie. Strike! Starve the leech out! Force his hand! Said Albie, whose father owned tenements.

Somebody pointed out that a sit-in would be hard to arrange in that snooty office amidst all the vellumed first editions.

But you could picket! Said Albie. Picket the bastard! Carry signs exposing his vicious labor practices! Call for boycotts, the works! Said Albie, who got an allowance from his slumlord father.

What'd Porn Worker Senior Grade think of *them* direct-action apples? He was really pressing, Albie was.

"Are you being entirely realistic?" I said. "Suppose he doesn't recognize your union and won't deal with you, where do you have recourse, the NLRB? What'll you tell the NLRB about the kind of work you do for Roster? So far as anybody knows the guy deals in Americana, that's all, what're you going to claim, that you're being underpaid for first editions of Alexander Hamilton you write?"

"All right, wiseguy, if you're so sure we can't nail him with a direct union confrontation, then what's your idea of how to approach it? Just for purposes of discussion let's assume you don't want to sabotage the whole push, for once you're not in favor of selling the workers all the way down the river, then where's the alternative to strike, what's your strategy here, boycott?"

"Well, I'm not sure any direct-action methods are going to accomplish much in this tricky case. Look, a boycott would be fine, but have you thought through just what you'd like to boycott, and how? You can't get up a boycott against Roster without knowing who his customers are and I don't think they'll come forth to be counted if you issue a call for them. Frankly, I don't even see how you can get any kind of effective picket line going. You can march up and down in front of the Time-Life Building, sure, but what would your signs say, BARNEYBILL ROSTER UNFAIR TO DIRTY WRITERS, BARNEYBILL ROSTER PAYS STARVATION RATES FOR DIRTY WORDS? See what I'm getting at? There's really no way to get your message across to the public—and without public support for your action, see what I mean?"

"Your whole pattern's coming out here, buddy," Albie said. "Any move any branch of labor makes to better itself, strike a blow for human rights, you're right in there making a pitch against the action, looking out for the boss's interests. Maybe there are some technical difficulties in picketing, all right, but the fact remains we've got to cut off the man's sources, unless we keep him from getting his finished goods for the market we've got no bargaining power, he'll tell us to go whistle. So how do you feel on this subject, Mr. No To Everything, you against any move to starve him out by cutting the supplies off?"

"You can quit work, sure, but I don't know how far it'd get you. You all belong to one shop, Zo-Zo's. All right. How many other shops are subcontracting for this guy? If you close down your own production, can you be sure a dozen other shops won't step in and fill the demand?"

"Where's the proof there're these other shops working? All we've got is your word for it and for all we know you're making it up because that's what Roster pays you for."

"He pays me for my pages, and he's paying plenty of other people for theirs, people you'll never track down. From all I've seen and heard I'm dead sure he's got a more than ample labor supply so there's no way you can hit him by turning off your typewriters. Do a home sit-down if you want, it'll overnight turn into a permanent lockout, I'd be lying if I told you otherwise."

"The way I read this situation you'd be lying if you told us you once spoke the truth when you opened your mouth here or anywhere, my friend," Albie commented. "For you everything's wrong in our plans and nothing's right. What do we do, then, by your lights, cave in and just take all the anti-labor shit this guy's dishing out? You've got to be advocating some measures so you won't be taken altogether for the fink you are. What's left, sabotage?"

"I'd be in favor of that, I certainly would, if I could think of a way to sabotage the man. Maybe there is one way. Find out where his outlets are, break in in the dead of night, remove all the pages from all the bindings and substitute typescript of *Little Lord Fauntleroy*. Frankly, I don't think that's a feasible plan. Frankly, I think you're stuck."

Realistic words; but a few of the boys, those close to Albie, didn't take kindly to them. There were even some grumblings about strikebreakers and sellouts and stooges for the bosses. The atmosphere was strained when I left. But in speaking out against Albie's battle plan, shot through with the infantile sickness of adventuristic ultra-leftism as it was, I'd done the one thing I could do.

If a union got going I would as a matter of principle have to join it. I couldn't have lied to my fellow porn workers. I would have had to tell them I was geting two dollars a page, which would have established me as an elite of exactly one, with resultant hard feelings that had to become explosive. And a work stoppage or even slow-down would have queered all my plans. My earnings were just then being eaten up by a backlog of family debts but I figured that if I could keep Barneybill's dollars coming in for another few months I'd be enough ahead to quit porn for good and maybe try my hand at writing another kind of book, a revolutionary book, a totally, undeviatingly, daringly, titillatingly, *un*dirty book.

Good sense did in the end prevail. Most of the boys realized soon enough that there was simply no way to use above-board labor methods against an under-the-counter employer, even the most potent flamethrower is powerless against a mole. Albie was voted down, and was stewing about it. It wasn't bad enough that I'd brought Hitler to Leningrad, now here I'd gone and killed an honest union drive, I just couldn't keep my saboteur's paws off workers' causes.

In the following months, as I learned, some of the worst soreheads just got fed up with Barneybill's high-handed procedures and one by one quit the game. One fellow took an English instructorship in a Toronto college. Another became an editor in the juvenile department of a Madison Avenue publishing house. A third went off to write a novel about mountain climbing. A fourth left Barneybill's office one day fuming, took the elevator up, and talked himself into a staff job with Time-Life. We were told he wound up as a war correspondent specializing in the technicalities of military aircraft. Rumor had it that he piled up more flying time with the Air Force than any correspondent in the European Theater of Operations. That was *his* way of getting aboveground.

It was the only time in my life that I played blackleg in a union effort, but I had to do it to keep my green thumb employed long enough to get me well out of the red. I comforted myself with the thought that if the circumstances could be explained to my old man, who prided himself all his days on having been a personal friend of Samuel Gompers and Eugene V. Debs and Emma Goldman, he'd understand.

Some weeks after that meeting I ran into Albie on Eighth Street. He was wearing denim Levi's and workshirt. The more he wrote porn, I noticed, the more he was moved to parade in the uniform of the manual laborer, maybe out of an obscure impulse to convey that what he was doing on the typewriter was being done by his hired fingers, not him; in the social relations of porn production he had to feel he was a pair of hireling hands, the plight of all sellers of labor power under capitalism. It's startling, how many penthouse dwellers in these uneasy times work overtime to give the impression that they're lifelong residents of the bottommost pit.

"Hello, fink," Albie greeted me. "How's the sellout business? Selling much out lately?"

"Listen, there's something I've been meaning to ask you, you don't really think I started World War II, do you?"

"You had help, I'll give you that."

"Albie, I want you to know something, I looked the dates up and I couldn't have started it, I wasn't even in town, if you want to know my exact whereabouts on that crucial day I was working in the engine room of a banana boat approaching British Honduras."

"I want you to know something, buddy, you're so full of shit the municipal sewage system couldn't handle you."

"Albie! This is exciting! That's the longest and most complicated sentence I've ever heard you speak, it's more complicated than any sentence in Mike Gold, you keep on growing like this, really thinking out some advanced word combinations and it's bound to improve the quality of your porn, you could in time get up to the buck-a-page level and become a Jew with some money that doesn't derive from those Lower East Side tenements that made Mike Gold so mad! Stay with it, kid! You're really getting to make sentences! Who knows? One day you might even write a book about how you came up out of the ranks of the millionaires on the Lower East Side and wound up discovering Literacy and filling out a membership card in the English language! The conversion of conversions!"

"I'll conversion you, boy, I'll conversion the whole fink to hamburger, I swear, the day the barricades go up I'll be coming for you—"

"I'll be waiting, Albie. Bring your dictionary along if you're not entirely at home in the language yet, I know it takes a while to get over the effects of somebody like Mike Gold. . . ."

I know something about Albie's later life. Roosevelt, being an accomplished dialectician, did find a way to get some millions of our soldier boys onto foreign soil in the interests of avoiding foreign entanglements.

Albie did get his Second Front. He was an inveterate Popular Fronter, and here he felt was a Front that was bound to win all the popularity contests, thanks to its popularity with the Stalins and the Roosevelts, all the strange bedfellows that the politics of universal grab had suddenly made; so he naturally enlisted.

Not to go overseas, though. Maybe, after his experiences in saving the popular people of Spain, it had finally dawned on him that he didn't do so good on fronts, even those he was frontman for. So he pulled a few strings through his old man and some of his Party contacts, and was assigned to a film unit of the Army's Signal Corps.

This shift from words to images is worth a careful look. Quite a few of Albie's friends, ones more or less literary in bent, had finagled this film-unit assignment for themselves when they got drafted, in fact, there was a sudden rush on the part of mobilized Stalinist and Stalinoid intellectuals toward military film-making. Two decades before McLuhan, they had decided to desert the written word for the moving picture as their message medium.

It may have been that, swept up in the Sandburg-MacLeish hysteria, they'd been convinced that the products of intellectuals have to function as bullets or they're just petty-bourgeois games. Why they didn't try to make their words into bullets, though, is a knotty question. They may have been premature McLuhanites, inspired by the notion that images bit people harder than words. They may, on the other hand, have recognized that the words *they* were capable of producing were so lousy, so potboiler, so lead-footed, they would drive people to distraction, not war. Maybe they wanted to help Stalin by turning out bold, rousing images. Maybe they figured they could best help Stalin by turning out *anything* other than their usual insipid Mike Gold words.

So Albie spent the war preparing training and orientation films on the historical friendship between the Russian and American peoples and seven ways to detect a dose of the clap. When the shooting stopped he took inventory and discovered that he now had a vocation, moving pictures, which gave him an opportunity to escape from words, which in his hands were never moving. Logically, he joined the trek of the many Army-trained film-makers to Hollywood.

He never made it in Hollywood. Like so many of the Stalinoid newcomers, he had no more talent for images than he'd had for words, and relied mainly on his political connections to get him peripheral, hack assignments in the preparation of scripts. For a time his ideological buddies threw just enough work his way to give him a minimal income. Then Senator Joseph McCarthy decided to take on Hollywood, the new Red Scare was on, and filmic heads began to roll from Culver City to Burbank, though less bloodily and less irreversibly than did their counterparts in Stalin's purges.

The McCarthy Inquisition hit almost all the CP-oriented writers to some extent, but its impact on the no-talent ones was a lot more devastating than on the others. The competent script carpenters—"constructionists," as they're known in the trade—did a lot better than survive. After his term in prison Dalton Trumbo was busier than ever with assignments, though for some years he had to write under a pseudonym. People like Ring Lardner and Michael Wilson managed to come back all right. It was the fringe-writers, the dullheads, the hacks, who were wiped out for good.

Among them was that talent of pure Gold, Albie. It would be a misreading of history to see Albie's decline in Hollywood as one more vicious effect of the McCarthy-inspired blacklist. His career out there couldn't have gone down because it never went up. He had from the beginning been an expendable, and McCarthy got him spent not a day earlier than might otherwise have been the case. Besides, and this is the point, McCarthy didn't *want* to get Albie spent, he developed a great and enduring fondness for Albie.

It is said that Albie was left a bitter man, and I believe it. From the first he hadn't taken the McCarthy terror lying down. No, he took it standing up, and singing. He'd gone fast to McCarthy's investigating team and said he'd be glad to help them clean up the Hollywood scene (probably just to eliminate the competition) by providing them with the names of his comrades, if they'd agree in turn to deal with him in private, not make him take the stand in open court and do his singing openly. They'd agreed. Albie was small fry, they wanted big names to parade for the public. He informed to the best of his ability, behind doors the McCarthy people were glad to keep closed.

And they gave him a clean bill of health. And still Albie was locked out of the industry. The one thing McCarthy couldn't give an informer was a modicum of talent, enough to get him to work.

Film assignments were hard for Albie to get before he ever met up with the ax-wielding Senator. Once it got around that he was singing in private his scripting goose was cooked. There were a lot of liberoids left in the film industry. They didn't dare to gang up on McCarthy's well-known and much-headlined informers. It delighted them to make a Hollywood non-person of Albie after his vocalizing, and it was easy— he'd been close to non-existent all along.

What I've never understood is that one of the names Albie chose to give to McCarthy's legmen was mine. Apparently he let them know that I was one of the most dangerous writers in or around the Hollywood scene. That didn't make sense from any angle, since I'd had just about no connection with Hollywood aside from letting this or that literary property be optioned by this or that Hollywood producer. Besides, this interpretation of my role as one of the most insidious far-left dangers to the United States government hardly gibed with Albie's earlier insistence that I'd been Hitler's foremost agent this side of the Atlantic.

A couple of McCarthy investigators rang my bell in the Village one day. They wanted to question me about my political connections and my undercover doings in Hollywood, they said. I told them to go away, and they did. I was never subpoena'd to testify before any hearing, maybe because I told the men who came to see me that I would out of principle refuse to answer any questions before any forum they might name since I didn't consider them to be a legally constituted body. They couldn't have gotten any information out of me if I'd been willing to sing as operatically as Albie. I didn't know anything they could conceivably be interested in. All I was involved in was the English language, which they couldn't speak, much less investigate.

That was the best and only barricade Albie could find to summon me to. One readymade for him by Joseph McCarthy. Which shows, doesn't it, that the taste for barricades may come from sources deeper than politics, and at times outdistance any politics you claim you live by.

Albie, I was told, eventually drifted back to the Lower East Side and took over his father's lively realty business. He was one Jew from that dramatic neighborhood who finally made his peace with a whole gang of money carved out of the hides of other Jews chronically without the stuff. If there were any barricades in Albie's life after that they must have been ones the cops put up around his offices to protect him from angry demonstrations of the moneyless Jews obliged to live in the ratholes he rented to them for exorbitant prices.

We begin to see the weakness in the conversion that comes in the last paragraph of Mike Gold's quasi-novel. Gold took the signing of the Party card to be the end of the story, where in many, many cases it's just the beginning.

Never mind where Gold himself went after he signed his card. (Though he was always well provided for by the CP bureaucracy, a form of security that in the lush years of the Party was as good as money.) Consider where Albie, and such as Barneybill Roster too, managed to get to after they joined up with the vanguard party. To money. To Americana and Porn. To Joe McCarthy. Their joining began a lot more processes than it ended. They experienced all sorts of conversions after the big conversion, landed on battlefields unimagined.

Ah, barricades. Ah, humility.

CHAPTER 12

KISSERS, TELLERS

Another occupational hazard of the porn worker: he can, after pro-tracted exposure to the typewriter, become de-sexed. The more you ver-balize about libidinal matters it would seem, the more you find Libido becoming *purely* verbal.

There's the old putdown about the adventurers of the mouth to the effect that they talk a good game. If the game under discussion is sex and if the main body of your talk is done on paper, it may turn out after a time that paper is just about your only playing field, you've become a paper tiger.

Here is new and startling evidence to confound the WWII Sandburg-MacLeish notion that words are bullets, grenades, missiles, with real piercing and detonating power. I suppose that theory orig-inated with writers who wanted to go marching off to war with the gunbearers, and saw to their dismay that they had no guns and had to convince themselves that their words, which they had in abundance, could accomplish as much in the world as guns, and who with a premise like that about the military value of their gibblegabble could justify their joining up with the Office of War information and other propaganda agencies that specialized in putting words into uniform and insisted that this had more effect on the world than to turn certain orders of writers into stenographers.

The martial-minded writers of WWII, the literary warriors, liked to think words can take ballistic wing. But longtime laborers in the musted vineyard of porn know from experience that highly potent forces can get *reduced* to words, and stay reduced for notable periods.

It's a mysterious process: head departing from body—in the exact measure that it memorializes bodies for departing from heads; and taking the organism's vital energies with it—while applauding bodies that drain the life force away from heads and back to the lower centers, where it presumably belongs. It will probably never be fully explained, this head-strong tendency in heads that make their living by eulogizing body-strong tendencies in bodies.

All the same, I have a few ideas as to how it happens, ideas formed while on the porn firing line. I'll set them forth here not as dogmas but as possible guidelines for future students of the phenomenon.

We start talking somewhere along in Year Two. But we start wanting in Minute One of Day One.

That is to say, yen antedates yap by a goodly number of months, though it doesn't fall away when verbalization appears, it merely finds a voice. It's the prime psychogenetic fact that the first, and maybe the most rampant, gimme's are experienced pre-verbally, therefore non-verbally.

I suppose this can be put less technically. Let's agree that want is first felt without being put into words, without being labeled with words and formulated in words, because it first comes up at a time when we have not yet become word-makers. If the first wants are associated with any mouth sounds at all, it's with a strident, unshaped, unpatterned howl, which tends with gratification to taper off into a gurgle, sometimes a terminal coo.

The initial fund of wants is often designated as the Id. The fund of body-serving pleasure drives, sensual demands, some call the Libido.

All right. All I'm saying is that Id is there before we have words to blab it out with. Libido is pumping away long before we have the oral tools to take the floor about it. We insist on being pleasured years before we can spell or even say—or even think—"pleasure."

With no more theoretical base than this, we can see how inherently ridiculous is the literature called Pornography. Because Pornography is a verbosity about the pre-verbal, an eloquence about what can properly be only monosyllabic, oratory about matters for which there are no formalized sounds.

So long as Id and Libido antedate spelling and grammar, any patterning of mouthed sounds, a literature of Eros must at the moment of inception turn into a parody of itself.

Those of the Sandburg-MacLeish inclination, those who believe in the endless trajectorizing majesty and impactive power of words, may argue that Eros is an *adult* form of the gimme's yen in its last and highest phase, and can therefore be given utterance in the words available to adults.

Sure, the specific form of Libidinizing Id called Genital Eros does not rear its slobbering, satyrish head all the way until the individual is well along, at least far enough to sense that Mummy and Daddy are having fun together and to express his righteous indignation over the monopolistic, exclusivist nature of that fun in all sorts of barbed words, a true malicious chatter, whose chief aim is to keep Mummy and Daddy too busy to go funning.

But Eros is not all of a piece, chronologically speaking. It may first appear wearing knee pants, and later slip on full-length Ivy League trousers, some in banker's gray, some even in the midnight black of evening wear. But it never quite kicks off the diapers. Strip away the diplomat's stripes and the full-dress sombers—there, underneath, are the indomitable swaddling napkins, fastened tight with the safety pins of nursery imperiousness.

I am trying to say no more than that the erotic desiring of adults comes with a built-in underside of brattish, all-out gimme. At the heart of the suavest, gentlest, most civilized "please" of grown-up Eros is the howling "gimme it all right now and forever" of the crib.

So the slobbered appetites of the cradle hang on undented and undaunted in the sophisticated eroticisms that infantile Libido ultimately gets channeled into. Those first self-service grabbings and monopolizings of all that feels good were pre-verbal. There are no words for them because there were no words for them. Though smoothed over and elaborately camouflaged, they remain at the core of the adult's erotic grabbing and monopolizing of the sexual objects that feel good.

So there are no words for what lies at the core of adulthood's Eros. Because there were no words for the gimme's that flowered into this Eros and feed it forevermore.

Though lovers can wax most eloquent. They run at the mouth something terrible. There could have been no entertainment called the "love story," from *Tristan* through James Gould Cozzens to Eric Segal, otherwise. Not entirely in jest have lovers' rhetorical flights been called "sweet nothings."

It follows that Pornography is much ado about nothing much. Because those aspects of sex that can be put into words are the ones least germane to it and the ones least worth talking about.

Lionel Trilling once told me that he'd never read a description of orgasm in a novel that didn't seem entirely a literary exercise rather than an adequate transcription of a truly and fully felt experience. After having made my living for almost a year from writing such descriptions, I have to say, hear, hear.

The thing always seems composed, never a time oceanicism truly passed on. Of course: that's not what words are for. That's not what the oceanic's for, either. You reach for the oceanic to get the hell away from words for a while, dodge the chatter.

This is one emotion you'd better forget about recollecting in tranquillity. In tranquillity it becomes schizoid-cold verbiage.

We can sense the problem here. Words came into existence to deal with trouble, not with ease, well-being, the sense of rightness. It follows almost by definition that words can capture what's *wrong* with sex, what *interferes* with it and *distorts* it and *frustrates* it and pumps *tension* into it; but never sex that goes smoothly and with its own marvelously silent efficiencies.

If people had never had problems they most likely would never have bothered to learn to speak and proliferate vocabularies. Those who want to write and read about sex must know it only as Problem, and dream of grasping the infernal Problem through words, those problem-graspers.

Sex is—apart from sleep and trout fishing—our enduring sanctuary from words and the cerebration that generates them, from the wordy world of problem-facing. Sex is a draining of vital energies *away* from the cortex, that hive of words, to the thalamus and other non-conceptual, non-verbal centers. At sex's highest point you are all but unconscious. Blessedly.

The hardest thing of all is to itemize the ineffable. Down through written history, down through the history of writing, even the literary giants have not been equal to the self-contradictory task of cross-indexing transcendentals. But I will venture this, if Casanova had had less urge to hold forth at length about his sexual adventurings he very likely would have had more to say about sex.

Words are problem-tongs, tension-tools, not transmission belts for the all too fleeting experiences of total inner harmony and oceanic lapping through barriers beyond the skin. It's a distortion of the very nature of verbalism, a semantic non-sequitur, to try to *say* the authentically Eros-ive.

The moment you grant the silent, not only *non*-verbal but intrinsically *anti*-verbal, nature of sex, you see the impossibly false premise on which Literary Pornography rests. Because Pornography is an attempt through the vocabulary for the sick, which is expressible and cries out for expressing, to convey the healthy, which defies voicing.

When we finally develop a true science and art of communication, one of its first miles will be: where sexuality is concerned, the more sensed, and the less said, the better. The genitals are almost as far away from the larynx as they can be, and should stay that way.

This is all by way of explaining, perhaps too conceptually, that, the more I threw myself into the world of New-Sexology, the more remote I felt from All That. I knew—and the recent flood of pop-sexo manuals has proved again—that you can hold forth interminably about what's *wrong* in sex, but there's precious little you can say about what's *right*. But it was my assignment to compose volume upon volume about the sexo wrongs, for which there is indeed a language, in the guise of the gloriously *right*, for which you can't find one communicative syllable.

In the end, the sick and the healthy were hopelessly mixed up in my mind. And the more sex got tinged with the pathological, the less I felt drawn to it in my non-writing hours. A paxadox. If I continued as Barneybill's fair-haired proser, the top-seeded chronicler of the post-Lady, I stood in grave danger of winding up a monk.

The biggest lesson I learned from my porn period was that St. Simeon Stylites' flagpole had no phallic significations. No more do the pillars of rhetoric on which rest, however shakily, the ivory towers of writers. The stilts of Literature, if employed and accommodated to more than ironically, will in the end lift you up from the flesh entirely; even if the message in all you write is the primacy and supremacy of flesh. There's something in word-making, doubly so when it's in the area of sexo exploration, which is ineradicably Manichean.

Distrust the Casanovas, the De Sades, the Frank Harrises. They wrote too much to have done much; well, anyhow. Kissers generally don't tell, especially in print—why bother?

Consider this Reuters dispatch, from Belo Horizonte, Brazil, under the headline, CASANOVA AN ALSO-RAN, OLD DOCUMENT HINTS:

An ancient document has been found in state archives detailing a list of crimes committed by a Portuguese priest that suggests he even outdid the famous Italian lover Casanova.

The document, signed by King Joao II of Portugal in 1481, annulled a death sentence passed against Father Fernando da Costa, 62.

The priest had been convicted of fathering 299 children by 59 women, including his own mother, five of his sisters, 29 adopted daughters and three slave women.

Note that Father da Costa, as nearly as can be determined, never wrote a line, about his exploits or anything else—unlike Casanova, he never had the time. Presumably he was even too busy to offer his services to whatever Offices of War Information were around. We can on the basis of the evidence assume that he didn't pass many of his hours in the verbal medium at all, aside from an occasional hasty sermon.

Barneybill Roster was a lover of hot words, sure. Because he could trail his heats only on paper. Where temperatures can never get even luke-warm. Because the pathological is nothing but chilling. Except to ice-cold psychopaths. Who take fire at the drop of a four-letter word.

Gimme, gimme, gimme, cried his iguana eyes, fixed forever in Day One. Nobody would give. Besides, he couldn't take. There was this deficiency on the receiving end, too. One-day-olds have such short reaches and are such butterfingers. The most they can grab hold of and hold on to is one more hot pastrami sandwich.

Such, often, are the roots of the literary interest, on both the production and consumption ends.

CHAPTER 13

SOMEWHAT RAW MATERIALS

I was riding too high, too high. We know from the Greeks—before, up to, and including Onassis and Agnew—how dangerous that is: he whom the gods would destroy they first make solvent.

Disaster had to strike. It did, through the good offices of a Czech we can, and will, call Jaroslav Hatchek, or Yar.

Yar was 10 years my senior. From his bearing you got the impression that he was 10 years everybody's senior. He'd been the senior secretary-bodyguard in the Trotsky household when I was its most junior member. From his chronically supervisorial approach to matters big and small, his managerial slant on the cosmos, you gathered that the human race could not organize for any project unless he was there to preside and edit the minutes, or any body, personal or political, be safe unless he was watching over it.

In a surprising number of cases, I am obliged to say even at this late date, this may very well have been true. I've seen any number of affairs not under his thumb go down the drain these last decades.

Yar, to give him his due, was a handler and overseer without parallel. He approached every endeavor, every situation, from the angle of how it could be controlled, if not manipulated. He was the most brilliant behind-the-scenes organizer I have ever known. I have not the slightest doubt that if Trotsky had placed his household entirely in Yar's hands, allowed the tough security measures Yar fought for, he would not have been killed, certainly not by slipshod, hysterical borers from within.

Yar belonged to the peculiar breed of professional conspirators who get spawned with depressing frequency in Mittel Europa, particularly in and around the Balkans. In his teens and early twenties, he conspired into being the Stalinist youth militias which fought blusteringly on the streets of Prague. Note that Yar himself did no street fighting, he hardly ever went outdoors. His peculiar genius was to map strong-arm tactics for muscle squads while himself shunning all manual exercise.

When he became disenchanted with Stalinism the Trotskyites, who knew his conspiratorial talents, dispatched him to Trotsky, then beginning his exile in Ankara. Yar remained in charge of Trotsky's security as he moved to France, to Norway, and finally to Coyoacán. He was handling all the ménage's practical affairs when I arrived and was pretty much my boss.

There was something deceptive about this small, ramrod-straight, crinkly-haired, blade-nosed, blue-steel-eyed, fast-talking, dandyish man. From his teens on he had been associated with highly conspiratorial movements; and, as a leadership personality among the cadres of the Revolution, he was expected to make himself a master of offstage scheming. Nevertheless, people supposed that his conspiratorial side was transitory—related to this occupation, not rooted in his nature. A surprising thing came to light when Yar's political ardors abated and he decided to work for his own improvement rather than the proletariat's. His taste for conspiracy in no way diminished.

It became stunningly clear that the man had not been molded by the politics, no, indeed. The man had *sought out* the politics which would with the most flash validate his conspiratorial leanings, which had existed in him long before he ever heard of politics. Now that the conspiratorial politics was gone, the conspirator remained, in all his attic, shades-drawn glory.

What changed was not Yar's life style but the area in which he put that hyper-efficient style to work.

First, Yar conspired himself into a marriage. An intelligent and attractive New York girl, vaguely associated with the intellectual fringe of the Trotskyite group, came to Mexico for a vacation. By this time Yar had privately decided to leave Trotsky and seek his non-political fortune in the States, but he did not lay out his plans that nakedly. Rather, he gave the girl the impression that political exigencies dictated his move, and with his headquarters authority convinced her that she had to help him to help the cause.

There was a simple way she could help him. She could marry him. With an American-born wife, particularly one from an old, well-established family, Yar's entry into the States would be facilitated and his naturalization papers would come through much, much faster.

The girl agreed. She wanted to help any way she could.

Also, though it was a bonus she would not allow herself the petty-bourgeois luxury of dwelling on, she liked Yar.

They were married. They proceeded across the border to Milk-Honey Land. For some months Mrs. Yar was pleased to supply all the milk and honey needed to support Mr. Yar. Then it occurred to her that, sitting home all day as he was, reading *Esquire*, he couldn't be hatching many revolutions.

That being the case, she said tactfully, wouldn't it be possible for her hubby to take on some not too exacting gainful employment which would make it possible for him to pay some of the household expenses?

Out of the question, Yar explained. He wasn't just sitting, though it might to the untrained eye look that way. His mind was going a mile a minute all the time his body was in repose. He was occupied round the clock, conspiring which fields he might next conspire in. It was a full-time job. He could not be lured from his true calling by attachment to this or that irrelevant payroll.

Mrs. Yar ultimately left Mr. Yar for companions with less vocation and more earning power. It was a stunning blow for Yar. In his scheme, and I do mean scheme, of things, his marriage had been part of an ongoing program for slipping smoothly through the world, no more. Once his wife was gone, he discovered that he missed her, and the realization almost undid him, suggesting as it did that he'd entered into wedlock as much out of sentiment as scheme, a thoroughly unprofessional and middle-class motivation.

He tried to explain away his wife's renegacy on the grounds of ideological deficiencies, of the sort all too often found in white-collar workers. It was hard to do, since he had lapsed away from his own class commitments. He still missed her, and not only because he could no longer use her. He had planned for her to be only an instrument in his life and she'd become a presence, a fact brought dramatically home to him by her absence.

For a time he was more than bothered. Here was evidence that he had a heart, the professional conspirator's Achilles' heel.

But Yar was not too unnerved to stop his conspiring. He conspired some wealthy Czech-refugee Trotsky sympathizers into financing him in a course in commercial Portuguese and Portuguese shorthand. He conspired some Trotskyite college students into researching economic journals which reported on the current commercial situation in Brazil and tendering him digests. He conspired the New York Board of Trade into inviting him to address their august body on the trends in Brazilian commerce. He conspired himself, in short, into the New York business community as an authority on Brazilian trade particularly as it related to American exports. As a result, he soon conspired himself into a plush job with a leading American plastics firm as vice-president in charge of Latin-American exports.

Soon after, he was traveling through Latin America for this firm, on a lavish expense account. It was a triumph for the conspiratorial way of life.

In two short years, Mr. Yar had conspired himself from a no-income position as Trotsky's ranking secretary-bodyguard to an upper-echelon post in the cutthroat world of American business and finance, at a salary of $40,000 a year, with many expense-account pluses. This may be a tribute to the fluidity of America's class lines, or it may only signalize one man's unique agility at the high jump.

After a very few months on the summit of American capitalist enterprise, Yar quit his job. For the simplest of reasons: he was bored. Why bored? Because he relished his conspiratorial virtuosity, not its fruits. Having maneuvered, plotted, schemed, juggled, toe-danced, high-wired, smooth-talked, wheeled and dealed his way onto the very peak of the pyramid of the managerial élite he found that life had lost its zest.

Yar was fully alive only when spinning intrigues in a peripheral attic, with the shades drawn. When the intrigues worked out so spectacularly well as to catapult him to fame and fortune, he was miserable.

Soon after his fling in and flight from the plastics vice-presidency, Yar Hatchek came to see me. He listened with interest to the story of my own more modest business activities in the less orthodox manufactories of Barneybill Roster.

It was easy to see that the whole smell of the backstairs industry I'd gotten involved with excited him. Our commodities were in every way more rousing, more challenging, more imagination-firing, than the plastic soap trays and doggie dishes he'd lately been wholesaling to the Brazilians.

His eyes, as our talk proceeded, regained their old sparkle.

Like a researcher for Fortune or the *Wall Street Journal*, like a field analyst from the Harvard School of Business Administration, he plied me with questions about Barneybill's entrepreneurial M.O.: plant over-head, personnel policies, labor relations, size of payroll, bonus incentive schemes, liaison arrangements with subcontractors, cost-plus formulas in wholesale pricing, warehousing facilities, distributive channels. I had very few answers for him, none, in fact.

The interrogation over, Yar sat for a long time, pursing his lips and nodding his head.

"I like it," he said finally. "Has structure. I approve, yes. Man knows what he's doing. There's planning. He sees that in the period ahead the challenge to industry is to diversify. Therefore Americana in the home plant and this porn, call it Europeana, from the subcon-tractors, for national distribution. Up and down the Tulsa nation. Good sense there. Get into different fields, open up new markets. All the better when the diversified products have something in com-mon, relate. Obviously you don't want to merchandize steam engines and slingshots, no tie-in. He's not fooling with steam engines and slingshots, no. Integration within diversification, that's his pattern, yes. Anybody can see Americana and Europeana have something in common. Maybe appeal to somewhat different markets but they're parts of a larger whole. Cultural bonds between them, as between America and Europe. Possible in time to unify the markets too. You couldn't sell steam engines to slingshot buyers, no. But with smart marketing you might eventually sell a lot of Europeana to buyers of Americana, yes. Though maybe not the other way around. In any case, a solid operation. The man has vision. Hasn't over-capitalized either, stays flexible."

Yar had a tendency to talk in telegrams, especially when working up to some connivance. He kept you occupied in one corner with a spatter of phrases, verbal feints, so his quick mind, undisturbed, disengaged, could map terrains and plan campaigns. Just then his style was getting very Western Union. It worried me.

"You want to get the dealership for Brazil, or Latin America as a whole?" I said uneasily. "I'm afraid I can't help you there. As I told you, this fellow doesn't admit he has dealers. He doesn't admit to any kind of distribution. He denies he's even in business."

"You mistake my meaning," Yar said. "I'm looking for a connection, yes. I'd like to get into this venture, yes. But not on the marketing end, no. I know he won't take a stranger in at that end so long as he keeps up the story of one subsidizing customer in Oklahoma, no. I'm thinking of getting in on the production end, yes."

I was startled. Yar had not before shown any writing proclivities. He'd never shown any *working* proclivities. He'd had experience in the production of nothing but street riots in Prague and free courses in Portuguese shorthand.

"You want to write books for Roster?"

"I want to write *halves* of books for this Roster," he said. "Let me lay this out for you. I've got a plan that could be profitable for both of us. I'm proposing that we collaborate on some books. Don't flinch, please. I know at first hearing this sounds farfetched because you're a writer and I'm not. But look at all the facts. You're a writer, I'm sure a very good one, I always had high regard for your literacy. But at the moment you're a writer who's running out of things to write about. You have to write about sex dramas and you've used up all the sex dramas you know first-hand or second. You're at the point of total depletion of raw materials. There's where I can be of help, yes. I'm older than you, yes. I've knocked around more, yes. I've had many women of many varieties, yes. I have a rich supply of sex dramas in my head, fresh ones, never been processed for commercial purposes. I propose that I put down some of the most dramatic of these sex dramas in, say, 150 pages. You're a fast and facile writer. You dress up these pages and add the connective tissues and we'll have 300 pages easily. This would be a fair division of labor, I hope you can see that. I provide the sex, you provide the words. There would be an equity to justify a 50-50 split. Remember, also that if I give you all the juicy stuff you won't have to bother your head with inventing any, so your writing can go much faster, because the connective stuff must be easier to write than the juicy stuff, so with a 50-50 split you'll actually come out ahead, you'll be getting full pay for writing 150 pages in much less time than 150 pages ordinarily take you on a project you have to create from start to finish, including all juicy materials. What do you say, yes? Shall we do one book together so you can see how much you stand to gain from a collaboration that taps for you a rich new supply of raw materials? I assure you that the materials I have stockpiled are of grade-A quality, and not easily duplicated, especially on this more naïve side of the Atlantic. Shall we give it a try, yes?"

He was putting me on a spot and he knew it. He'd done things for me in Mexico. For example, his alert eye was the first to notice that I was turning pale and losing weight after my first months in Coyoacán, and his alert mind told him this was because I couldn't swallow another mouthful of the foul and flabby kasha cereal which because it was the staple in Trotsky's diet because of his nervous stomach, was heaped on our plates three times a day.

Yar promptly took over an unused storage closet off the backyard, put a lock on the door, and installed in that cubicle a secret commissary for the two of us, a cache of spiced hams, potato chips, bolognas, bonbons, and other goodies designed to assuage the bohemian palate, one held to be counter-revolutionary in our circles, as were all non-organizational appetites, but which sometimes cropped up there anyhow. It made no difference that Yar, who had developed gourmet tastebuds after years of conspiring himself through the best restaurants of Central and Western Europe, ate as much of this glorious provender as I did. He was the one who conceived the idea, bludgeoned sympathizers into putting up the moneys, and with his organizational genius established this beautiful larder that became an underground to our already subsurface household.

I was indebted to Yar on several scores, including the gastronomic. He knew what I owed him, and he was asking for this collaboration as payment. He now meant to conspire himself into my bonanza. He was going to get himself a dipperful of my gravy.

I agreed, with reluctance, yes, and more than one anticipatory shudder, yes, yes.

Three weeks later Yar handed me his 150 pages. The moment I read them I knew I'd been had, and wished I hadn't.

The story opened promisingly, with a man in bed. From the Roster point of view, though, it was a somewhat limited situation: there was nobody in bed with him. But there was a potential here: a girl was close by, as unclad as the man was. However, the girl was in the next room, which was the bathroom. More discouraging still, she was doing nothing more stimulating than relieving herself. Worse yet, the man was doing nothing more provocative than studying her through the open bathroom door. Still, you could hope that things would pick up.

On page 1, the man was flat on his back, studying this girl. On page 150, the man was flat on his back, studying the girl. In the course of the 150 pages of narration the man had not stirred from his spot, nor the girl from hers. The man had not mobilized himself to the extent of reaching for a cigarette or scratching his ear. The girl, perhaps because of some obscure genito-urinary disorder, had remained similarly statuesque. There had been absolutely no commerce between them beyond the occasional exchange of insubstantial glances.

True, the man had been, from page 1 through page 150, observing the girl's anatomy in scrupulous detail and engaging in rich fantasies, á la Molly Bloom, about each item in her structure. But, considering the girl's proximity and presumed availability, these flights of fancy had a chilling rather than suggestive quality. You wondered why, if he was so fixated on the lady's parts, he didn't get the hell off his ass and go for them. You wondered if possibly he was a paraplegic. You wondered if she should be treated for catatonia.

The situation, in dramaturgical terms, lacked conflict, dynamic, confrontation, involvement. It was definitely deficient in pace and plot advancement. It suffered from what a Eugene O'Neill or a Barneybill Roster, though with very different frames of reference, would both call an insufficiency of movement. To be sure, Barneybill was after a Sexo Literature that boldly opened doors. Yar Hatchek had undeniably opened a door, the one to the bathroom. But he had quite forgotten to direct any traffic through in either direction.

Yar's offering was a stroke, not of inspiration, but of doom—for me. I was done in, done to a turn, undone.

The price I was about to pay, belatedly, for those marvelous furtive Coyoacán feasts of prosciutto and chocolate-covered cherries was to be thrown out of the one industry in which I'd gained a footing, black-balled for life. Barneybill had to rise up in all his lopsided wrath at this look-but-don't-touch version of the New Sex. The jig, my jig, was up.

You may ask why I didn't just tear up these static pages and write another book from scratch. Well, under less pressure-cooker circum-stances I would have. But there was no time. When I agreed to this collaboration I informed Barneybill that another work would be forth-coming and promised delivery in a month's time. He was a-drool to get my new offering, wouldn't hear of a more remote deadline. Three weeks of our period of grace had elapsed. Yar was over a week late in giving me his pages, which left me exactly one week to get the whole book ready. In that limited time I couldn't possibly work up 300 pages on my own—it would be a murderous job simply to prepare the 150 connective-tissue pages.

I was stuck. I was boxed in. I had to dress up this miscarriage as best I could, and be prepared to run for the hills. But around Manhattan, I should point out, the terrain is very flat.

Exactly one week later, on deadline day, I brought the finished manuscript to Barneybill. With my awesome talent for working to fine tolerances on my Remington portable grinder, I'd managed to eke out exactly 300 pages. Barneybill was jumping with enthusiasm over the birth of another masterwork. Luckily he didn't browse through the pages in my presence, as he sometimes did—I'd so whetted his appetite that he wanted to get rid of me and settle down to savor in privacy this newest and best hot pastrami sandwich of all.

He pressed $300 into my hand. It was the right sum: because Yar badly needed cash I'd gotten a $300 advance weeks before and turned it over to my lethargic collaborator who opened doors so blithely but couldn't summon the energy to pass through them.

"It's a joyous day for me," Barneybill bubbled. "I've told my secretary I'm accepting no calls, I'm going to hole up and read, read, read, I know you've surpassed yourself this time, you're always surpassing yourself. Go out and have some fun, see a French movie, row a boat in Central Park, get a rubdown, buy a hat, you've earned it. Now beat it, wonder boy!"

Wonder boy wondered less and less boyishly through that sleepless night about just when and how the ax would fall. I was not long to be kept in suspense.

Bright and early next morning, the phone rang. Barneybill. Sounding like a man choking on a fishbone with rich ciliation.

"Can you get up to my office right away?" he said without ado or how-do. "I've got to have a long talk with you."

"I don't think I can make it," I said.

"I think you can," he said. "I think you will. I'm not asking you, I'm telling you."

I began to talk very rapidly, listing all the pressing business on my agenda that day. I explained that my grandmother was in Winston-Salem with hepatitis and sinking fast and that I would have to catch the next plane out if I was to get there in time. I said something about being due for an electroencephalographic checkup myself. I think I added a word about having received an urgent summons from my draft board.

"Don't bother me with details," he said. "Arrange your day any way you want, so long as you're here in exactly one half hour. If you're not in my office precisely at the stroke of 9:30 our business association is at an end, you swindler, you footpad."

He didn't have to spell out what would happen if I failed to show up. It would have been laboring the obvious to warn me that I'd be black-balled from the industry—he *was* the industry, all balls of all colors were in one sweaty hand, his.

"I guess I *can* juggle my schedule a bit," I said. "I'll be right there."

All the way uptown in the cab I studied the handwriting on the wall. It was stark, it was unequivocal, it was terminative in both substance and form. In bold black letters it conveyed such messages as, NOTICE OF SEVERANCE, DISCHARGED FOR CAUSE, KEEP THIS MAN OFF COMPANY PROPERTY, CLOSED FOR THE DURATION, APPLICATIONS FOR WELFARE ACCEPTED HERE, BREADLINE FORMS TO THE RIGHT, etc., etc.

That finagler from Prague, that doggie-dish promote boy, that one-man cabal, that single-o junta. He'd sure fixed my wagon with square axles and cooked my goose to a sad mess of charcoal. Yes.

CHAPTER 14

ANIMAL SOUNDS

"What's the matter with you anyway! Gone off your rocker entirely! This swill doesn't sound like you! Fellow who can Stigglee up a junior-high prom in an upper-middle suburb, build orgies around a Tinker-Toy, talent like you turning in water-closet cameos painted in swamp colors and calling it an effort! Passionate looks through the bathroom door! Takes a truly dirty mind I'm telling you! Erotica of the toilet bowl! Ugh! C'mon!"

He was shaking as though a thousand runaway Buicks were bearing down on him and some practical joker had folded up the sidewalks. Every feature of his botchily assembled affront of a face was in independent motion, creating an effect of physiognomic hurricane. He was in the mood to murder but the maximum violence he could allow himself was to punch himself repeatedly on both inflamed cheeks, as though all the Francos had made their headquarters high up in his sinuses.

I couldn't stand the zoo sounds he was creaking out in between and all around his words. I was faced with an identity crisis—his. The man creaked out animal sounds between and around his words, the heeings of the horse, yowlings of the pup, but his eyes remained the eyes of the iguana.

"Usually you congratulate me on my changes of pace," I pointed out.

"When you *change* pace! Not when you *lose* pace altogether, boy! For Christ's sake! Not when you come to a total and permanent halt and give me a whole book's worth of stop-action and call your stall Literature! Where's the unfolding, where's the upshot, tell me that! Who told you to cook up a hot affair between paralytics! These cripples couldn't take liberties! This broad can't even take a leak! You don't hold my interest, dear sir, with a broad who stays riveted to the toilet seat for 300 pages, we might as well get that clear right now! Couple of jerks eyeing each other up and down through the john door and this by your standards is a stimulating work! Thirty chapters of tepid looks and you have a sense of accomplishment! Sex is for you a running battle of the eyes! Can't think of any other organs to enter the fray! For people looking each other over from head to foot and making slow-motion inventories I don't pay two good dollars a page! If nothing's happening make it not happen in one succinct page, don't mess up another 299 with ditto marks! A five-foot-shelf of staring contests and the world's supposed to get hot pants! Since when are looksees orgasmic! Some bedroom athletes that bear nothing but witness! People who mate through scrutinies don't need Freud, they need a good oculist!"

In a blaze of revelation I saw everything. This man, his clients, the inner logic of Pornography, the essence of all Literature, High and Low. A moment of, yes, epiphany, which I can set forth in a series of propositions:

(1) What is Fiction? I don't mean to knock my own profession but facts are facts. Fiction is Peeping. The writer peeps at a bunch of care-fully selected people then invites others to join him. His work provides a window, if not a proscenium arch, through which readers can ogle the cast which the writer has screened, placed in position, and set in motion for just such ogling purposes. Literature is a form of Spying and Eavesdropping which violates none of the constitutional rights (those that are left) protecting privacy and the sanctity of the home.

(2) But nobody likes to own up to being a Peeper. So the consumers of printed-page voyeurism need a face-saving formula for their Peeping.

They have one, artfully worked up for them by critics and other literateurs. To wit: "Who's peeping? Sneaking furtive looks into the private lives of others is furthest from our minds. What we're doing is indulging our curiosity about human beings in all their wondrous guises—a humanistic immersion."

(3) That's a white wash, and the fictive element that gives Fiction its name—remember, our synonym for lie is fiction.

You get your first training as a Peeper the moment the grownups' bedroom door is slammed in your face. (If not, to get more elemental still, the sad day Ma's amples, that snuggly no-charge yummiest soda fountain of all, shut their doors in your startled face for good.) Your body is confined to the hallway but your eyes bore holes in that killjoy door and pass right through. The first peeping impulses are directed in wrecking activities against that crucial door. (If not, indeed, against the killjoy textiles that willed you from Ma's fabulous founts.) Later they get sugarcoated as "curiosity about all the wonderful doings of all the wonderful people in all the wonderful areas of this endlessly engrossing human existence."

It's this sugarcoating that made Storytelling, and then Literature, possible. Peeping may get disguised as Insatiable Intellectual Curiosity about Everything, but that barricading bedroom door's never entirely out of sight.

(4) In that Infra-Lit called Pornography, as in the parent body of Above-Board Lit, the first lure is the chance to peep. But there are significant differences.

Pornography provides the peeper, not a window or proscenium arch, but a keyhole. It directs the peeping impulses away from Humanistic Considerations back to that accursed bedroom door where the eyes first got mobilized. The panting, slobbering quality of the peeping is naked and much more narrowly focused, as it was in the beginning. All the new-brain rationalizations are stripped away.

(5) The Pornography Peeper has no facesaving formula about "curiosity regarding people in all their wondrous forms and activities." The Pornography Peeper acknowledges a salivating curiosity about people in one form, naked, in one place, the bedroom, in one activity, the coupling of bodies which the child's hungry eyes were not allowed to see.

Pornography cracks off the sugarcoating, brings the sophisticated and subdued and rechanneled "wonder about the endless variety of life" back to the primordial "gawking at what naked bodies do together."

(6) But a lot of Pornography Peepers feel uncomfortable. Their hobby smacks too much of the infantile. Why bother? Since those once taboo doors have swung wide open for you in adulthood, why paste your eye to the old Keyhole—unless you've reverted to kid games?

A disturbing question, never far from the mind of the Porn Peeper. So the true nature of his hallway gawking must be fancied up. Pornography can never be fully and convincingly decked out as Serious Literature but it can be given some of the guilt-easing whitewash of Literature. Hence the strictures that *Serious* New-Sexualist Writing must "take up where Lawrence left off" and "fulfill the revolutionary promise in Freud."

Some Porn Peepers will indeed lap up undisguised Filth and Trash and exult in the stuff, in a kind of polymorph-perverse "slave revolt" against all taboos. But many need the window-dressing of Seriousness, the slogan of "a salutary frankness that will help to usher in the new and long-overdue Sexualist Enlightenment."

(7) Therefore, the Pornographer with a true calling, a genuine appreciation for his craft, knows that he must at all costs avoid one subject in his work—unhumanistic, pansexual Peeping in its original, undiluted Keyhole form. Reduce the sex dramas in your pages to nothing but Peeping and all the high-flown pretensions about carrying on the good Freud-Lawrence work fall away. Then you're not letting your

uneasy Peeper-Readers off the hook, you're heaving their quintessential Peeping back at them, smack into their flushed faces, like a custard pie.

Instead of allowing them to Peep without calling it that, you're rubbing their faces in the muck of their own Peeping-Tomfoolery. You give them no outs. You pillory and parody them by presenting Eros under the rubric of the ocular. When you feed undisguised voyeurism to voyeurs—the game's up. A deadly dull game. A deadly game, maybe. If it is a game.

(8) Barneybill Roster was a Peeper Deluxe, urgently and sweatily needing to hide his Low Porn under the fancy robes of High Lit.

In cooking up a sex drama in which people did absolutely nothing but ogle each other, Yar Hatchek had stripped away all of Barneybill's facesavers and sent his ugly over-heated head slamming against the one door of all doors he couldn't bear to acknowledge, the door to Mummy's and Daddy's bedroom, wherein the sound effects are not of Lofty Literature but only the groaning springs of a bed forever beyond the reach of the impotent snotnose prowling the hallway.

(9) No wonder Barneybill accused me of having a dirty, dirty mind. . . .

"Even your style's turned rancid! Drab! Makeshift! You, who showed you could make words dance, writing sentences awkward as a one-armed paperhanger, flat as dishwater! D'you know what dribble this is! Don't you have any idea at all how your phrases that used to sing now sag, how your prose has been deboned! My God! Up until the day before yesterday you could hear the most delicate tinkle in a word, now you've suddenly developed a wooden ear! This isn't writing, boy! This is throwing gobs of unsifted words in the air with a shovel and calling it a new lyricism! Damn you! Damn you seven times around the equator to Hell! I pay good coin of the realm for raptures and you give me some moronic hands-off babble! If a high-school kid turned in such a composition I'd give him an 'F' and shove him quick into a remedial reading and writing class! You don't shortchange *me* with such shoddy merchandise, no, my dear fellow! I demand value for my money! I don't buy rejects and seconds in *my* business! For such bargain-basement words you don't get *my* good dollars! Yah! Yah! Sure!"

He was working himself into a kingsize frenzy. His cheeks were the color of borscht without the toning-down effect of sour cream and his lips were in the sort of all-out agitation that's usually the forerunner of a maximum temper tantrum. If you've ever seen a baby screwing up all its features and straining all its blood to its head preliminary to total conniption, you know the kind of facial storm I'm describing. Clearly I, Porn's fair-haired boy, had metamorphosed into another Franco, and Barneybill was pained.

I knew my latest effort was a bit breathless, helter-skelter, perhaps too hastily Scotch-taped at the joints, but I rather resented Barneybill's recourse to exalted esthetic standards in his textual analysis of the thing. I somehow had the feeling that all those painstaking academics had not gone to all the trouble of devising the New Criticism to provide Barneybill Roster with a way to separate that offal which was acceptable to his turdy mind from that which was not.

"I don't think you get the point," I said. "The whole secret of the stylistic flexibility you used to admire so much in my work is that in each case the rhetoric is cunningly adapted to the people, the setting, the atmosphere, the mood. My aim in everything I write is to let the words find the exact emotional level of the characters."

I was listening to my mellifluous phrases and marveling. Fresh from Bolshevik-Leninist hole-ups, marine engine rooms, and machine shops, I sounded like William Lyon Phelps updated for the *Partisan Review*.

"In this instance we're dealing with two people at a moment of stasis in their lives. You can't work up a dynamic, flashing, darting, surging prose when you're concerned with people who for the moment can't find the energy to rise to their feet or even to a sitting position. They necessarily have to look at each other at some length, and think turgid thoughts, which means that the prose conveying those thoughts has to be somewhat turgid too, unless we abandon all pretense to a hard-hitting realism, which I assumed was the quality you're after in all the books you commission. If you've changed the esthetic by which you operate without informing me you can't hold me to blame, I can't read your mind."

"It never occurred to you that you might get these two bums up off their asses and speed up your realistic thought-conveying prose a little, huh! Your inventive mind never hit on the revolutionary idea of making remote-control lovers with the sleeping sickness sit up straight and get a little unturgid in their thoughts! Maybe even wake up and show some life and spunk for a few pages! Don't give me that malarkey about words having to be retarded when you're dealing with retarded schnooks! The masters could make their words do somersaults no matter if their characters were in a coma or being laid away in coffins! Here! Here! I'll show you! Listen to this! I'll open to any page!"

He was doing his own version of the gandy-dance between the duded-up cobblers' benches. In the course of his spastic ballet he'd come to a bookcase in which he kept a few modern novels, his favorites.

At random, with fluttering hands, he'd pulled down one of the volumes, Thomas Mann's *Buddenbrooks*, and pawed through the pages. He now read several lines from a passage about mercantile practices in 19th-century Lübeck, in a pellmell, quavery voice.

"You see!" he raved on. "See! There's a style all glory, has majesty, resonance!"

He grabbed for another volume, André Gide's *The Counterfeiters*. He riffled the pages until his demented eyes lit on something that interested him. He read some of *that*, the brooding thoughts of an old music teacher whose chief ambition in life seemed to be to do away with his spouse in some extremely violent manner; I thought this, too was rather tangential to the matter under discussion.

"How's that for a word magic?" he ranted. "Pure song on the printed page! Every phrase has a movement all its own! Every syllable hits you in the eye!"

As I would have dearly loved to hit him.

"Do you suppose we could dispense with the reference works?" I said with a great deal of mildness I did not have. "Thomas Mann and André Gide were writing to other specifications. These quotes are fascinating but they don't relate to our special literary problems. What I mean is, this isn't getting us anywhere."

"I'll show you something else!" he babbled on. "Here's the master of masters! Here's Henry Miller himself! Listen to how he builds and soars even in a little thing like *Max and the White Phagocytes*! I happen to know this book backwards and forwards! It just so happens that Mr. Miller presented this book to me himself, and wrote a personal inscription in it! See? You're not talking to some illiterate you can lead around by the nose and con with your fancy writer's talk! I know a few writers myself!"

Saying which, he shoved the open book in my face, so I could see the flyleaf.

I hew this work of Miller's. It was a shattering description, I remembered, of a wretched little tailor whom Miller had known in Paris, a bloodless, whiny, sniveling, cadaverous parody of a man who made a career of trotting along lugubriously in the wake of other people's lives trailing laments. To indicate the dried-out, shadowy nature of the man's existence, Miller had nicknamed him "White Phagocyte."

I studied the inscription Barneybill was holding proudly under my nose. It was indeed in Miller's breezy, rambunctious handwriting. The exuberant words were: TO BARNEYBILL ROSTER, THE WHITE PHAGOCYTE, FROM HENRY MILLER, THE RED BLOOD CORPUSCLE!

"You do know some eminent writers," I said, "and some eminent writers know you."

"Here, I'll give you samples of real writing!" he ground on. "Let me find something, there're gems on almost every page, just a minute, I'll get a good passage—"

"No," I said, "let's not do any more reading." I took the book from his moth-lively hand. "Let's try to get our voices down very low, and let's try to talk very slowly about the problem that seems to have arisen between us, which isn't discussed anywhere in the works of Mann, Gide, or Henry Miller. As I see it, the issue is simply—"

"Don't tell me what to do!" Like a snapping wildcat he pawed at the volume, slashed it out of my hand. "Don't you give me orders, you intolerable and thieving snot!" He'd really lost all vestige of control. "*I'll* tell *you* what we're going to do, and I assure you it'll be done, exactly as I say! What we're going to do is, you're either going to return the $600 you got out of me under false pretenses, by slimy con, or we're going to consider that sum an advance on your *next* work, which you will write for me *immediately*, and not at special rates either, at the standard rate of one dollar a page! *That's* how we're going to handle the problem that's arisen, friend, you deliver another book that's more than a dirty, insipid joke *or* the moneys you hoodwinked me out of! Is that perfectly clear?"

He had the book raised high, he was swinging it back and forth for maniacal punctuation. His face was going through one implosion after another.

Oh, it was an unappetizing face. To unveil such a face anywhere in the presence of humans was an act of sheer malice, the insult direct.

"I'm afraid I can't do that, Mr. Roster," I said. "If I agreed, it would mean that my work for you is on a speculative basis, that payment is subject to your approval. I never write on speculation, it's unprofessional. It's not the money I'm concerned with *primarily*, there's a principle involved that goes beyond monetary considerations. I would be a traitor to my craft if I didn't take the strongest possible stand against speculative work, so—"

"You *won't* give back my money! You *won't* give back my money! You *won't* make restitution, that's your final word, ah!"

"That's the general idea I was trying to get across, Mr. Roster," I said. I felt safe enough in my stand. Where could he go to register a complaint against me, the Better Business Bureau? The National Institute of Arts and Letters? "I'm afraid you'll have to whistle for that money. It'll be a nicer sound effect than the animal cries you're making right now."

And he was. A sort of blubbering sequence of growls, unlikely though the combination sounds, was issuing from his throat, as his off-center Adam's apple bobbed in a direction that deviated noticeably from the plumb line.

"Snot!" he cried. "Bummy bastard!" he yawped. "Dirty little! Rotten filthy! Scum of the! Stinking piece of!"

"What've you got against people looking at each other anyhow?" I said. "For a man who spends his whole life sneaking peeks, trying to crawl into keyholes, who makes a business and a hobby and—"

He stared. His mouth was caverned. His eyes were flurrying. His cheeks were in flames. He was still holding aloft his copy of *Max and the White Phagocytes,* in a Statue of Liberty pose.

The book began to move. Downward. In the direction of my head. At an alarming speed.

I don't to this day know for sure whether he truly meant to conk me with that volume in which Henry Miller had had the geniality to issue to Mr. Barneybill Roster a charter membership in the Fraternity of White Phagocytes. But it certainly looked like it. Besides, I'd gone for months, much too long, not depositing my fist in that foul cheesy chubbiness of a face that was designed for such deposits.

I hit him. Once. Not with such force as to cause lasting damage. But smartly.

It probably did hurt some, because when I made my hand into a fist I forgot to remove from it the micrometer I'd been carrying in my pocket ever since my Bridgeport grinding days, maybe as a reminder that there are worse ways to make a living than Porn. But my full weight wasn't behind it any more than my stomach was.

It was one of the four or five occasions in my life when words became so unequal to the task of making a point, so obscenely irrelevant, new brain so swamped by old-brain urgencies, that communication seemed possible through only one organ, the hand. I hit him, feeling my stomach dismally dwindle.

It would somehow have been as fulfilling as appalling if he'd chosen to continue the conversation on a manual basis. He didn't.

He simply regarded me with a cosmic surprise. Sank slowly to his knees and buried his face in the colonial hooked carpet, to devote himself with full energy to an exercise in the dry heaves.

He sobbed, but no tears came. If he wasn't eating the carpet he was certainly giving his jaws a thorough workout on it, like a puppy chomping on a beloved blanket.

He whimpered, "Say what you want, Thomas Mann is a superb stylist."

That seemed to wind up our discussion with awful finality. There was nothing more to say. I stepped over the inscribed copy of *Max and the White Phagocytes*, circled around the spinning-wheel lamp, proceeded across the Monticello rug, between the shelves of Jefferson and Franklin first editions, wondering if our founding fathers ever were handed such shoddy goods by the many they dealt with and by the cosmos encompassing them all that they simply dropped to the floor and gave out the distress calls of colicky pintos and flea-crusted airdales—and out the door.

I never saw our Porn Patron again, except on nights when I jolted awake with a hee and a yowl and an overriding curse, clawing the air to comb out assorted incubi with wet Barneybill faces. I won't conceal it from you. I didn't like the man.

CHAPTER 15

FAMILY MAN

But I wasn't through with him. Not yet.

There was trouble in New Haven. My father was on another sabbatical from the half-there ranch. He was this time staying with my mother. Their quarters had all along left something to be desired. What they were now about to leave to be desired were quarters.

For a time my mother had been running a little grocery store on the edge of the Dixwell Avenue ghetto and living behind it. The store had folded but she was still occupying the rear. Now my father was with her. I called them, as I did from time to time, and found that the old wooden building was going to be knocked down and they'd been served an eviction notice.

They had no idea what to do, they were just sitting there, the old man examining the walls, the old lady examining him. I told them to stay put and not to worry, I was on my way to Grand Central and I'd be with them by early afternoon.

When I arrived it was as I suspected, he had his eyes on the wall, she had her eyes on him, no love in any eye I could see, no program, either. I told them not to worry, I was going out for an hour and when I got back we'd take hold of the situation.

Being not at all convinced we'd be able to, I said it with total conviction.

. . .

I went to a neighborhood bar and had some fast drinks. I was thinking hard, trying to match resources to needs at a time when resources were down to nothing and needs up on the final crisis level.

The trouble was, I had no capital to finance any bold moves. I'd made good money these last months but all of it had gone to pay my folks' long-standing debts, arrange some much needed medical attention for them, buy them some clothes, etc. Two or three months from then I'd be ahead again and ready for any emergency but at that point I was ready for nothing but to have all hands kept off me.

Something had to be done, done in the next hours, and whether it was big or small, bold or cautious, I was in no position to underwrite it. Just to find another place for the old folks, a couple of modest rooms in this low-rent neighborhood, and move them in was more than I could pay for. I had something like 12 dollars in my pocket and no further income to look forward to unless I could trick Barneybill into some more deals.

It was, I announced to myself, a moment of truth for me, *the* moment. There were just two courses open.

I could go to the railroad station and catch a train back to New York and leave the folks to whatever might or might not turn up. I could, in other words, greet the problem with my back, on the grounds that life in these times was tough for everybody and in the jungle it's got to be every man for himself and if the old and weak have to drop along the way, well, that's how it goes some years, I didn't make the world, I just try to keep going in it.

I could just walk out on the problem, telling myself that if two people are destined to go down the drain it helps matters not at all to throw a third in with them, especially when the two doomed ones are very old and played out and the third, the optional sacrifice, has long years ahead of him.

That was one way to go. The other was to take the old folks with me on the train back to New York and assume total responsibility for them, on the wild chance that before my 12 dollars gave out I'd find some way to make more money, enough to feed and house the three of us.

But I saw no way to make money, none at all, unless I could somehow get to Barneybill again, and that would not be easy. And even if it turned out to be possible it couldn't be fast. I'd have to write at least part of another porn work, then get it to Barneybill, before there was a chance of any payment from him. That was going to take time, more time than 12 dollars could be stretched to cover even if there were only one mouth to feed.

There'd be three.

I drank fast, wondering why some people go out of their way to find moments of truth in wars, bullrings, body contests, all those spectacular places off the beaten track and not touching the mundane at any point.

The real moments of truth, I told myself, hardly listening, the moments that count, tell you who you are and who you aren't—come to you in your daily rounds, in familiar settings. You really don't have to reach for tests if you're at all plugged into the world, they present themselves on the job, on the street, at home, in bed. The results of such tests, the truths that come to you through them, will serve you better because you're going to be spending much more of your life working, walking the city, sitting with your family, going to bed, than on battlefields and football fields or in bullrings. I told myself.

You might learn a great, a stupendous truth about yourself around a bullring, it's possible, and then never have occasion to visit another one in your lifetime. You can avoid bullrings. Try avoiding an eviction notice.

I tell you, as I told my face in the bar mirror, the people who keep finding out big truths about themselves in the dramatic far-off theaters often turn out not to have much of a life with fellow-workers or close relatives, in fact, at times they seem to be looking for the wars and spectacles in order not to spend much time at a job or with a family. Maybe the truths about themselves in those undramatic areas are harder to live with than the ones they claim to turn up in the places of fireworks and pageant.

I gulped those shots of sour mash in that Dixwell Avenue bar and considered the question of who I was and who I wasn't in relation to work and family, just what obligations I was ready to assume because I truly wanted to apart from what the usages of morality tell us, since for a very long time morality had been telling me nothing.

If it were just the old man in this spot, I'd have said, you're on your own, Pop, let it go as it chooses, I won t intervene.

Not that I didn't feel for him, not that I wished him anything but well. But he was a loser by makeup, a has-been before he tried his hand at any being, a constitutional also-ran, and if that was his destiny, well, I didn't see why I should share it and thus be burdened with it. Get involved in a loser's life and you can only lose yourself.

I wasn't ready to knock myself out, take courses I would not otherwise take, to feed and house him, there was just no point to sacrificing any considerable portion of my life to his, which was already sacrificed, had been from the beginning.

Besides, to look at the practical side, there were agencies to see after him. If I didn't provide the walls for him to stare at, other people were standing by ready to service him at that end. He hadn't been discharged from the Middletown hospital, only given a furlough, he could go back at any time.

The Boss was another story.

I was never impressed by the universally fostered notion that any son not totally and permanently at the service of his poor old ma, that hallowed gray angel of mercy who worked her fingers to the bone to do for him, is an ingrate, more, a monster. I'd always thought that among the sons who kick their mothers aside there are many sick ones, and among those who've never cut the umbilical, who worry about ma's every sniffle, wait on ma hand and foot, there must be an awful lot of very twisted specimens too.

I don't see, and never did, that you can work out your dealings with your mother by any guidelines laid down in official sentimental blood-line morality, you've got to take each case on its own merits.

I examined the case of the Boss on its own merits, there on the fly-shat bar mirror.

The examination, it was clear, had to be conducted without any reference to the blood bond—the mere circumstance that an old lady had brought me forth didn't make her anything special, admirable or despicable, she could be my mother and still neither witch nor guardian angel, or either one, or both. The test was, how would this particular woman add up in my eyes if I had no blood connection with her at all, if she hadn't given birth to me or, for the matter of that, anybody?

There was no doubt about the answer. As anybody's mother, or as no mother at all, this woman in my eyes had significance, dimension, a toughness I respected, a fierce will to get through it and help others through, a fighter, in short, and in her own contained way heroic.

My old man was forever quitting, and my old lady didn't know the meaning of the word quit. Maybe it was none of their own doing, maybe it was just their respective DNA's at work, but who says you're obliged to be equally amiable toward all DNA's?

I'd let the old man go, but I was moved to keep a woman like the old lady from going, not just in the spirit of tit for tat, with the idea that I had to sacrifice for her because she'd sacrificed for me—no, because she had worth, she had spunk, fists she could and did all her life use—that it was much of the time in my behalf was beside the point.

I'd seen her use her fists for neighbors too, even for total strangers who came along, against landlords, relief investigators, social workers, bill collectors, cops, in behalf of people of all colors and shapes, and beat back the world of officialdom and property rights for at least a moment, and that was a sort of fighting that was inspired by something larger and better than the sense of blood kinship.

I, too, was drawn to kinships that passed over bloodlines, so I had to admire this family-augmenting trend in her. How could I not?—I got it from her.

I wasn't much of a family person in the usual sense, ignored birthdays and holidays and the sentimentalized special home occasions, and this in good part because the Boss was that way. She wasn't stingy, she was very much a giver, but she never saw much reason to coordinate her giving with dates on the calendar, to let her generosity be institutionalized and routinized and tagged to times without personal meaning.

I was glad to move away from home the first chance I got, to be on my own, but not to dodge my mother; in fact my mother not only approved the move, she urged it on me.

I don't think I was much beyond 15, starting college, when she began to say to me in private that the back of this store was no place for me to live and that if I wanted to do one thing in the world for her I'd move out and never come visiting. I did get my own room as soon as I could, but of course I went back to visit from time to time.

You want to visit an old lady like that who insists you stay the hell away and forget about the family. You want to keep your connection with a woman like that, whether she's related to you or not.

No, I wasn't much of a family person, I saw as I took inventory of myself in that bar, but this was a time when I had to give some thought to the family, not because of its existence as a family, because of the Boss.

I put it to myself this way. When I came to the last day of my life, and looked back over the things I did and didn't do, and remembered not lifting a finger for the old man on the day he faced eviction as a full pauper, how would I feel?

I knew the answer—sad, but in no way guilty. I was, in other words, sure that I felt no responsibility for him and would go on feeling that.

It was different with the Boss. If I let her be evicted, placed no doubt in the hands of the relief people, her life to become from there on in a thing totally in the hands of the welfare bureaucrats, she to become totally a thing, a computer datum, I wouldn't be able to live easily with that memory. On the last day of my life, I was sure, I would not be pleased with myself if I had such a memory.

I reminded myself of the old lady's feelings about relief. She despised it. For years she'd been eligible for it, and to have taken it would have improved her life in several ways, but she wouldn't think of applying. She had to rely on the efforts of her own two hands to keep going; the knowledge that other hands were serving her, that hers had been retired, put in storage, would have killed her.

There was a time when *I* had to get approved for relief. The job with the WPA Writers Project had opened up, but before you could get on WPA you had to be certified for municipal relief.

I remembered how the Boss took the news that I was a relief client. It made no difference to her that I wasn't going to draw a penny of relief money, that it was just a formality to get me started on the WPA job. There was a spasm across her face. She flinched. It was as if somebody had hit her hard on the cheek.

She didn't say a word about it but I knew what she was thinking. One of us had thrown in the towel, somehow. One of us had given in, given up. We couldn't do it entirely with our own two hands any more. I'd gained a job, but in her innermost thoughts she took it as a loss to her, a black mark, a taint. And in a way I agreed with her but I didn't take it so much to heart, I was much more ready to maneuver through and around the enemy than she was.

In her absolute refusal to accept any form of charity, any hand-out from any source whatsoever, the Boss was no doubt an extreme masochist. Sure she was. There are times, especially in a depression, when your own two hands, no matter how much guts are backing them up, are just not going to make it. In bad times the survivors are often those who can swallow their pride and open their mouths to whatever comes along, including government doles, any scraps from any table. Who if they get small and infrequent mouthfuls chew each one 32 times, then 32 more, counting all the way.

But, you know, I said to the mirror, heard from the mirror, there are masochists and masochists. Some, the whiny ones, the complainers like my old man, you want to boot down the stairs. Some can be exasperating in their stubbornness, but leave their brand on your brain with their sheer gallows guts—such are to be made room for, always respected, frequently learned from, at times hugged.

I found the man I was looking for down an alley off Dixwell Avenue and brought him back with me. While he was itemizing all the articles in the place I explained to the folks that he was a junkman, he was going to buy the stuff here, for how much I didn't know, he'd give us his offer in a minute.

They must not try to save anything, we were going to be traveling light. The idea was for them to throw a few clothes in a valise, that was all, and after the junk dealer paid us we'd get on the train for New York and *go* to New York. For a short time we'd have to put up with cramped conditions, we'd have at first to live in my room on Barrow Street, but I promised that in short order I'd find a decent apartment for them and get them set up in their own place. It would be rough for a few days, but things would work out.

The idea was to forget about the past and not cling to any of the articles that represented it, make a clean sweep, let the junkman take all this junk, just put together a few needed clothes, in a world like this it was the best policy not to live your life as though it were one big junk pile and you the junkman building it up and up. One suitcase. A minimum of clothes. Keep your needs down. A toothbrush, yes, a sewing machine, no.

I was being this talky because I wanted to keep the Boss's mind off one article in particular, not the sewing machine, though that was what I mentioned over and over. The stove. I saw that her eyes were on the stove, and that they widened, went to fullest, when the junkman in his scrutinizing tour came to it and lingered, peering analytically into its insides.

The man finally came over to us, shaking his head.

"You won't take it the wrong way if I lay out the facts as I see them," he said. "What you got here ain't the furnishings of a mansion."

"No, we sold those last week," I said, "along with the mansion. We needed the cash to fix up this place."

"You should of held out for another million. With an extra million you could maybe fix up this place fine, starting with tearing it down to the ground. Look, what a junkman has left over once he's sold all his stuff that's got value above two cents, that's what you got a whole lot of. Only two items could bring something on the market, the sewing machine, it's old but in good condition, and the stove. You throw those in and if I stretch a point more than it's my habit to stretch I could maybe offer you a hundred even for the lot. The hundred is mainly for the machine and the stove, the rest of it you can consider I'm paying for but most I'll leave, it wouldn't pay me to cart it away, I got no room down to my yard for stuff that'll do nothing but hang around."

I said, "Sounds like a fair offer, but could you wait out in front for a minute while we talk this over? We have to have a quick family conference, no reason to involve you."

He went to the front. I didn't want to but I looked at the Boss.

"The stove too?" she said.

"It's got to be. We have to get rid of everything we can't carry, Boss."

"That stove's been in the family a long time," she said. No complaint, she was simply citing facts.

"We all have, Boss. Sometimes to save a family you've got to give up one of its favorites."

That stove was a favored member of this family, all right. It had been acquired at a crucial moment in our lives: the old man had lost his job and had his breakdown, as a result they couldn't keep up payments on the house they'd bought years before, they'd lost the house and moved to a rented place. The old man started his stays in the hospital, first in the institute of Human Relations, then in state retreats, the Boss became the breadwinner, scrubbed floors, tended drooling paralytics, whatever came up. The places we lived in were cold in the New England winters. The Boss put away nickels and dimes until she was able to make the down payment on that big, dancy-legged, claw-footed, shiny tan stove. It wasn't just for cooking, though it had all the facilities for that. On its left side was an arrangement of burners with rests for two big glass bottles of kerosene, a heating unit that would maintain at least two rooms nice and warm. We kept a steel barrel filled with kerosene in the cellar, we were forever going down to fill those bottles in the winter, no matter how tough things got we were always warm.

That stove was for years the center of the Boss's existence, the axis she revolved around, the focus of all her big pushes. It was the arena of our eating and our heating, from it we were fed, thanks to it we didn't freeze. Of course, it didn't belong to us outright. The Boss had made some minimal down payment and was giving the dealer two or three dollars a month on it, barely enough to cover the interest charges. But though it didn't belong to us clear and free it was working for us around the clock, we ate around it, slept around it, got our energy and our peace of mind from its presence.

One afternoon while the Boss was out wiping the droolings and drop-pings off the old paralyzed woman she was taking care of, the man who sold us the stove came calling. He had an assistant with him, a fellow as burly as himself. I was the only one home. The dealer announced that we hadn't made any payments on the stove for three months and he was repossessing it.

He wasn't impressed when I told him to go away. He seemed not to hear when I informed him we needed that stove more then he did, because in our house it kept people warm and back in his place of business it could only make more money for him. He pushed me aside, he and his helper started to take the stove apart.

I kept trying to stop them, they kept shoving me away. It was just no contest. Then by a stroke of wild luck the door opened and the Boss came in.

It so happened that the husband of the paralyzed woman, a man who ran a window-cleaning business, had decided to take the day off and hang around the house. When he gave himself such a vacation he usually brought a girl home with him, the girl who looked after his office and answered the phone. When he spent the day home in bed with this girl he didn't want my mother around, so he'd let her go home early. Of course, the paralyzed wife was there, and could hear what was going on in the other bedroom, but she was paralyzed, she couldn't butt in, she couldn't even talk, much less walk, she could at best make gurgling sounds far down in her throat and the window-cleaner didn't mind that, he just turned the radio up. It was a break for us that the window-cleaner had gotten hot pants this day, otherwise the Boss wouldn't have made an appearance until hours after the stove had been carted off.

She took one look at the scene and understood everything. She was good at drinking the essence of a situation with one quick survey.

"Oh, no you don't," she said. "Some things are allowed, and some things are entirely forbidden, what the law might say go tell lawyers. This house is warm, and it stays warm."

She flew across the room. She leaped at the men. She was clawing, scratching, using her tight little body as a battering ram. She got tossed away, she came right back.

In a second I was with her. By myself I was no match for either one of these bruisers, but the old lady and me, we made a fine team, we had, what do they call it, spirit, drive, the will to win.

They gave up after a time. They just got tired of heaving us against the wall and having us bounce right back at them. They picked up their tools and left muttering something about putting this in the hands of the law, they knew their rights. We stood there by the stove, breathing hard, laughing into each other's face.

Maybe the idea behind American sports is not who wins but how you play the game. Well, this game we'd been playing was not in the American grain, the boasted one anyhow, the idea behind it was to win, to win at all costs, by means fair or foul—and we'd won. We'd so trounced the other side that they never came back.

We were so delighted with ourselves, not for the way we'd played the game but for winning, that we took the coins out of the old coffee jar where we saved for payments on the stove, and I went out and bought us two double-scoop maple-walnut ice cream cones to celebrate with. We lapped at our cones and laughed like hell.

That stove followed us everywhere after that. It was the one absolutely staple item in our ramshackle household. Whatever other possessions fell away as we moved around, it was all right, so long as the stove traveled with us and stayed on good terms with us. I think I've established that that stove meant a great deal to the Boss, and that if the time had finally come for her to part with it, she felt she was losing an arm, a lung, an emblem, a history. . . .

"One point is, we can't carry the stove," I said. "There's another, all the money I have in the world is 12 dollars, if I don't get the 100 from this man we can't make a move, we'll hardly have enough for train tickets, if we go to New York we'll arrive without a cent. The stove's served us well, Boss. Let it serve us one last time, by buying our train tickets and feeding us for a while in New York till I get you settled. If you could ask her I think she'd say she wants it this way, she's a good old stove."

The Boss made no objection. She was above all a realist, she knew when sentiment was out of place and a drag on people who have to move. But her eyes stayed very wide, and set, and I didn't enjoy seeing them like that. If you've ever whipped your family dog for some wrong-doing, and he never knew from beginning to end what this punishment was all about, just stood there and took it because his feeling for you overrode all the hurt you were giving him, if you've ever done that, and seen the look in his eyes as he stood still and took it, you'll know the expression I'm talking about.

We put up in my room on Barrow Street for a couple of weeks, the old man and I sleeping on the double bed, the Boss on the couch. It was a fine old brick building at the point where Barrow west of Seventh crooks to the north, converted from a turn-of-the-century firehouse, and I was satisfied to live there, but three in one medium-sized room was impossible.

I scoured Lower Manhattan until I found an apartment for the folks in Knickerbocker Village just east of Chatham Square, got them set up there with some furniture bought on the installment plan, used up most of my nest-egg to pay a month's rent. Now I was called on to keep up *two* households, in addition to paying for my parents' medical bills, which were hefty. I had to go to work, and fast.

I began to answer handfuls of help-wanted ads, but the business world was still not bidding for my services. I had to do a couple more quick jobs for Barneybill, no two ways about it, and I could hardly arrange that myself—I needed a go-between who wouldn't give my identity away. Bright idea: Zo-Zo the Generous would come to my rescue.

No soap. Bettina learned that Zo-Zo was no longer available to artists in need. Her husband, the Rumanian wheat and coffee factor, had found that with Hitler overrunning all his markets business was falling away to nothing. He'd skipped out of Paris in the nick of time and made his way to New York and a reunion with his wife. This was Zo-Zo's moment of truth. All along hubby had had the idea, fostered by her, that she'd gone off to New York to give harpsichord concerts and in general foster her musical career. Zo-Zo wanted to make this man happy. She had feeling for him, also felt guilty about having neglected him for so long to help a truckload of other men she wasn't even married to. To make amends, she began, as soon as her husband arrived, to solicit bookings for harpsichord concerts. Now in the thick of the concertizing world, and caught up as she was with traveling and rehearsing, she'd moved out of Barneybill's orbit entirely, had no contact with him. Under ordinary circumstances she'd have been only too happy to front for a talented New-Sexualist like me. As it was. . . .

Bettina and I held a council of war. It was clear enough that none of the Blooming Boys could do liaison for me, even if they wanted to—none of them was in that solid with Barneybill, most of them didn't even know him personally.

For a while it looked like we were stymied. Then Bettina came up with an inspiration: what about the newcomer, Jason Orroway!

CHAPTER 16

CLIFFHANGER

For years Jason Orroway had lived in Amagansett, near the eastern tip of Long Island, where he put out a little magazine of Tolstoyan-Reichian pacifist-anarchist persuasion. Its name I remember as something like *Bustout*.

Finally his wife came into a little money. Jason had always dreamed of making his way deep into the unspoiled country, like Thoreau, and working the primeval land, like Tolstoy. With his wife's inheritance he bought a small farm in a remote corner of New Hampshire. He installed his wife and several kids on the farm and instructed them in how to live in a natural, Tolstoyan symbiosis with the good earth, tilling the soil with their bare hands or at best a hand-hewn chunk of wood, growing only organic vegetables, raising only organic livestock, all without the benefit of befouling chemo-agriculture: in short, folding into Mother Nature's arms instead of constantly poisoning and choking and mauling the Old Biddy. This simple life was not only Tolstoyan, it would build sturdy bones, strengthen teeth, flush out the liver, put iron in the blood. Mens sana in corpore sano, etc.

Two years passed. One day Mrs. Orroway said to Mr. Orroway:

"Jason, Tolstoy isn't working out for us. It's fun scratching the soil with bare fingers, though it tires you out like a coolie, but we don't seem to get much of a crop that way. I'm all for the natural life, dear, but part of being natural is eating regular, and we just aren't, if you don't mind my pointing it out while I still have the strength. We need money, Jason, there's no two ways about it. We need seed. We need a cow. We need a pig. We need a few chickens. All that takes money. Also, though I know it's against your principles and that pains me, we need a real store-bought metal plow, and a tractor to pull it with, not to mention a truck so that when we get some stuff raised we can get it to where it can be sold. That takes money too. I don't much care how and where you get this money but you've got to get it. If you don't the need for it will disappear fast because you'll have no more family around requiring minimal support from you. I'm as fond of Tolstoy as the next farmer's wife but I want to point out something you may have overlooked, Tolstoy had an inherited income, he furrowed the soil with his bare fingers for a hobby, not a livelihood. Also, he didn't have a family to feed and look after. I mean, he had a family, all right, but he didn't have to stick around and provide for their daily needs, he was happy to hit the road and get away from his wife, who spat at him a good deal and thought he was a revolting nut. You go arrange an income like Tolstoy's and I'll scratch the soil with you all day long for the fun of it, so long as the freezer's full of contaminated foods and there's a fulltime lady serf in the kitchen preparing meals for the family out of all that lovely store-bought poison."

So Jason Orroway came down to Manhattan to make money for seed, cow, pig, and chickens, against which he had no principled objection, plus plow, tractor, and truck, which violated all he stood for. Jason knew some of Barneybill's Boys from earlier days around the Village. They set him up in porn. He moved into a basement on Leroy Street, over near the Hudson, and went to work. He figured he needed $1,200, so he knew he had to write 1,200 pages. The question was, what subject within his ken was worth 1,200 pages? The answer was, himself. There was nothing else he knew so well, and nothing he found anywhere near as interesting.

Jason Orroway took the post-Lawrence mission seriously. He meant to write such a New-Sexualist autobiography as would dynamite the fat and lazy vested-interest world of Letters and break ground for the anarcho-pacifist orgone-rich soul now begging to be liberated from the human breast. His plan was simple. He made a list of all the girls he'd had in his life. It was amazing, how many girls he'd managed to turn up in and around Amagansett, Long Island. He made copious notes as to the many ways in which he'd had them. The program was to devote one chapter to each girl, going down the list chronologically. He estimated that would add up to 1,200 pages easily, even if he omitted family and educational backgrounds.

Of course, the upshot of this writing would be to make him one more agribusinessman, at the mercy of the fertilizer manufacturers, a pawn of the produce markets, tied irrevocably to this vicious supply-and-demand, buy-and-sell profit economy, with no time ever again to squat in classic farmer style on his haunches and run his gnarly, honest-laborer's fingers through rich, uncontaminated loam. But this was the price of becoming a family man: under the pinched and earthbound auspices of a wife the mundane has got to triumph over the millennial. Having mouths to feed forces certain compromises on you. Today no Pangloss can cultivate his own garden; instead of a mess of optimism a man needs a mess of sowing and harvesting machinery and fleets of vehicles to get his produce to the wholesalers in town. Not without an inherited income of Tolstoyan proportions. Simplicity takes capital. The natural life requires heavy underwriting.

Jason Orroway had already put on paper the first 37 sex dramas of his adventurous Amagansett life. He had 63 to go.

Bettina went to see Jason. She told him that she had this very dear friend from Salt Lake City who was a gifted concert pianist. Unfortunately, this friend had had an accident. He'd been playing tennis one day recently and broken his finger. Obviously he couldn't go back to the piano until the finger was fully healed, all his concerts for this season were canceled. This friend also happened to be a very intelligent and literate fellow, tuned in on the most up-to-date literary trends. He could write well, too. He'd heard about the practitioners of New-Sexualism and was fascinated. He wondered if he could get into this thing himself. He'd love to write some of this stuff, partly to make money, partly because he felt he had something to say along these lines. He had the time, while his finger was healing. He wondered if there was anybody close to Barneybill Roster who would be nice enough to sponsor him with Barneybill.

Sure Jason Orroway said. Bring the guy around. He'd talk with this piano player, size him up as to genital-orgonotic orientation and things like that, and if the guy sounded promising he, Jason, would be glad to bring anything the guy wrote to Barneybill. There was a big job to be done here. It needed as many hands as could be recruited. Revolutions take teamwork. There had to be a place in the taboo-toppling Sexualist Enlightenment for piano players too.

Bettina arranged for me to meet with Jason. I did my best to discuss New-Sexualism with him from the rather specialized point of view of a concert pianist from Salt Lake City with a broken finger and a lively interest in where the genitalia might be heading after D. H. Lawrence.

Jason Orroway was impressed with my spirit. He was also impressed with my authenticity: I was wearing a fat bandage on the little finger of my left hand, which I assured him would not keep me from turning out reams of New-Sexualism since I typed by hunt-and-peck rather than touch. He said, fine, great, splendid, go ahead and do up an opus and he'd serve as agent for it with the Boss.

I went to work with zest. A plot had come to me out of the purple. This one was practically writing itself, it was pretty much a collaboration between story and typewriter, with me providing the stationery.

There's this real Don Juan of a concert pianist. There's this veritable Juno of a concert harpsichordist. He has satyriasis and an
extensive wardrobe containing over 100 pairs of trousers, all kept
considerably above room temperature, and his hot pants are all for
her. She has a gazelle neck and nymphomania and pants equally
hotly for him, that is to say, her pants are equally hot for him.
The trouble is that their concert itineraries never deposit them in the
same town long enough to allow the consummation devoutly desired by
both parties. They meet only fleetingly and supra-genitally in railroad
stations, airports, banquet halls, the lobbies of auditoriums: one's always
going as the other's coming, which is not the way of Eros. Each is ber-
serking with the thought of what will happen when fate drops them in
the same place for an hour or even, for a consummation too tornadic to
have anything devout about it, a day, a week.

It is quite clear that when satyr and nympho finally do merge in
some remote motel or presidential suite the rafters will quake, it will
be Jericho time. They are trying frantically to get the impresario who
handles both their bookings to arrange some joint concerts for them so
that they can make beautiful and prolonged music together offstage,
and certainly off-color.

The impresario, who knows them for the appetitious blowtops they
are, with the disruptive horniness that seems to be chronic among string
instrumentalists, and who takes a dim view of such passion because he's
a bit gay, is determined to keep the two prodigies and their prodigious
appetites apart.

They manage nonetheless to have moments together, though always
on the run, at a clip which excludes any consummatory horizontalism.
They spend a hot minute in the dim recess of a BMT subway station.
Their fingers brush tantalizingly as the Superchief pulls out of the
Albuquerque depot with one of them aboard and the other running
frantically alongside. Appearing as guests on the panel of an early TV

quiz program, sitting side by side they grope each other abominably and interminably under the table, only to be whisked away afterward in separate Cadillacs to separate engagements in widely separated cities. . . .

This marathon tickle continued for exactly 300 pages, exactly half of the novel I had planned. I decided to turn in these pages as the first volume of a two-volume work. My eagerness to get my hands on more of Barneybill's dollars was only part of the reason behind the installment approach.

What I was writing was the cliffhanger of all time. Never in the history of our Popular Culture, from *Uncle Tom's Cabin* to *The Perils of Pauline*, had anyone dared to build such a space-taking head of steam, to suspend without promise of early or even eventual drop, to let tension mount with no least hint of easement in the offing. On page 1 our two feverish tumescents were hanging by their fingernails from the genital cliff, and on page 300 they were still agonizingly in midair.

You may deduce that I was trying to tease Barneybill in some especially provocative manner. Quite right. But if you assume that there was unconscious malice behind this you'll be wide of the mark. The malice, which was Gargantuan, was all quite conscious. I hoped to do more than just tantalize the man. I hoped to frustrate him entirely.

With such unprecedented buildup, Barneybill had to expect equally elaborate payoff. 300 pages of preliminaries could be justified only by the certainty of 300 additional pages of sheer orgiastic aftermath. I wrote this first promissory volume with all the porn cunning I'd acquired over the months, precisely to whet Barneybill's appetite to the point of hysteria. I wanted him to be aching for the second volume, in which all the author's obligations, and all the protagonists' gonads, had to be discharged.

I wanted, further, not to deliver the second volume. To help-wanted advertisers in the *Times*, I was sending off massive quantities of letters, hoping against hope that there would be a response to one of them and that I would finally get a salaried job somewhere and not have to finish this opus. I wished to leave those two musicians clinging to that cliff forevermore. It would teach Barneybill Roster a lesson. Aside from the fact that, with luck, I would have outmaneuvered him in his determination to reduce my rate from two dollars a page to one.

I knew I could get $300 for my first volume. But I was also going to plead for an advance of another $300 for the second volume, on the grounds of extreme need. I was pretty sure that the first volume was provocative enough to get me the advance. If I collected *$600* for the first volume, and never wrote the second, I would have been reimbursed at my old, special, rate of *two* dollars a page. This was the consummation *I* desired, with a devoutness which bordered on the saintly.

I gave my first volume to Jason Orroway, explaining that there was a thoughtful esthetic behind the master plan for this work. It was my conviction that only Trash Porn threw in a lot of bedroom scenes without motivation, creation of an atmosphere, and careful establishment of character. I knew that the New-Sexualists didn't want Trash any more than I was prepared to write it. So what I was after here was Serious Porn. I was so intent on making my P. absolutely S. that I had taken 300 pages to get all elements in place and all motives squared away before the rollicking began. With this painstaking buildup we could now have meaningful and untrashy payoffs. The second 300 pages would consist entirely of payoffs. After being apart for 300 pages, our lovers would now be together for 300 pages, and I did mean together. I had provided a most sturdy erotic springboard. Now the piano player and the harpsichordist were going to jump. Into bed. The second whole volume would jump. Never leaving bed. Statistically speaking, the book in the overall would arrive at a balance that had to please any Serious-Porn fancier. If the 300 nookyless pages were to be offset by 300 pages of nothing but nooky, a quick breakdown would show that for every no-sex page there would be a corresponding all-sex page: one word in bed for one word out, 50-50, a perfect ratio for those after more than Trash.

Jason was a bit troubled. He thought the 50-50 formula might work, but he wasn't sure that you could put the establishing 50 in a long volume and only then get down to the second, and perhaps more germane, 50.

I argued that the precise mixture had to depend on the temperament and tactics of the individual artist. *He* apparently mixed on every page. *I* had to do it volume by volume. I reminded him that in *War and Peace*, that many-volumed work by a man he held in high regard, the scrambling was done with massive 100-page units rather than in quick sprinkles.

Jason readily agreed. He wondered, though, if the interminglements we were after were precisely the same as those Tolstoy had been after.

I said, certainly, isn't the aim of all Serious Writing the rich delineation of character? What about Jason himself? In his very long catalogue of all the women in his life, listed chronologically, was he only trying to titillate or was he hoping to capture the full and revealing flavor of personality?

Jason acknowledged that I had a point.

Then he read my pages. All his reservations flew out the window. He was overwhelmed. What I had done here was masterly, masterly. The buildup while it *seemed* at moments to be dragging its feet and other organs, was bound to pay rich, lush dividends. He felt I was striking a new and unprecedentedly profound New-Sexualist note.

He thought I was a tremendous find. He would be most happy to rush the manuscript to Barneybill and petition him in the strongest terms for the $600 payment I was requesting. He did so rush and so petition that very afternoon.

And that very evening, filled with the solemnity of the occasion, deeply moved, he folded $600 into my hand. Barneybill had read my pages in Jason's presence. He had become so emotional over the text as to break down at three different points. He had found on all these words the stamp of total inspiration.

"You've got the touch, all right," Jason said to me rather awed. "Barneybill says he's seldom come across a writer in our field who can make his people so real."

"Maybe it's because I'm the kind of artist who works with real-life models," I suggested. "You can see that I didn't invent much. I know the music world intimately." Sure: I once saw Zo-Zo's harpsichord out of the case, without a stitch on.

"Barneybill says you're one of the few guys working for him that he'd like to know personally. He wants you to come up and have a long visit."

"I'd certainly like to, when I get back. I'm leaving town first thing in the morning. I have to go to Minneapolis to see a specialist, an osteo man who's going to give me a new heat and radiation treatment for my finger. It's not healing at all well, unless this man can help me God knows when I'll be able to concertize again."

"You will be back?" Jason spoke with some anxiety.

"Oh, sure. They'll keep me in Minneapolis for a while but Barneybill doesn't have to worry. This treatment won't interfere with my typing. I'll have my typewriter with me and work on the second volume every day I'm in Minneapolis."

"That's good. That's very good. Barneybill's dying to get it. He says that only twice since he's become involved with this New-Sexology has he come across writers who could be classified in the full technical sense of the word as geniuses, and the first one let him down badly, turned out to be a bunkoman and a Judas, and you're the second, and he's got high hopes you may develop into a replacement if your book winds up as marvelously as it begins."

"It's a challenge. I'll try to do as well as this other fellow, whoever he is and however he acted up. It's hard to follow in the footsteps of a full genius but I'll certainly make the effort."

"I only hope Barneybill thinks half as well of *my* stuff when I turn it in. Boy, I don't know how you do it, what's your secret?"

"It's simple, Jason. I just don't mix on every page, I think in the larger units. Mixing the non-genital with the genital on every page suggests a little anxiety, maybe, implies that you're not entirely sure of yourself, maybe because you're in such a hurry to get your cow and your tractor."

"I don't know. I just don't know. I have to mix fast because I've got to get some genital stuff in with each girl and I've got a lot of girls to cover, 100 all told—and as I see it it's incumbent on me to tell all. Yes, I'm planning to make it an even 100, and I'm past page 400 and I've only covered three dozen and one."

"That *is* a problem. Ever thought of cutting down the number of girls to 50, say, or even 20? That way you could mix a little more slowly, and more thoroughly too, maybe. You might even do a whole page here and there without any genital orientation at all, but building up a richer background *for* the genital stuff, if you see what I mean. If you're interested in that kind of pulse in your work, I mean. I don't want to suggest that such a pulse is necessary for good writing, I've known some excellent writers who had no pulse at all. But Christ, you don't want all this free advice from a newcomer."

"No, no, I'm glad to get your slant. I just don't know how I could get reoriented along your lines, though. I work true to life too, you know. I want to tell the naked truth in every respect. I *had* these 100 girls and it would be a falsification, just the kind of phony note I hate in today's fiction, to pretend it was only 50 or 20. If experience is ever going to be truly conveyed in an artistic work we've got to get rid of the idea that we've been given this artistic license to distort the facts. No, it's got to be 100, no more, no less. I guess I'll just have to forgo that pulse effect. I'm the kind of writer that's more interested in content than in form."

"Well, Jason, I certainly didn't mean to lay down any laws, and I'm sure you know what you're doing, so please forget the way I've been shooting my mouth off uninvited. I can well believe that if you've got 100 girls for content you don't have to worry much about form, in this case I think form will just naturally follow content, and form following a content of 100 girls will have to be pretty shapely. It's been good talking with you, Jason, and I want to thank you for all you've done, this $600 may have saved my finger, thanks a lot."

"Don't mention it. Listen, shoot that second volume to me the minute it's ready, will you? Barneybill's going to be breathing down my neck for it, particularly since he's already paid for it, and besides, he's dying to know just where the story's going."

"The minute I hit Minneapolis I'll get to work on it, that's a promise. See you, Jason."

"Stick with it, genius."

The next day, literally the next day, I got an answer, my first, from one of the *Times* advertisers. I went for an interview. Two days later I was on a payroll, an honest, respectable, nine-to-fiver's payroll, as a fund-raiser in the annual campaign for the non-sectarian Denver Jewish Hospital for the Tuberculous Poor. I was getting only $75 a week, but I didn't have to think up any dirty stories to earn my keep.

CHAPTER 17

TURNCOAT

I plunged into fund-raising with a vocational focus the Time-Life people didn't think I had in me.

One thing that excited me was that it was completely non-genital, which immediately put me in a holiday mood. But its mechanics were fascinating, too. Fresh from a world of total fall-short lust, I found myself in a world of total peak-performance blackmail.

Most professional charity solicitation revolves around one cunningly conceived institution, the testimonial banquet.

The laying-out of the campaign which is to culminate in the banquet is a simple enough operation. You decide which areas of the business world you want to put the bite on. You then choose as the dignitary to be testimonialized a man who is so important to those business areas that the mere mention of his name strikes terror into the hearts of the businessmen involved.

You seldom have any trouble lining up the dignitary. For one thing, he can't very well express indifference toward the Tuberculous Poor or whatever group of unfortunates you want to be nice to. For another, he generally has a deep, though unvoiced, conviction that the world has owed him a testimonial for some time.

Once you have your testimonialee, you're in business. All you have to do is make the rounds of the many businessmen who deal with this magnate, tell them about the banquet, and let them know that the magnate is looking forward to seeing them on that happy occasion. They can arrange to be seen by him through an absurdly simple device. All they have to do is buy tickets for the banquet. Tickets not only for themselves, of course, but for all their top officers and associates. Say, 25 tickets, or 40 tickets, or 50 tickets, for a medium-sized firm.

These tickets, I should perhaps mention, cost $25 each. So, for the modest sum of $500, or $1,000, or $1,250, which will go a long way toward making the Tuberculous Poor less tuberculous and somewhat less poor, they, all the important executives of the particular firm, will be seen at the banquet by the magnate being fêted, who will be damned grateful.

There's a corollary, of course. If the magnate *doesn't* see them, he's bound to feel disappointed. Hurt. Badly let down. May take to brooding over the slight. May very well look over his business connections and reconsider the matter of dealing with this particular firm in future.

The businessmen selected as targets in our drive were the leading figures in the leading firms of the fashion world, designers, cloak and suit makers, perfumers, cosmeticians. The magnate we planned to testimonialize was a fellow whose name was magic to these businessmen— the owner of an enormous department store in the commodity-craving heart of Middle America, which sold cloaks, suits, perfumes, cosmetics in whopping quantities.

My job was an incredible cinch. I dropped in on the leaders of the fashion world, men and women alike, my briefcase loaded with packets of banquet tickets, and terrorized them.

It was a heady experience. Like many folk with Marxist background, I could philosophize with quite some eloquence about the mechanics and dynamics of power; but, again like many of my Marxist confréres, I had never in my life had one taste of the power I understood so profoundly. Suddenly, though I was being paid only $75 a week for my terroristic services, I was ensconced on the topmost seats of power in our national power complex, squelching the mighty with the utterance of one charismatic name, making millionaires quake.

My trousers were about to come through in the rear and my shoes needed resoling, but I could strike the fear of God into the hearts of empire builders wearing cut-aways and diamonds. What clearer proof did I need that ours was still an open society?

Understandably, I forgot about writing dirty books for the Barneybills of the world, who were small potatoes as against these satraps of the domains of dress and smell and coif and skin-conditioning.

But there were those who did not forget.

One day, about a month after I went to work as a soft-spoken mus-cleman for the lung-sore poor, I was crossing Seventh Avenue at the corner of Barrow Street. I heard a voice calling agitatedly, "Bucklin! Hey, there, Bucklin! Now, Bucklin, listen, wait a minute!"

I paid no attention: my name is certainly not Bucklin, and I was reasonably sure I would be less than interested in anybody whose name was Bucklin or who knew anybody by that name.

But halfway across the street I pulled up short. Bucklin was not *my* name, no. But it *was* the name of the Salt Lake City piano player with the wounded paw who for a brief period I had in certain circles alleged to be.

I looked around in what I imagine was a harried, perhaps even haunted, way.

There on the corner, waving his arms wildly at me, was Jason Orroway.

I was trapped. I got to the other side and waited for him to catch up. I greeted him with a pretty sickly smile. "How're things going, Jason?"

"What the hell happened to *you*?"

"Happened? Nothing's happened, Jason, just been kind of busy."

"Where's that second volume you owe Barneybill? The one I was sucker enough to get you an advance on?"

"Oh, well, now, Jason, some things came up. Some things came up and, well, I just haven't had a minute."

"You had an oral contract for a certain job of work. You took the money for that job and beat it. I'm left holding the bag because I was sort of your sponsor, I was practically guarantor of the contract, I'm the one getting shafted because you ran out on your commitments."

"Well, I wouldn't call it running out, exactly, Jason. See, what happened, some people asked me to help raise funds for this hospital for the tuberculous poor. I couldn't say no, the tuberculous poor need all the help they can get, so that's what I've been doing, raising money for the tuberculous poor, and it's been taking all my time. I know I have a commitment to Barneybill but you can see that my commitment to the tuberculous poor has got to come first, they're needier than Barneybill is. That's the way it is with charity work, it gets to be a full-time thing."

"You said you were going to work on that second volume the moment you got to Minneapolis."

"Well, I meant every word of it, Jason, that statement was made in all sincerity. The fact is that I never did get to Minneapolis so there wasn't any way I could work on that book in Minneapolis, my plans were changed due to factors beyond my control."

"What do you mean, you never got to Minneapolis? What about that doctor who was going to treat your finger?"

"Well, when this thing with the tuberculous poor came up it was urgent, so my finger had to wait, I couldn't think of my own needs when others were worse off than I was. The way it looks now, I probably won't have to go to Minneapolis at all. As you can see, the bandage is off, my finger's really a lot better. See? I can move it fine, it's practically healed by itself. Maybe a good part of the trouble was psychosomatic."

"And just when *do* you plan to get that book done?"

"Well, that's hard to say, Jason, hard to say. I've been finding out there're an awful lot of tuberculous poor. They need a terrific amount of money. I may be at this thing for some time."

"I swear I don't get you, Bucklin. This thing you were working on was a real trail-blazer, it was probably going to revolutionize the whole field, be *the* big contribution. And now you're saying you don't know when you'll get back to it, if ever. How can you abandon the most important thing in your life, what might be your life's work, this eye-opener that only you can write, as though you were just slipping off a pair of gloves or something?"

"I don't think you ought to use a word like abandon, Jason. I'm not abandoning anything. The fact is that I began to have second thoughts about that book anyhow. All things considered, it's probably a good thing I backed away from it, though I certainly wouldn't have if the tuberculous-poor thing hadn't come up. You see, what I never got around to mentioning was, I had rather different ideas about how that second volume was going to turn out than you and Barneybill may have assumed I did. The second volume was going to bring those people together, sure. It was going to take place entirely in the bedroom, I wasn't kidding about that. But I know these people better than you and Barneybill could. I knew what had to happen once they got into the bedroom. I've been around the music world a long time, Jason, and I am very familiar with musicians of this type. That satyriacist was going to turn out to be impotent, Jason, and the nymphomaniac had to be revealed as absolutely frigid. That was the only way I could write the thing, Jason, and be true to the facts, because that's the way things are with musical satyrs and musical nymphos, and as you yourself have said to me on more than one occasion what's the sense to writing this stuff at all if it's not brutally honest and in the best realistic tradition? But if I wrote it that way I knew Barneybill was going to be quite disappointed, maybe even upset, and I didn't want that to happen, so I really didn't know how to finish the thing, and the more I thought about it the more stuck I was. All in all, it's probably a good thing the tuberculous poor came up. I just couldn't bring myself to do another 300 pages in which these two people got together only to find that the man had insurmountable erectile difficulties and the woman equally crippling ones in the area of vaginismus and non-lubrication. I just couldn't do that to Barneybill. Besides it's practically impossible to get 300 pages out of a vaginismus and non-erection situation, I think you can see that, Jason."

"In other words, you're stealing $300 and thumbing your nose at everybody in the bargain. What am I supposed to say to Barneybill? Just how am I supposed to get him off my back?"

"Give him this message for me, Jason, I'm sure once he understands it he'll let up on you. Get the phrasing absolutely right, it's important. Tell him Vico's cyclical theory of history has gone to work very dramatically in his life. Tell him that if the first authentic genius invited him to whistle for his $300, it had to follow, according to Vico, that the second authentic genius would similarly invite him to whistle for his $300, especially since the kinship between the first genius and the second genius is very, very close, the second genius is practically a projection of the first. Tell him, too, that the second genius, because of his rich communication with the first genius, knows a great deal about Barneybill, and is therefore confident that Barneybill can finish that masterwork out of the depths of his own slop-pail of an imagination much, much better than any run-of-the-mill peepingtom genius ever could. Think you can remember all of that, Jason? Try to repeat it exactly the way I said it. And don't take any of this personally, Jason. I like you, and I'm truly grateful for the way you helped me out, and I wish you all good things with your 100 girls, and I hope you get the dandiest cow and pig and tractor around, and my regards to the wife and kids up in New

Hampshire. Goodbye, Jason. You'll never be far from my thoughts. Mix well and be well. So long."

He made no move to stop me as I took a couple of experimental steps away from him. It looked like I was going to get out of it all right.

My pace quickened. I almost broke into a trot as I turned the corner.

But I heard his voice, which he'd found at last, battering after me. One harsh, spat-out word of the ultimate vituperation meant to expel me permanently from the human race:

"Turncoat! Turncoat!"

If he hadn't meant Bucklin Something, not me, and if in addition I hadn't been doing positive things for the Tuberculous Poor, I might indeed have felt like one.

CHAPTER 18

HENRY'S IN TOWN

And still I wasn't through with Barneybill Roster. The screw, the one
loose in his rattling head, needed one last turn.

Unlike TB, which knows no tassel-time, banquets against TB are
highly seasonal. Once our Denver Hospital banquet was held, and all
funds raised, my usefulness as a fund-raiser was at an end.

I was again without a job. I was again without prospect of a job. I
was again direly in need of Barneybill's inexhaustible dollars. But there
was no ready access to them. I refused to take that as final.

Jason Orroway could not be called upon for further intermediation.
Nor was there any other Blooming Boy to front for me. Zo-Zo was
gone from the scene entirely. The Rumanian had moved to Caracas
to set himself up as a sales representative for Moroccan architectural
tiles and Swiss decorating machines, and Zo-Zo, reveling in the newly-
found role of loving wife, had packed up her harpsichord and gone with
him. I knew I could somehow work up another New-Sexualist identity
worthy of presentation to Barneybill. But there was nobody around to
do the presenting.

Until Bettina Tokay burst upon me one day with stimulating news:
Henry Miller was in town!

· · ·

Henry had been knocking around Greece for some months with Lawrence Durrell, Katsimbalis and others. Then the war situation had taken a turn for the worse: Hitler's goons were poised for an invasion of the Aegean lands too. Henry had wanted to get back to Paris but the American consular officials insisted on sending him home to the States. Now here he was in Manhattan, memorializing his Greek vacation in what was to be the magnificent *Colossus of Maroussi*, and preparing for a voyage of bilious rediscovery around his homeland which was to result in the work called *Air Conditioned Nightmare*.

This news was of interest to me on more than one count. Barneybill Roster stood in trepidatious awe of Henry Miller. Henry Miller could get to Barneybill Roster any time he wanted. The Red Blood Corpuscle could make the White Phagocyte jump to any tune. Where the Parkinsonian ballets of the one were concerned, the other was Head Choreographer.

Henry was not in the least a standoffish man. When I got word to him through mutual friends (the Kenneth Patchens, I think or maybe it was Anaïs Nin) that I urgently wished to talk to him about a matter relating to Mr. Roster he said sure, let's get together and have a drink.

We met in one of those fine seedy Third Avenue bars that the chic had not yet thought to take over and spruce up as neo-Georgian trysting places for Georges who dote on other Georges. This was a joint where they still served free lunches of smelly cheeses and raw Bermuda onion to go with the beer. The time of hot deviled-crab hors d'oeuvres, served to boys by boys by candlelight, was not yet upon us.

Henry was not what I'd expected.

We Village malcontents had worked up a lively image of the berserker who'd concocted the *Tropic* bombshells. Such a prancing bull of the prose pampas had to be out-dimensional in every aspect: a brawler in rude denim jeans, defiant locks snapping in the Seine breezes; a debaucher on the grand scale who, singing all the way, consumed Gargantuan daily rations of wine and women; an expatriate Johnny Appleseed standing, at conservative estimate, 12 feet tall. We knew a giant when we read one; the deeper undergound a book was driven, the taller grew its author.

Well, the Rimbaud of Myrtle Avenue, the Villon of the 14th Ward, was neither big nor loud nor rambunctious. He was slight and bone-thin. His voice was soft, mellifluous. The gray hair that fringed his bold bald pate was neatly crew-cut. His jowls were as clean-shaven as his nails were clean and manicured. He wore impeccably tailored Bond Street tweeds and a natty plaid ulster.

He was kind, courteous, considerate, mild, modest, gentle, and all but old-worldly in his gallant manners with the womenfolk—the very antithesis of the capering, carousing cutup called Henry Miller in the books of Henry Miller. The rapacious desperado of *Tropic of Cancer*. I found to be everybody's Dutch uncle.

But with something added—something not just avuncular, some special clear unblinking light in the deceptively mild blue eyes half draped by slanty mandarin lids, some special husky vibrant sound in the misleadingly gentle voice that had never deviated from the flat Brooklyn tones of his birth. You couldn't pin a name on this laxed electricity in him, but you knew when it was turned on.

You stood with the unstagey man at the Third Avenue bar, talking easy about nothing in particular. The barflies would stop mumbling into their boilermakers and perk their ears to Henry's homey sound. They would raise their eyes from the sawdust to study his good-neighborly, ostensibly bland face. They would gather up their beers and drift toward the source of that ingratiating sound and stand in a circle around that good-guy face, asking mutely for something—benediction, warming, the gift of such energy as tightens no muscles, a shot of some unnamable balm.

It was impossible to carry on a conversation with Henry in a public place. Too many winos made their mothlike way into the glow that emanated from any bar stool he graced.

Somehow we shook the winos. I told Henry the whole history of my involvement with Barneybill. I laid forth the practical reasons why I badly needed to work up still another New-Sexualist incarnation and grab me still another chunk of the New-Sexualist loot. I asked if by any remote chance he could see his way clear to helping me pull some more conspiratorial wool over Barneybill's unsavory iguana eyes.

"I think we can work things out," he said genially. "I think something can be done, yes. Give me a day or so to look into it. Let's meet on Friday, say, and I'll try to have some news for you."

His eyes were very lively. He looked like a man who smelled a challenge and had every intention of meeting it head-on. My hopes were high.

It was from Henry, by the way, that I finally got the facts about Barneybill's operation. Henry knew this man well. He knew a lot about how he worked.

Barneybill *was* involved in the buying and selling of pornography. Maybe there'd been a genitally under-par oilman out in Tulsa who got him started in this line, or maybe the bug-eyed oilman was in Barneybill's own oily head, maybe his whole head was a yearning Tulsa, the only one he knew—but his hot materials were being consumed all over these United States. Profitable though it may have been, his rare-book business was a cover for his New-Sexualist trade, and small potatoes alongside it.

The manuscripts put together on Barneybill's assembly line were never published. Several dozen typescripts of each novel were made. Each was bound in hand-tooled Moroccan leather. Each was sold discreetly for something between $300 and $500.

Barneybill's main outlets were through certain book-dealers in New York, Chicago, New Orleans, and, most particularly, Hollywood. At a conservative estimate, the gross annual take from this back-room trade was in the vicinity of five to 10 million dollars.

Barneybill Roster was in porn up to his mismatched ears. Behind his elegant façade of first-edition Tom Paines and Thoreaus, with his feet up on his decorator-veneered cobblers' benches, Barneybill Roster was overseeing what was very likely the biggest and most profitable quality porn ring ever to operate in this country.

When we met the second time Henry's eyes were not only lively, they were dancing.

"Well!" he said. "Well, now! I think we're getting somewhere! I think we can report real progress, yes, indeed!"

"You fixed it for me to write some more?"

"Barneybill's not only willing, he insists on it! He's expecting great things from you!"

"That's marvelous, Henry. You've saved my life, no kidding. But just how did you sell me? Better give me some idea of what my identity's supposed to be this time, so I can work up an appropriate approach and style."

"Here's how I put it. I told him one of my best friends in Paris was a very talented surrealist poet, big with the ladies and equally big with the words. My friend came to feel that Western Civilization was going down the drain, that it was genitally paralyzed and morally kaput. One day my friend got so disgusted that he pulled up stakes and took off for Tibet, which we'd talked many times about doing together. My friend made his way to the highest peak of the Himalayas and took up residence in a lamasary whipped by glacial winds. Here he's been sitting for some years now, looking down over the decadent and moribund West from the crow's nest of the Orient, evaluating in particular his very rich and variegated sex life in that dying neck of the woods. And he's been recording it all, his vivid memories, his new visions, as they come to him in that thin and bracing air. I've explained that he sends his pages to me as they're composed and that they're the most profound and inspired sex writing I've ever seen. Barneybill's more than anxious to get those pages. You write them, turn them in."

I had by this time a considerable sense of my own competence in porn; but all the same Henry's blandly delivered description of my new personality left me blinking.

"I'm supposed to write a whole book of erotica from the viewpoint of a French surrealist poet turned lama who's surveying the decline and fall of the West from his eyrie somewhere in the Himalayas? Swell. Thanks a lot."

"What's the problem? If you're a writer, hell, you should be able to write anything. D'you know that for some months in Paris I was turning out a column on men's fashions for a monthly magazine for gentlemen golfers?"

"I'd be a lot easier in mind writing this book from the viewpoint of a men's-fashion columnist on a golf magazine. I think I could capture the essence of the moribund sexuality of the doomed West better as a men's-fashion columnist than as a surrealist lama. Well, O.K., I'll do my best. I'll try to think sweeping Himalaya thoughts. By the way, where *is* Tibet?"

"That's beside the point. Tibet is where you want it to be. Look, this is worth your best effort. I've told Barneybill he can't expect to get these pages at his regular rates. I've given him to understand that these scripts have to be carted down the Himalayas by yak-pack, brought to Hong Kong, placed in diplomatic pouches by a friend who's cultural attaché over there, flown to San Francisco, picked up and carried by private parties overland to New York. All this, Barneybill understands, is damned expensive. He's ready to pay *three* dollars a page for this stuff, and is convinced it'll still be a bargain."

"Forget what I said, Henry. I'm beginning to get a real feeling for Tibet. I've suddenly realized that it's been there under my nose all along, right in the shadow of the Time-Life Building. Those bracing winds are making me tingle all over. I'll write the definitive work on the slow genital death of the West. I'll describe it inch by inch."

And I did. The new and unprecedented page rate Henry had arranged for me slipped my imagination into high gear.

In less than a month I had a novel of some hundreds of pages ready for submission. It was a thing of obscene beauty. It covered all phases of the creeping ossification of the Occidental groin, graphically, mercilessly. It was a cunning admixture of Oswald Spengler, Ouspensky, Swami Prabhavananda, Thorstein Veblen, Pierre Louys, and Zen, liberally sprinkled with Céline and Henri Michaux. Nobody had ever gotten this high on the Himalayas. Nobody had ever gotten this high on the prospect of three dollars a page.

Barneybill was enchanted. He was bowled over. He let it be known that the *third* authentic genius of porn had shown up, or the second, depending on the degree of separation between the swindler of the Stigglee period and the apostate-dropout of the musical cliffhangers. He paid the plump sum for the latest masterwork and begged for more.

I wrote three more books in different keys but all with the Himalayan slant. They were all received with ovations and much jumping for joy. One thing was fine about my Tibetan-lama identity, Barneybill could hardly ask to meet his new prodigy in person.

Tibet had turned out to be money in the bank for me, literally. My capital assets were growing at such a pace that I was thinking seriously about consulting a good investment counselor.

I bought some more furniture for the folks' place, got it fixed up. I took them shopping in Wanamaker's for some clothes. The old man appreciated the new duds but the garment he liked best of all, one he really cherished, was a Bond Street nubby-tweed hunting jacket that Henry had found he had no more use for and turned over to me. He'd earmarked it for my old man, who moved him though they never met.

The old boy was honored to have that spiffy hacking jacket, he was proud that the thing on his back had once graced the back of this great writer, he sat for hours, before his sight went, wearing that jacket and reading all the books written by its previous owner. He loved the books as much as he loved the jacket, thought they were the straight goods. I believe he was wearing Henry's old jacket when he died up there in Middletown, trying to say something about his false teeth.

My last contribution to the annals of porn deserves special mention. By the time I sat down to write it my sexological imagination, Tibet or no Tibet, bank account or no bank account, was running thin. Again I looked around for an existing literary property to pornographize. Again I found the ideal work, a practically unknown novel by a practically unknown European who, happily, had many Zen-Tibetan leanings highly adaptable to my purposes.

The original was hardly more than 200 pages in length. I quickly and expertly pornographized it into a fat and profitable 500. My *established* rate was now three dollars a page. Thanks to the assist from this talented but abysmally neglected European novelist, my rate went up to something very close to *six* dollars a page. For sure better than what Dostoevsky got in his best week.

Years later I was to be given dramatic vindication of my literary taste. The obscure European whose fine novel I had fleshed out was awarded the Nobel Prize. His novel was hurriedly put out once more in an American edition, and this time it sold rather widely. Whereupon a peculiar thought occurred to me.

Around these United States there were certainly many dozens, perhaps some hundreds, of people who had first encountered this work in its Rosterized form. Some of them must subsequently have caught up with the thing when it got officially reissued. They must have recognized the considerable overlap of the two versions. What could these well-read folk have said to themselves?

Something like this, possibly:

"This is a magnificent work. We appreciated its magnificence years ago, when we read it in manuscript, and it is deeply gratifying to see that the Nobel people have finally come to share our enthusiasm. But what in hell is wrong with the American publisher who got the book out in this butchered way? The published book is less than half as long as the original, all the juiciest parts have been chopped out! What kind of miserable prudery is this, anyhow? To perform such a philistine hatchet job, such literary vandalism, on a masterpiece like this! And they cut out all the best parts, the pigs!"

My last creation for Barneybill Roster was *Steppenwolf* by Hermann Hesse.

CHAPTER 19

Up and Out

That's the story. At the end of my eleventh month in porn, on December 7, 1941, the day of Pearl Harbor, I got another job through another *Times* ad, and this one launched me on something approximating a career. I mean, a kind of work I could do, and could get hired to do consistently enough so that not too critical observers might take it for a calling.

My interest in all this went beyond money, though that was my continuing need. In those days people with certain callings didn't get called up. After Pearl Harbor a lot of people began to get called up.

I became a roving reporter for *Popular Science*, covering technical stories having to do with the war effort. Pretty soon I shifted over to *Mechanix Illustrated*, first as correspondent, then as editor. I bought war bonds. I was a frequent visitor at the Pentagon. The Air Force arranged flights for me here and there. Fathers asked me for vocational advice for their college-age sons. I began to be invited regularly for jury duty. I was, to an appreciable degree, Up and Out.

I was given a draft deferment. The sort of journalism I was doing was classified as "essential to the war effort."

During my 11-month stint at porn I earned something better than $10,000. This was six or seven times what I'd made as a grinder in defense industry and as engine-room wiper in the merchant marine, 10 times what I'd made on the WPA Writers Project, several thousand times my remuneration as housemate to Trotsky. Porn was my launching pad into the respectable brackets.

It provided me with a status salary, it gave me something like a vocation.

In 11 months I wrote 11 novels; and when I finally crawled out of Barneybill Roster's salt mines I'd acquired the work discipline of a professional writer, capable of a solid daily output. Having whipped through as many as 60 and 70 pages of that scented bilge in a single day, I could face any more regular writing assignment, which rarely calls for more than three or four pages of copy in any 24 hours, with equanimity.

I'd come into the House of Words, that regal hostelry, through the cellar door, but I had come in. Mine was not the first literary career to be inaugurated in the sewers. You have to start somewhere. Nobody invited me to start at Time-Life. (Everything considered, Time-Life probably did me a good turn by keeping me away from a staggering variety of jobs. Who's got the time to consider everything.)

But for a long time I carried my old Bridgeport micrometer in my pocket, a reminder that whatever payroll you land on you have to work to close tolerances and allow for the degree to which even the best grinding wheels get ground down. At the commercial writer's grind there's a lot of early wearage.

You keep that committee-established margin of error up front in your mind, you engrave it on the reverse side of your dogtag. Until the great day when you kiss all the committees goodbye.

The day I finally got down to writing my own books I laid away the micrometer for good and all. When you're in business for yourself you don't have to measure your words, your output needn't be checked as to length, breadth and depth. You go to any lengths you want (as several of my editors will affirm), travel as high and wide as you feel is handsome, dig as deep as you've got the shovels for. When you go to work for yourself you can throw out officialdom's calipers.

During that porn year the Kenneth Patchens were living in the Village, we saw a lot of them. The atmosphere in their Bleecker Street apartment was congenial, the wine was plentiful, the talk was easy. We kept them informed almost day by day about the gnarled doings in the Roster nether world. Years later Kenneth published a novel more or less suggested by Barneybill and his Blooming Boys—*Memoirs of a Shy Pornographer.*

I was disappointed in the book. It had the sharpness, the sprightliness, the quick verbal footwork, that distinguish all of Kenneth's writing, but I felt he hadn't done justice to the subject.

Why? Because, instead of developing the astonishing facts, he'd used them as springboards into surrealist inventions which were nowhere near so astonishing. Yet, it seemed to me, the situation was one in which Reality so far outstripped Art in unlikelihood and outrage that the artist's job was merely to record, not make up anything.

How make up a liblab slobberer to equal Barneybill Roster? A New-Sexualist grande dame of Zo-Zo's stature? Bolshevik-Leninist beaver of Yar Hatchek's ilk? Not to mention a Reichian seeder of the sod like Jason Orroway? It would take a touch of genius to capture such originals in *all* their gaudy sights and raucous sounds—a job, really, for the photographer and phonographer. The surrealist's flights of fancy simply won't work here; with a roster of people like Roster, reality itself turns surreal.

It's a new ballgame: daily life has become so incongruous, so contrary, and so hurtling-fast as to leave the traditional vanguard people in the lurch, bringing up a laggards' rear. Business-as-usual has nothing either businesslike or usual about it, each day's round brings more of the inconceivable. Your Minister of War turns out to be Profumo.

How schoolboyish Jarry's *Ubu Roi* sounds alongside the *Warren Commission Report* or the transcript of the Eichmann trial! How quaint is Dali's melting watch against the first close-ups of the moon or photographs of the patternless webs woven by spiders made psychotic with injections of some schizophrene's blood! How insipid the plonks of John Cage's prepared piano, now that we have recordings of the telemetered pulse and respiration of a John Glenn in orbit, of computer burble, of dolphins no doubt trying to tell us something important, of radio signals from unseen galaxies!

Can Blake's best visions hold a candle to the hallucinations a thousand people have recorded under the spell of LSD? Are you honestly going to put Gide's playboy counterfeiters up against Bobby Baker and Billy Sol Estes? Genet's stagey blacks against Lumumba, Nkrumah, Kenyatta, Mboya?

Forget it. The job of the decimated avantgarde is to catch up with the ordinary, which means learning to move with the speed of light.

Don't waste your time or mine writing Kafka's *The Trial* still another time. Get down on paper, if you can, some of the ambience of Jack Ruby or Charles Manson in the courtroom. I dare you. Get all the Barneybills down. You can't invent Barneybills anywhere near as stunning and stomach-turning as those who are running around all over the place, often as prime ministers and commissars.

No, Kenneth Patchen's book bothered me. And it made me think about what I might have tried to say about the fantasy world of Barneybill Roster. Something along these lines, maybe:

All Peeping is One. Not a noble phrase, but a notion worth holding on to, to keep a good balance and a clear eye.

All Peeping is One: minor but valuable footnote to the underbelly of American Letters.

It's well to remember that Literature *does* have an underbelly. Its head can sometimes, under favorable circumstances, rise to the heights, true. But some of its nether portions remain planted in mucky subcellars. The Barneybills hold them there.

Sometimes—with luck—the siphoned-up scum dosn't kill off the topmost blossoms but actually nourishes them. Roses from dungheaps, etc. If and when that happens, it's least of all the fault of the Barneybills. Their horizons will never reach out wider than that primordial Keyhole, which tries to squeeze all Literature down to Gawk.

Gawk it will remain in some aspects, even in the best of cases, because Gawk it was in the beginning, and to Gawk it must from time to time return. But all Gawk is *not* One.

Gawk can go down to pander and up to wonder. You don't respond to a Tijuana Bible the way you do to Goya's nude Maja. There's no Keyhole framing Maja. A Proscenium Arch, maybe. Bemusement is something beyond amusement. Wonder is different in kind from slobber.

Not that there's anything inherently wrong with slobber. It's just that you'd do less of it, and so have a more varied life, if from time to time you stretched the Keyhole to an Arch or, better still, passed through the Keyhole and joined the party on the other side. Watchers slobber, musers get wet in the eyes, doers get wet you-know-where.

When Literature fights its way out of and beyond the Keyhole, all the way to the Arch, as it can, as it sometimes, miraculously, does, it's in spite of the Barneybills and against their best efforts. But don't kid yourself that the Barneybills are a breed apart, some malodorous lunatic fringe.

They're everywhere, right, left, center, burrowed deep into a great array of institutions and ideologies, atop the very pinnacles as well as in the back alleys, cringing and strutting within all sorts of dragon-slayers and Buick-dodgers.

There are lots of them among the respectables. It was no accident that led Barneybill into the Americana business as a front for his porn operation. Very likely it happened the other way, he dealt in the Americana first, and through this came to porn.

If the Mormons could go in one generation from polygamy to a flinty killjoyism, it's possible to begin with love of country and grand old flag and wind up a porn dealer. For some it may be necessary: every cloud must have a silver lining, and vice versa.

Too much patriotism about anything can inspire a lapping undercurrent of prurience—among other things, a form of nose-thumbing—the nihilistic undercoating to the inspirational. It may have to do with the sexual loss that accompanies prestige gain. Some losses you can't take gracefully. Devote all your energies to the scramble into respectability and when you heave yourself all the way up there you may find your neglected gonads aching. Overworked new brain gets nostalgic for overlooked old brain.

Waste no tears on the prestige-gaining, sex-losing Barneybills. You can't blame a man for his sickness. But you can abominate him for ideologizing and institutionalizing that sickness: a favorite pastime in the world today. Otherwise the woods would not be full of toy tigers and paper pumas. Whose teeth, unfortunately, can be sharp.

It's not always wrong to hit a Barneybill. They asked Freud if to understand all was not to forgive all. He said, no, sometimes there's a son of a bitch you have to hit in the mouth.

When you come across a Barneybill with a gun, duck. Run for cover. People like that are dangerous with guns. They can't train on any one target. Their fire tends to scatter. Since their only real target is themselves, and they can't quite turn their guns around. . . .

Some 20 years after all this, Henry Miller and I had a reunion in Hollywood. I reminded him of our little gambit with Barneybill. He enjoyed the story hugely but claimed he couldn't remember any of the details of his own involvement.

Well, much fermented water has passed under many dental bridges. Wars, revolutions, and all manner of upheavals have come and not by any manner of means gone. The human race has tottered a long and devious way since those innocent days when our determined band of scribes did their best to help Lady Chatterley take her next step. Barneybill Roster bulks petty and well-nigh irrelevant on today's wobbly horizons, he was not of the stuff that sticks to the mind's ribs over the years.

All the same, as I've pointed out to Henry, the physical fact is that I have in my possession, in a safe place, under lock and key, 11 most Erosive manuscripts, among them a fat retrospective on the waning eroticism of the Western peoples, spelled out in steamy detail, composed from the point of view of a French surrealist poet who has journeyed the footsore way from Montmartre to a lamasary high in the Tibetan Himalayas to get the long Spenglerian perspective on his blighted origins.

A manuscript like that doesn't just grow. It has to have a history and a raison d'être. I never wrote from the viewpoint of a lamasaried Rimbaud-qua-Kinsey before I met Barneybill Roster and Henry Miller, and—this is a matter of record—I haven't since. Whose memory is to be faulted?

What happened to Barneybill? I haven't the slighted idea. My jobs took me away from New York for long periods, then overseas. When I got back toward the end of the war I opened a Manhattan phone directory and for the fun of it looked Barneybill up. His name was not listed.

I stopped by the lobby of the Time-Life Building and checked the business directory there: no trace of the man's name. None of the alumni of my old alma mater, Blooming Boystown, had the foggiest notion as to Barneybill's whereabouts. He seemed to have disappeared from the face of the earth.

Of course, a war of some proportions was on. War spews up unexpected career possibilities for a lot of people, it can be a vocational door- and eye-opener. It may be that in the stress and heave of the times

Barneybill Roster found himself and as a result found new areas for his entrepreneurial talents. It may even be that he woke up one fine day and realized that if he was ever going to take that poke and that potshot at the Hitlers of the world this was the time—he could engage in the bellicose exercise under the auspices of the Allied Command.

But I rather doubt that this man ever reached for that gun he had such a verbal fondness for. Not this man. I can't picture him on a battlefield, where the traffic is indeed heavy and all the half-track Buicks and twin-engine Buicks are indeed bearing down on you, you personally, you in particular.

I can't picture him crossing the bloody Fifth Avenues of Bastogne or Iwo Jima. Barneybill Roster would not adjust well to a situation in which the traffic is runaway and the pastrami, not hot, has to be gulped out of a C-ration can.

It's one thing to talk up cojones so People's-Frontally from behind a barricade of cobblers' benches and Jefferson first editions. But in a real live war you can get hurt. Your cojones too. Very, very often the lads who most value the manly assets called cojones do not have the cojones to go out and do battle in defense of their cojones. (In the ways that truly count, which are least of all martial. Hemingway kept going to wars to make the most dramatic spectacle of his cojones. And having nightmares, out of which he fashioned books, about the wars shearing his genitals off. What really drew him, the demonstration—or the ongoing nightmare?) You begin to wonder whether with some of the loudest dragonslayers the scrotal opulence is not more for display than for use.

What happened to Barneybill? Nobody knows. But I have a recurrent vision. . . .

Barneybill Roster is walking, walking. Up hill and down dale he walks, ever on the sniff. He's questing for something he thinks is the all-hot post-Lady but he's wrong.

What he's looking for, though he doesn't know it, is—benediction, warming, the gift of such energy as tightens no muscles, a shot of some unnamable balm. A few red blood corpuscles to keep his over-abundant white phagocytes company. The Holy Grail of No-Thought and No-Lit, the ease which is wordless because it needs no words and there are no words for it. Less ooze on the palms and seepage on the cheeks.

He walks. He crosses continents, quaking at every column of red ants caroming his way. He navigates oceans, pausing on the crest of each wave to look right and left—whales have no brakes.

In the distance, fringed with mist, an island looms. It's a completely uncharted island but Barneybill knows its name. Amohalko, revered by the natives as Backward Oklahoma. Amohalko, where the sperm-oil wells shoot a thousand feet into the air and the tumids grow as high as an elephant's eye.

Here in friendly, tropical Amohalko, Barneybill settles. In the town of Aslut, a Backward Tulsa. Here he meets the woman he thinks he's been searching for high and low. She calls herself Amelia Earhart but he knows better, he knows she's really Lady Chatterley with the pelvis finally mellered up.

He and Amelia get married. Judge Crater performs the ceremony. Glenn Miller plays the "Wedding March." B. Traven and Isaac Babel sing "O Promise Me." It's the cultural event of the Amohalko season. Burgess and Maclean serve as ushers.

But the marriage doesn't turn out too well. Barneybill finds that post-Lady isn't all she's been cracked up to be. The trouble is that none of her heats is on paper—you can't turn the pages. Also, she's not framed by a keyhole. Barneybill isn't used to looking at post-Ladies outside of the keyhole framework. Amelia seems incomplete to him. And it's frustrating, you just can't turn the pages.

He feels somewhat let down. He has a sense of being less than whole. Something vital is missing.

He moves into his own bedroom in the opposite wing of the bamboo castle. He sends for Martin Bormann. Martin is dressed up in the Iberian generalissimo uniform. He's given his assignment: to stomp up and down the room, screaming imprecations, slights, and threats against polity and pubis alike.

Good: Barneybill's got his Squelcher back. A definite improvement. He feels deliciously threatened in all sorts of hotshot Falange castrational ways. Now there's one other thing to arrange, to make life full again.

Barneybill sends for Ambrose Bierce. He puts him to work in the opposite corner of the room, writing steamy, sizzly, polymorph-perverse prose. Ambrose's fingers fly over the typewriter keys. He writes fast, the typewriter is well-oiled, it's Alger Hiss's. As the pages leap from his machine they are conveyed by an assembly-line belt to Barneybill's lap, which, naturally, is tenting.

Barneybill reads and reads, his eyes wide. This stuff would be damned good even in the gloomed quiet of the reading room of the 42nd Street Library. Here, somehow, it's still more rousing. Because, you see, there's Marty goosestepping up and down, making great Squelcher sounds.

Barneybill's got his world in order again. Squelcher in one corner, Porn-Proser in the other, who could ask for anything more? The keyhole frame is back around the post-Lady, and she's suddenly luscious in the right number of dimensions, two, and you can turn her pages, turn as you finger yourself.

Barneybill's billowy cojones are once more in a cosmic boil, ready for anything so long as it's on paper and you can turn the pages. It's better than being cooped up with that Amelia. She can't even make a good hot pastrami sandwich, and her pickled tomatoes taste like cojones marinated in crypto-fascist pizzle grease.

Barneybill summons the little Negro boy who did all that good work for Irving Berlin. He commissions the talented tike to compose a national anthem for Amohalko, along the lines of the spirited song Rodgers and Hammerstein turned out for Oklahoma. As a matter of fact, the Negro boy writes the ditty to the tune of the original "Oklahoma," which he penned for Rodgers and Hammerstein in the first place.

Burgess and Maclean stand on the balcony as Marty rants and Ambrose types and Barneybill reads and reads and reads, completing himself. They accompany themselves on a couple of Zo-Zo Borracha de la Ciudad's old harpsichords as they serenade the boss with Amohalko's new anthem. It goes something like this:

"A-A-A-Amohalko, every night my Lady-Post and I, drool alone and peek, and breathe the reek, through lazy keyholes on the sly, we know we belong by Mum's door, and the door we belong by's no bore."

But Amelia's not drooling alone. She doesn't have her husband's political and literary resources, she can't make herself self-sufficient in the bedroom. She needs unpaged comforting, and Judge Crater's in her bed, unpagedly comforting her.

Barneybill's oblivious to this development. The keyhole of his wife's bedroom is the one keyhole he never thought of gluing his eye to. The keyholes Ambrose Bierce supplies him with are better all around, in their handy pocket editions, with Martin Bormann's realistic sound effects in the background.

Years pass. Camillo Cienfuegos lands on Amohalko. He's still dripping wet from the dunking he took in the Caribbean somewhere off the Cuban coast, due to malfunctions in the engines of his plane that have not been satisfactorily explained (though Fidel's hand has a long reach when any of his old pals questions whether all the fighting in the Sierra Maestra was for the purpose of producing one more Squelcher Deluxe).

Camillo makes his way to Barneybill's bedroom, trailing Carib waters. He pounds on the door. He shouts:

"Hey, Barneybill, listen to me! We've got to chop down the Squelchers, all of them, the Squelchers to the right of us and the Squelchers to the left of us, and those of the center too, the Squelchers of all colors, yes! But not on paper, you know! Not by turning pages! This way the State will never wither away but all cojones will, that's for damn sure! Listen to me, Barneybill, we got enough real generalissimos Out There, and enough real ladies with real heats, we don't have to make them up, that way we sure as hell don't get anywhere! Amohalko's very backward as compared with any real Oklahoma! Ask any oil millionaire in the neighborhood! Come on Out and Up, Barneybill! Let's go after some real targets politics-wise and pubis-wise!"

Nobody hears. It's a busy household. . . .

CHAPTER 20

POSTPORN/THAT'S THAT

Leftovers. . . .

I don't respond to porn, never did. If it's on a page I begin to parse the sentences. If on a screen I find myself studying the arrangements of bodies to see if the composition's good.

Little gets roused in me but, in the one case, the grammarian, in the other, the art critic.

Before I got into the porn game I preferred to see this inappetence as merit. Not a falling short but a rising above.

I sad, look, a principle of the conservation of psychic energy is no doubt operating here. I said, see, my bio-economy just isn't going to waste emotion in the head on what's not available to the hands. I offered myself a number of congratulations.

They were not accepted. After my stint in porn they weren't even listened to.

It wasn't presence of mind after all. Just absence of mind's eye.

Something was left out of my makeup, the apparatus to see and feel what's not there. If I have any inner eye at all it's very glaucomatous. My year in porn proved that.

You're supposed to *see* the couplings you read about in printporn—all I see is words. You're expected to *feel* what you see in picporn—I feel only that what these energetic people are up to has nothing in common with what I'd be up to in like circumstances. First of all, because I wouldn't have a cameraman present. Not to mention a *stenographer* or tape recorder.

Bob King, top-seeded San Francisco pornfilmer:

> And dirty films are really made for people whose level of fantasy is very low. They don't have any imagination at all, which is why they need something explicit. It's like TV, you know—the *Beverly Hillbillies* and *Bonanza* and all are made for people with no imagination, too. Pornography is just dirty television. And who needs that?

Graphic porn may be for low-fantasy types. Literary porn has got to be for grandmaster visionaries—given dirty words, they have to supply their own dirty pictures. Into which they can trancewalk. Each man his own McLuhan.

Without a visual or tactile imagination—not even the amount needed to imagine what things must look and feel like to people who do have it—how could I write porn?

Not being able to visualize, let alone empathize, I made a mighty effort to *realize* my scenes—in words. I couldn't shoot the dirty television for my readers. I *could* go out of my way to give them detailed shooting scripts, with all camera angles spelled out.

The result was hailed as a hauntingly lush, vivid evocative prose. Leaving little to the imagination. Sure. What imagination did I have to leave anything to.

So lack of qualification led to my meteoric career, sequence of careers, in porn. My gift was a product of my impoverishment.

By such a twisty dialectic does luxuriance arise from paucity, lushness from lack. Even, let's face it, in areas of art endeavor far removed from porn. Even in areas of life far removed from art.

My blind spots gave me a sort of steampipe perspective on Eros.

Tunnel vision doesn't make a man a seer. But blocking off certain orders of distraction as it does, it can make you see things. What I see is a race of men (and women) with a steady indisturbance in the face of all porn incitements—due to bioeconomy, not facultative voids. Men (and women) expending their libido energies in a tunnel sexuality, with no residues to need the seep of fantasy.

What would life be like with no mass erotic moonraking and stargazing? All heads clear for singleminded attack on other vital matters? How large would erotics bulk in esthetics? If at all?

Did Lawrence Durrell have such questions in mind when he pleaded with his old friend Henry Miller not to finish, in any case not to publish, the volume of the *Rosy Crucifixion* trilogy called *Sexus*, Henry's one truly pornographic work?

In a forthcoming novel a man encounters a porn movie, later delivers himself of these strong words:

> I see nothing *wrong* with people watching other people. What bothers
> me is that anybody would *want* the audience, or need it, or tolerate it,
> much less be in it. Turn act into performance. The escape pools are
> diminishing in number. Socialize fuck too and there'll be no sepa-
> rate heads left, you've finally produced massman. What's obscene in
> pornography is the McLuhanization of the to now unseen, therefore
> unmonitored. The massmediation of solitude. Imposing the commune
> logic of day on the anchorage of night. Making a freeway of the escape
> hatch. Safety in numbers, they say. Safety from what, in this case? Fuck
> if it's anything is the safety from the all too numerous. The liberty

to stop performing in front of other eyes and simply be, do, go. End to show, prove, project, image make. That was a highly political film, you see. Its politics, not its sex, was the abomination. Its message that what can't be done except in private isn't worth doing. Its overtone that socialization is the only valid life-style, not just a strategy to make life outdoors go smoothly and unobtrusively so life indoors can be lived with the shades drawn and the eyes turned inward. Yes. It was a political statement, reactionary to the core, fascist (even when dressed up as Reichist or Provoist or Maoist), to put it bluntly. . . .

I couldn't have put it better myself. God knows I tried, over and over, when I was writing that speech.

Marxism understands social entities better than it does persons one by one—understandably. Human units are individually so wildly devious, in such wildly individual ways; clumped together their deviations cancel each other out.

Social classes behave as though they're made up of interchangeable parts—Economic Man widened to a homogeneous mass. Their components, though, seem to be moved by a variety of impulses that have little to do with economics and are often the opposite of self-serving.

Nobody was ever more swamped by economics than I was in the year 1940. And yet—and yet—the strongest forces pushing me into porn were not related to the needs imposed by economics. Economically I was needy, oh, yes. But I had so many needs beyond money. For things that money can't buy.

I know a man named Kahlo. He's been trying to finish a novel for 30 years and it's still no go. But when he takes an assignment to turn out a pseudonymous porn paperback, to make some quick money, his blockage vanishes, he tears through the thing, gets a fat volume done literally in days.

I know another man named Browkaw. He has the world's worst stutter. But he's a devoted teller of Negro dialect stories—when he slips into that Tambo drawl his verbal stoppages disappear, the language flows, you can't shut him up.

You see what I'm getting at. Browkaw has one kind of stutter, Kahlo another. Porn is Kahlo's Negro dialect.

I had a stutter. I couldn't get a word out. Porn cured me, it was for one crucial year my Tambo dialect, my blackface, my pseudonym.

I was luckier than my friend Kahlo. I got to turning out words at such breakneck speed that when my porn phase was over and I starred to use my words for my own purposes, they kept on coming.

I am in major senses a Marxist but I can't see that my immersion in porn is in any significant way to be explained by a materialist interpretation of personal history. If porn hadn't existed I would have had to invent it, or something like it, to get the word machine in me started. Even if I'd inherited a million dollars and had to support nothing but a string of polo ponies.

The first rule in storytelling is that characters aren't supposed to wander off, never to be heard from again. If people just up and disappear you can't get them together toward the end for what in playwriting classes are called the *obligatory scenes*, the payoff confrontations, thematic hammerings-home, tidy wrapups.

Nine-tenths of the obligatory scenes cried out for in real life never come off because the protagonists simply disperse. The unsatisfactoriness of that is probably what leads us to fantasize about what might have happened if the cast could have been kept together to play the drama out to curtain—and from such fantasy, of course, are born theater and fiction, including their porn subdivisions.

. . .

The Boss wandered off—into herself.

After the old man died in the Middletown hospital she took to sitting on her dark rooms back in New Haven's Dixwell Avenue ghetto, shades drawn, considering the blackness on all sides. She was failing, fading. I was settled in Los Angeles. I decided to buy a house in the Santa Monica mountains with a little private wing that the Boss could occupy. I thought she might have a few months in a pleasant setting, maybe the toss of green and flit of birds roundabout would get her to look out the window a few more times.

On a Sunday in May, 1963, I called to tell her I was getting the house ready and would have her put on a plane in a couple of weeks to fly out to a new life. My brother answered—he'd found her on the bed that morning, fetally hunched, fingers to mouth, whether to keep something outside from entering or something inside from leaving it was impossible to say. Sammy had been dead less than a year. She never could abide his presence, she couldn't survive his absence. She was 82, 83, nobody quite knew.

I stopped talking about Bettina Tokay on page 243 because at that point she stopped being around. One day she just packed a bag and went back to Provo. I guess the uncertainty of moving around the world never knowing if and when her father would come down on her bedpost got to be too much for her. She moved back home, where she could at least be sure of the visitation every night.

I got a note from her one day saying she'd married a nice young fellow, a sort of pioneer poverty lawyer. A little later she wrote to tell me she'd had a baby, a boy. There followed years of silence. Then in 1963 I got out a book. Bettina came across a review of it in a magazine, and it prompted her to communicate again, via my publishers, as follows:

We've been here for some years now, in this fellowship of some 100 washed souls. Our retreat is God's country, over 400 acres of fertile hills ringed by miles of unbefouled pine-thick wilderness, over a day's ride by horse from the nearest towns with their brassy lurings. Our days are serene. All of us in this Eden are too busy to feed egos and let the sins of self take us from the Path. What material things we own—they're minimal, and simple—we own in common. We work the land 10 hours a day and with an hour's prayer at sunup and another at sun-down you can see it makes for a full, filled, fulfilled life. I am content to the depths to have found my Jesus and opened my heart to His Glory Visitation. This is why I'm trying to reach you, to tell you you too can have the Shining Gift. The Savior is there, waiting for the least signal that He's wanted. Only invite Him and He'll come, all smiles. I have to pass this news along to you, my eyes have been opened. I see now that pornography is a wider thing than you and I once supposed. This new book you've written is every bit as much pornography as those vilenesses you were making for money long years ago. All your writing is pornography. All writing is pornography. All the benighted doings and reachings of city people in the dark cities are pornography. All acts of pride and amassing and accomplishing and asserting and self-featuring and ego-feeding. There is another Way. You can breathe clean air again, if you will only turn away from your petty self-servicing and show Him He's welcome. . . .

The letter was from some religious community in Saskatchewan, roughly between and vaguely north of Moose Jaw and Medicine Hat. The "we," further passages made clear, had reference only to Bettina and her son—no mention of the nice young poverty-lawyer fellow who'd once been around in capacity of husband.

I could only guess at how and why he fell by the wayside. Bettina had at least symbolically tracked back to the domain of her ancestors, where her father would (at least symbolically) be permanently installed on the bedpost. The husband probably began to feel crowded on such promises. Maybe he took off. Maybe he was jettisoned. When you go back to the Salvation Road that I presume was the Path Bettina referred to, you want to travel light.

Whatever the mode of travel, go back she did. Geographically she may have settled in remote Saskatchewan but spiritually she'd returned to Tanganyika, to the work of summoning the flock she'd once strayed from and now was happy, and lightened in heart, herself to rejoin for good.

I couldn't help wondering whether in making her prodigal way back to the spirit of her Mormon-pioneer ancestors Bettina hadn't violated that spirit, at least muddied it. Those raspy, jut-jawed, defiant early westerners had been in their own time revolutionaries, they'd injected such a fund of protest into Protestantism as to unnerve most of their co-religionists. Bettina's re-entrance into the fold in her own life signaled an end to protest, fight, opposition, departurism.

It's the dilemma of every revolution that gets anywhere. The straggling, sore beset, pariah cadres become an army, then an armored nation. The originally chancy movement begins to put on snappy parade drills headed up by high-stepping marching bands. It's fun for the bystanders to fall in. The once embattled cause has blossomed to a popular pastime, the thing to do. People tend to forget that what is now a bandwagon was in the beginning an underground railway. Nobody stops to ask how much these holiday-mood new recruits can have in common with the old-timers—they being devout joiners where the old ones, the best ones, were rude leavers.

But the human nervous system just can't take a lifetime of displacement and nay-saying. Sooner or later people get tired of wandering, and want to go home. So it is with revolution in our day, and perhaps in all times—and that's the enduring headache, for those who are moved to revolt and know that beyond their own personal needs it's the enduring need of the world.

Bernard Wolfe (1915–1985), dramatist, television writer, and novelist, graduated from Yale in 1935 and after service in WWII worked briefly as secretary and bodyguard to Leon Trotsky during the revolutionary's exile in Mexico (he was off-duty at the time Trotsky got plugged) before settling in New York to become a writer. Among his many books are the novels *Limbo*, *The Late Risers*, *In Deep*, *The Great Prince Died*, *The Magic of Their Singing*, *Logan's Gone*, and *Lies*, the short story collection *Move Up, Dress Up, Drink Up, Burn Up*, and the influential jazz memoir *Really the Blues with Mezz Mezzrow*.

Jonathan Lethem is the author of seven novels including *Fortress of Solitude* and *Motherless Brooklyn*, which was named Novel of the Year by Esquire and won the National Book Critics Circle Award and the Salon Book Award, as well as the Macallan Crime Writers Association Gold Dagger. He has also written two short story collections, a novella, and a collection of essays, edited *The Vintage Book of Amnesia*, guest-edited *The Year's Best Music Writing 2002*, and was the founding fiction editor of *Fence* magazine. His writings have appeared in *The New Yorker*, *Rolling Stone*, *McSweeney's*, and many other periodicals. He lives in Brooklyn, New York.

MORE TITLES FROM PHAROS EDITIONS

The Fan Man
by William Kotzwinkle
SELECTED AND INTRODUCED BY
T.C. BOYLE

Wintergreen
by Robert Michael Pyle
SELECTED AND INTRODUCED BY
DAVID GUTERSON

Still Life with Insects
by Brian Kiteley
SELECTED AND INTRODUCED BY
LEAH HAGER COHEN

Doctor Glas by Hjalmar Söderberg,
Translated by Rochelle Wright
SELECTED AND INTRODUCED BY
TOM RACHMAN

A German Picturesque
by Jason Schwartz
SELECTED AND INTRODUCED BY
BEN MARCUS

The Dead Girl
by Melanie Thernstrom
SELECTED AND INTRODUCED BY
DAVID SHIELDS

*Reapers of the Dust: A Prairie
Chronicle* by Lois Phillips Hudson
SELECTED AND INTRODUCED BY
DAVID GUTERSON

The Lists of the Past
by Julie Hayden
SELECTED AND INTRODUCED BY
CHERYL STRAYED

*The Tattooed Heart & My Name
Is Rose* by Theodora Keogh
SELECTED AND INTRODUCED BY
LIDIA YUKNAVITCH

Total Loss Farm: A Year in the Life
by Raymond Mungo
SELECTED AND INTRODUCED BY
DANA SPIOTTA

Crazy Weather
by Charles L. McNichols
SELECTED AND INTRODUCED BY
URSULA K. LE GUIN

Inside Moves by Todd Walton
SELECTED AND INTRODUCED BY
SHERMAN ALEXIE

McTeague: A Story of San Francisco
by Frank Norris
SELECTED AND INTRODUCED BY
JONATHAN EVISON

*You Play the Black and the Red
Comes Up* by Richard Hallas
SELECTED AND INTRODUCED BY
MATT GROENING

The Land of Plenty
by Robert Cantwell
SELECTED AND INTRODUCED BY
JESS WALTER

Printed in the United States
by Baker & Taylor Publisher Services